KIMONO

KIMONO
THE ART AND EVOLUTION
OF JAPANESE FASHION

The Khalili Collections

edited by Anna Jackson
with additional texts by Nagasaki Iwao, Timon Screech,
Christine M. E. Guth and Kendall H. Brown

Thames & Hudson

Contents

Preface

PROFESSOR DAVID KHALILI, PHD, KCSS, KCFO

Since 1970 I have assembled, under the auspices of The Khalili Family Trust, eight of the world's finest and most comprehensive art collections: Islamic Art (700–2000); Hajj and the arts of pilgrimage (700–2000); Aramaic documents (353–24 BC); Japanese art of the Meiji period (1868–1912); Japanese kimono (1700–2000); Swedish textiles (1700–1900); Spanish damascene metalwork (1850–1900) and enamels of the world (1700–2000). Together, the eight collections comprise some 25,000 works and each is, on its own merit, among the largest and most significant in the world. The Khalili Collections will be fully represented in a series of eighty-eight books, including exhibition catalogues, of which seventy have already been published.

And now, after many years of painstaking research and with the assistance of one of the most eminent scholars in the field, we are able to publish our superlative collection of kimono.

The art and style of the kimono has been of enormous significance to the cultural history of Japan. The striking visual beauty of these garments has also influenced generations of artists and designers around the world. In collecting kimono, I wanted to draw from a wide selection of techniques and forms, and include important examples of formal, semi-formal and informal kimono, worn by women, men and children. Represented in the collection are the sophisticated garments of the samurai elite and affluent merchant classes of the Edo period (1603–1868), the shifting styles and new colour palette of Meiji-period dress (1868–1912), and the bold and dazzling kimono of the Taishō (1912–26) and early Shōwa (1926–89) periods, which utilized innovative patterning methods and derived fresh stimulus from both past traditions and the modern world.

The form of the T-shaped, straight-seamed, front-wrapping kimono has changed very little over the centuries, yet the collection reveals an astonishing variety of designs. In Japanese dress, it is the surface decoration, rather than the cut and construction, which is important, and indications of gender, age, status, wealth and taste are expressed through the choice of colour and pattern. The kimono in the collection convey the remarkable creativity of designers who used the surface of the garment to produce a work of art that would enfold the wearer. They each form a sort of capsule, a personal statement as well as one of status and period, a representation of a world recorded in fabric. Much like *ukiyo-e*, the 'pictures of the floating world', kimono designs represent a way of life that moves between the serene, the provocative, the domestic and the public, and today the iconic garment continues to offer dazzling inspiration to lovers of Japanese traditional culture and contemporary design enthusiasts alike.

I would like to sincerely thank Anna Jackson, Keeper of the Asian Department at the Victoria and Albert Museum and Honorary Curator of the Khalili Kimono Collection, for her dedication, expertise and professionalism as main author and editor of this publication. My gratitude also to my dealer Shoji Tsumugi and curator Dror Elkvity; to the contributing authors Nagasaki Iwao, Kendall H. Brown, Christine M. E. Guth and Timon Screech; everyone at Thames & Hudson; and all those who have helped to bring my project to life and create this book that you have before you. As always, I have received great support and encouragement from my wife Marion, and our sons Daniel, Benjamin and Raphael, who have shown such enthusiasm for our collections.

opposite
Kimono for an infant boy (detail)
1920–40
K107

on p. 1
Unlined kimono for a young woman
(*hitoe*) (detail)
1860–80
KX187

on p. 2
Kimono for a woman (detail)
1920–40
K32

on p. 4
Unlined kimono for a young woman
(*hitoe*) (detail)
1800–50
KX236

Clad in the aesthetics of tradition: from kosode to kimono

NAGASAKI IWAO

Today, the kimono is perhaps the ultimate symbol of traditional Japanese culture. This distinctive form of clothing has a very long history, stretching back to the Heian period (794–1185), although it was not until the Momoyama era (1573–1603) that garments resembling the modern kimono in terms of shape and patterning were first worn. The Edo period (1603–1868) witnessed a profusion of decorative techniques and surface designs, particularly in the case of women's garments. While not identical in every way to their modern counterparts, the aesthetics of Momoyama and Edo-period dress are directly reflected in contemporary Japanese kimono culture.

Kosode and kimono terminology

Prior to the Meiji period (1868–1912), the type of garment we now call a kimono, meaning simply 'the thing worn', was known as *kosode*, or 'small sleeves'. This term did not refer to the overall size of the sleeve, but to the sleeve opening, which was just wide enough for the wrist and arm to pass through. In the late Heian period, the term *kosode* came to signify garments with tubular sleeves and narrow armholes, in contrast to *ōsode*, or garments with 'large sleeves'. At the time, plain silk *kosode* were worn by aristocrats as undergarments for wide-sleeved robes such as the *sokutai*, the formal attire of court noblemen, and *jūni-hitoe*, the 'twelve-layered robe' worn by ladies of the imperial court (fig. 1). Commoners also wore single *kosode*, often as hemp, both as inner and outer wear.

During the Kamakura (1185–1333) and Muromachi (1333–1573) periods, the political influence of the aristocracy began to weaken and power shifted to the warrior class, who wore *ōsode* on ceremonial occasions but *kosode* for everyday. Unlike the plain or simply patterned hemp garments worn by ordinary people during the Heian period, the *kosode* favoured by the warrior class were of richly decorated silk. Over time, the tubular sleeves of the Heian era were replaced by

fig. 1
Tale of Genji (Genji monogatari), scene from the Yadorigi chapter

Handscroll, ink and colour on paper
Heian period, c. 1130
Tokugawa Art Museum, Nagoya

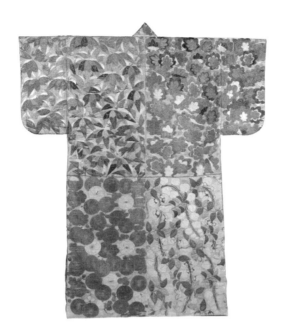

fig. 2
Kosode with flowering plants of the four seasons

Silk with embroidery and metallic foil (nuihaku)
Momoyama period, 1573–1603
Kyoto National Museum

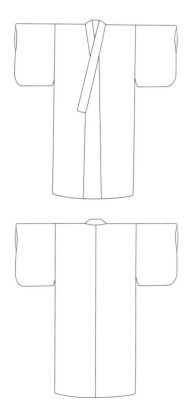

fig. 3
Basic structure and pattern layout of kimono

'civilization and enlightenment' (*bunmei kaika*) was initiated by the new government, there was a rapid introduction of western culture into Japan. This resulted in many significant changes, including the westernization of dress as part of a general trend to adopt European and American models. Western clothing was initially adopted by the Meiji ruling class, which emerged from the former aristocratic and military classes, who would have had occasion to wear *ōsode* during the Edo period. Since their adoption of western dress meant that the *ōsode* fell out of use, there was no longer the need to use the distinguishing term *kosode*. From the Meiji period onwards, therefore, only the term 'kimono', as used to signify *kosode* of the sort previously worn primarily by townspeople (*chōnin*), remained in use.

The adoption of western dress gave rise to the need for another term to mark the distinction from traditional Japanese garments. The word that emerged was *yōfuku*, a combination of the *yō* of *seiyō*, meaning 'western', and *fuku*, meaning clothing in general. In the Taishō period (1912–26), western dress and kimono were worn to a similar extent, particularly in urban areas, which meant that the terms *yōfuku* and 'kimono' became equally current. As a result of this yet another word, *wafuku*, 'wa' meaning Japanese, came into use.

Interestingly, just as Japan was adopting western dress, an influx of Japanese goods into Europe and America gave rise to the cultural phenomenon that became known as 'Japonisme', one aspect of which was a fascination with kimono. Western women clad in kimono were depicted in paintings, while the shape of the garment and the designs used to pattern it had a significant influence on western dress. The appeal of kimono in Europe and America that began in the late nineteenth century has continued to the present day.

longer ones, although still with a narrow opening at the wrist. During the Momoyama period a wealthy merchant class emerged, which also adopted *kosode* similar to those worn by their warrior counterparts. As a result, the *kosode* replaced the *ōsode* as the main form of garment worn by the ruling classes and the economically powerful. Together with the type of garment worn by commoners, this meant that by the end of the sixteenth century the *kosode* had become the principal form of dress for all sections of Japanese society, and for both sexes (fig. 2).

The term 'kimono' first appears in documentary sources of the thirteenth century, referring to clothing in general, rather than a particular form of dress. During the Momoyama period, the word appeared in the reports of Portuguese missionaries to denote the shape and appearance of a specific type of garment, suggesting that by this time kimono had become synonymous with *kosode*. This shift probably reflects the ubiquity of the *kosode* across all social groups, including the ruling warrior class, and the fact that the *ōsode* was disappearing from public view. It is likely that the term 'kimono' became more widespread during the Edo period, although because *ōsode* continued to be worn, it was still more common to refer to this type of garment as *kosode*.

At the beginning of the Meiji period, when the power of the Emperor was restored and an age of

Kosode and kimono characteristics

The most commonly noted characteristic of *kosode* and kimono is that they are straight-seamed garments. They are made from lengths of cloth, cut across the grain, which drape over the shoulder and hang all the way down the body to the hem. A

sleeve	sleeve	neckband	over-collar	body	body
		overlap	overlap		

central seam down the back joins the two lengths of cloth, to which sleeves are attached. Separate pieces of fabric are used to form the neckband and collar, and then the lining is added (fig. 3). The garment is wrapped around the body, left side over right, and secured with a sash (obi). The length can be altered for height by drawing up excess fabric under the obi, and other adjustments made to suit the wearer, but essentially all adult kimono are the same basic shape and size. This method of cutting cloth and creating garments is very unlike that used in the West, the result of different attitudes towards clothing. At the heart of this lie notions about the relationship between dress and the body, and whether garments emphasize the wearer's shape or lessen its presence.

With kimono, the emphasis is never on the shape of the wearer's body, but always on the garment itself. The method of construction, with the body and sleeves forming a continuous flat plane, means that from the back the kimono has the form of a large 'T', which provides a more suitable platform for the design than the front. Evidence that the back was considered the aesthetic focus of women's dress in the Edo period can be seen in surviving garments and in pattern books (*hinagata-bon*), which, with very few exceptions, contain designs that only depict the back of the *kosode* (fig. 4).

The implication is that, within the aesthetics of Japanese dress, little regard is paid to the presence of the body inside the kimono. It is interesting to consider the pose seen in Hishikawa Moronobu's *Beauty Looking Back* (fig. 5), in which both the face of the woman and whole of the back of the *kosode* she is wearing are visible. The painting demonstrates the ingenious compositional devices that Japanese artists used to allow both the beauty of the clothing and that of the wearer to be viewed. In western dress, there is great emphasis on the body. The focus of decorative attention is generally at the front, and women's clothes in particular have traditionally been constructed to emphasize the bust, waist, hips or buttocks, often with the use of supporting devices to alter the shape and accentuate the profile of the female form.

The formal and conceptual characteristics of Japanese dress make it unlike that of western and other cultures, the most distinctive feature being the significance, importance and sheer variety of surface designs. Despite, or indeed because of, the separation of the body and the garment, *kosode* and kimono offer great scope for the expression

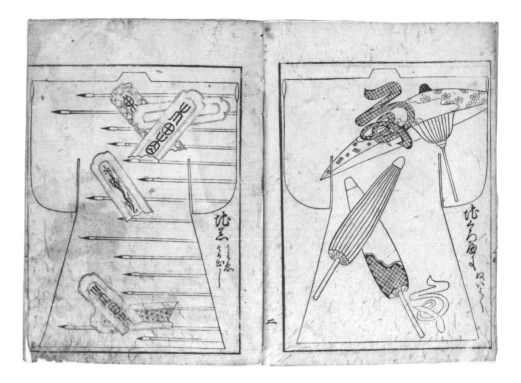

of sartorial beauty. The fact that the focus of interest is on the surface decoration, rather than cut, explains why, over the long history of these garments, their shape underwent almost no change. Gender, class, status and the spirit of the age were expressed not through modifications to cut and construction as in the West, but by changes in fabric, colour, pattern and decorative technique.

Women's kosode and kimono

Japan's long history of expressing status through clothing meant that in the Edo period, as before, men whose lives were spent in the public arena (*omote*) of officialdom had little liberty to choose what they wore. As the codification of clothing played such an important role in maintaining the class system, there was little scope in men's *kosode* for the reflection of individual taste manifested in the rich variety of women's clothing. The style of men's clothing changed very little over time, and fashionableness was of almost no concern.

The private arena (*oku*) was the opposite. Despite the existence of strict dress codes in the public sphere, women, whose lives were spent in the private realm, were generally allowed a considerable degree of freedom in their choice of clothing, as long as they did not overstep the boundaries of social acceptability. Women of

fig. 4
Hishikawa Moronobu (1618–94)
Hishikawa Moyō
(Kimono designs by Hishikawa)

Book, woodblock on paper
Edo period, c. 1675–80
Victoria and Albert Museum, London

fig. 5
Hishikawa Moronobu (1618–94)
Beauty Looking Back

Hanging scroll (detail), ink and colour on paper
Edo period, c. 1670–90
Tokyo National Museum

the Edo period were able to reflect their cultural sensibilities and aesthetic preferences in the *kosode* they wore in different ways, according to class and status. This gave rise to stylistic differences specific to particular periods in time and the development of an exciting fashion culture.

In the Meiji period, despite the use of key words such as *ishin* (restoration) and *bunmei kaika* (civilization and enlightenment), change did not always occur rapidly or uniformly. Westernization was spearheaded by the government, but the speed and degree to which it took place varied according to class, gender and realm of activity. In the case of dress, westernization began with men of the aristocratic and samurai class who stood at the centre of the new polity, followed a little later by women from the same backgrounds. Women of less elevated status, however, continued to wear kimono during and after the Meiji era for both everyday and formal occasions. The styles of kimono worn by women from the Meiji period onwards were essentially the same as those worn by female townspeople during the Edo period, although the late Meiji, Taishō and early Shōwa (1926–89) eras did see the development of bold colour schemes and dramatic design compositions that reflected the modern world.

Furisode

'Kimono' often conjures up an image of what is actually a more specific item of dress, the *furisode* (literally, 'swinging sleeves'). In its broadest sense, the term refers to garments with sleeves that swing because only part of them are stitched to the body, and therefore can include *katabira* (unlined bast fibre kimono worn in summer), *hitoe* (unlined silk kimono, also worn in summer) and *uchikake* (lined silk kimono with a wadded hem, worn without a sash as an outer kimono on formal occasions). While *kosode* would normally be the umbrella term to refer to all such garments, *furisode* refers specifically to a lined silk kimono with fine wadding – but not worn as a *uchikake* – and swinging sleeves, which in the Edo period grew increasingly long.

Furisode first appeared during the Muromachi and Momoyama periods. Documents and paintings of the time indicate that they were worn mainly by children. They were not, however, referred to as *furisode*, nor did they have particularly long sleeves. In *Nihon Furisode Hajime* (*The Origins of Furisode in Japan*) of 1718, Chikamatsu Monzaemon notes that *furisode* originated as a form of clothing for young men and women, in which the undersides of the sleeves were left unstitched and open to compensate for Japan's hot, humid climate. Similarly, Ise Sadatake's *Sadatake Zakki* (*Miscellaneous Antiquarian Writings of Ise Sadatake*) of 1846 mentions that part of the sleeve is left unstitched beneath the armpit. He explains that this was devised as a form of ventilation to regulate the body temperature of children aged seventeen and below, whose temperature was higher than that of adults. Sadatake also states that in the past garments of this kind were called *wakiake* ('open armpits') rather than *furisode*, and that they did not have long sleeves.

These descriptions indicate that at the beginning of the early modern period, swinging sleeves were a purely practical device and not the decorative feature that distinguished later *furisode*. Sadatake goes on to note how the sleeve length of *furisode* increased over time, from about 45 cm (18 in.) in the 1660s to 63 cm (25 in.) in the 1690s, and to about 88 cm (35 in.) in the 1750s. Late Edo-period *furisode* with long sleeves were worn by young women, as can be seen in many paintings and prints of the time (fig. 6). The format of clothing worn by young women and children was essentially the same. The only difference was decorative, with children's *furisode* usually patterned with designs that reflected parental wishes for good fortune and avoidance of evil spirits. By the late eighteenth century, the principal purpose of long sleeves in adult dress had become, as today, purely a means of enhancing the attractiveness of the garment and the young woman wearing it.

While the shape of the kimono remained largely unchanged during the Edo period, there was, as we have seen, a constant process of experimentation with designs appropriate for men and women of different ages. The same was true of the Meiji period and afterwards, when the introduction of western technology such as synthetic dyes expanded the colour palette, and the use of western-style motifs further broadened the design repertoire. The widespread adoption of western clothing after the Second World War resulted in the decline of kimono production. Yet the kimono's importance remains secure, and today it continues to be both a significant vehicle for the exploration of contemporary sensibilities and a potent reflection of Japanese tradition.

I
EDO

1603
–
1868

Governing, spending and wearing in the Edo period

TIMON SCREECH

Japan during the Edo period (1603–1868) may be considered a federal state. Some 280 regional lords, or *daimyō* (literally, 'great landholders'), governed a country known to most people as the Tenka ('below Heaven'), or, in contradistinction with the Asian mainland, Honchō ('this Realm'). Superior to the *daimyō* was the shogunal family, the Tokugawa, who controlled around a fifth of the Tenka as their privileged holdings, 'the lands of Heavenly Command' (*tenryō*). *Daimyō* states were of varying size – some about that of a small European country, others little more than a town and its environs – and they all had their rights, duties and skills. It is necessary to investigate the nexus of rule that pertained to the Tenka of the Edo period to establish how its cultures of dress, comportment and consumption operated.

Production and practice in the Edo-period Tenka

The cluster of collaborating and competing states that made up the Tenka differed widely from one another in terms of culture, religious affiliation, food, crops and livestock, and were as unalike in terms of terrain and weather as the furthest reaches of northern Europe are from the Mediterranean. From the snow-bound vastness of Tōhoku to the orange-growing south of Kyūshū, there was both abundance and variety. The different regional accents and dialects were all but mutually incomprehensible languages. It is wrong to think of the Tenka as anything akin to the modern nation-state of Japan, although, in time, the one grew out of the other.

But the Tenka was not just a mass of disparate units. It had a number of nodes that functioned like magnets, drawing the regions together. These were the great cities, foremost of which were the Three Ports (*sanga no tsu*), although of these only two were actually coastal. Kyō, also called Keishi (or more formally Kyōto, its modern name), was inland, while Osaka and Edo (modern-day Tokyo) were by the sea. The addition of the ports of Sakai and Nagasaki

created a group known as the Five Royal Cities. Collectively, these cities may have been home to about a quarter of the Tenka's population, indicating – importantly – a high degree of urbanization. These five cities were incorporated into the lands of Heavenly Command (hence the term 'royal'), as was the great city of Owari (modern Nagoya), making a sixth. It was recognized that no *daimyō* should be permitted to control an area capable of generating a Tenka-wide economic pull. But several regional cities were also large, and could boast sophistication and plenty, offering hinterlands and areas further afield enticing visions of art, goods, literacy, learning – and decadence.

The Three Ports were supreme, and they alone would have conjured up certain images to all inhabitants of the archipelago. Osaka was the entrepôt for most regional production, and was popularly known as the 'Tenka's kitchen'. Rice, also a unit of currency, was transported there for redistribution; cloth was imported from the weaving and dyeing centres; and lumber yards dispatched wood as required. Like most cities, Osaka was centred around a castle. In the *daimyō*'s capital cities, the castle was the residence of the ruler and focus of his administration, but in the case of the Royal Cities the castle belonged to the shogun, who was elsewhere, and so was unoccupied for much of the time. Some of the Five Cities had a governor, who was sometimes a shogunal relative. Osaka had a powerful castle representative (*jōdai*), who was not a relative and was given only a small support staff. The city thus had very few members of the military-bureaucratic class. While in other areas of dense population samurai might constitute one or two in every dozen people, Osaka had only a few hundred in total. It seemed, therefore, a more liberated city, where merchants were free to engage in unfettered money-making or in more relaxed pursuits.

Kyō, only a day's walk from Osaka, was very different. It was also built around a castle, although one perpetually unoccupied as the shogun never went there, nor did he assign a relative or representative to take up position in it. Kyō was governed by a plenipotentiary known as the *shōshidai*, one of whose tasks was to liaise with the court and the figure known today as the 'emperor', though at this time he had no imperium. Throughout the Edo period, this shadowy individual was known to most people as the *shujō* ('master above'). No one knew his name, but all were dimly aware that such a person existed, keeping alive the twin flames of ritual and tradition. Kyō had a carefully honed air of antiquity, although, like all the Royal Cities, it was new in material fabric. Horrific wars lasting for most of the sixteenth century and not a little of the fifteenth had laid waste to the city, and hardly any architecture, bridges, gardens, wells or ditches survived. People lived in an urban spread of recent erection. Antiquity was only tangible in outlying parts, such as Kyō's hilly outskirts, in chattels or in toponyms.

Thirdly there was Edo, the locus of the centralizing shogunal power. Created from nothing at the end of the warring period, by the mid-eighteenth century Edo was the largest city on earth. The Tokugawa, before their accession to shogunal rank, moved to the fertile Kantō region following the success of their allies at the Battle of Odawara. The area was potentially rich, but underdeveloped. The coastal plain stood in marked contrast to the precipitous slopes and uplands of much of Japan. The head of the family, Tokugawa Ieyasu (1543–1616), then a battle-scarred warlord approaching fifty, began to turn the unimpressive, dilapidated

town of Edo – set on a bluff where the River Sumida meets a wide bay that opens into the Pacific Ocean – into a city that would symbolize his aspirations to (re-)unify the Tenka. When Ieyasu died in 1616, he had brought peace to most of Japan, established the lands of Heavenly Command and forced the *daimyō* – some willingly, some grudgingly – to accept the priority of his house. Another aspect of unification under the Tokugawa was the controlling of overseas trade and the de-Christianization of the Japanese population, many of whom (though the number is uncertain) had been converted by Iberian and Italian missionaries during the chaos of the civil war.

In time Edo grew to rival the Osaka/Kyō region (the Kamigata), and by the second century of Tokugawa rule it was being referred to as Tōto, 'the Eastern Metropolis', in explicit contrast to Kyōto, 'the Capital Metropolis' (where the emperor lived). Moreover, to some, Edo was no longer 'eastern' but central, with the Kamigata relegated to the fringe. All government highways were said to start in Edo; the city centre (Edo being the first East Asian city to be given an iconic centre, probably as a result of missionaries' comments about the organization of European cities) was called Nihon-bashi, 'bridge of Japan'. Edo was the centre and the core.

The fact that Edo was a military city was to have a huge bearing throughout its history, even as it mutated from warrior base to a city of genuine culture. Upon arrival in Edo, a man from Kyō could

fig. 1
Procession to Edo by the Daimyō of Owari
*Handscroll, ink and colour on paper, c. 1800
Tokugawa Art Museum, Nagoya*

still observe in the early nineteenth century that, when he 'saw all the *daimyō* and lesser lords with their pikes and banners', he was tempted to think 'we were still in time of war'.[1] The streets of Edo had considerable bravura; 'men of the East' adopted a swaggering gait and were deemed necessarily rough and tough. By contrast, the anciently settled regions were 'effeminate'. This was cultural cliché: there was enough elegance in Edo, and enough rudeness in Kyō, to satisfy most appetites. But as the regions struggled to formulate their identities, a triple division was established: Edo was virile and strong; Kyō old and punctilious; Osaka financially absorbed. It was argued that children born in Kyō were more likely to be girls, whereas those born in Edo would be boys.[2] A traveller to Kyō from Edo in the late eighteenth century was intrigued to find that 70 per cent of the city's population was indeed female, whereas in his hometown it was the reverse.[3]

In a sense, our traveller was stating an empirical truth, even if the medical reasoning was wayward. Because of the shogunal presence, Edo had a congregation of officers and staffers unlike any other city. Samurai in direct shogunal employ (*hatamoto*, known in English as 'bannermen'), numbered in the thousands, but that figure rose in 1635 when the third shogun, Tokugawa Iemitsu (1604–51), instituted a system of 'alternate attendance' (*sankin kōkai*), under which all *daimyō* had to spend one year in two in Edo and to leave their principal wife and nominated heir there permanently. There was a colossal to-ing and fro-ing as retinues arrived in the city and returned to their country seats. Processions could take hours to file past and were made up of several hundred men at a minimum (fig. 1). Whereas the bannermen and other shogunal servants resided in Edo with their families, it made no economic sense for *daimyō* to permit their entourage to bring dependants with them. Edo thus became a city of interim bachelors; men were there to work, but they also needed their distractions.

How do you keep a city of bachelors under control? How do you retain the proprieties of the family in a town of 70 per cent men, most of whom are exposed to the liberating experience of being alone in a foreign city for a whole year? And how do you square this with the requirements of dignified comportment in (as they called it) 'the lap of the shogun' (*shōgun no hizamoto*)? From this dilemma emerged a culture of extravagance and showing off that, in time, created the 'Floating World' (*ukiyo*).

The Floating World

It was in Osaka, the merchant city, that a culture of unchecked hedonism first appeared. Osaka had a gender balance, and most men lived at home, but decent women did not stray far, and social expectations made cross-gender fraternization hard to orchestrate. In 1682, a wish-fulfilling bestseller set the tone for what was to come: *Life of a Sex-mad Man (Kōshoku ichidai otoko)*, by Ihara Saikaku (1642–93).[4] Over the course of the book the hero, Yonosuke ('man of the world'), an Osaka merchant, sleeps with hundreds of women and a good few men; to make the story more convincing, the author tells the reader he has done about as much himself. To achieve real success Saikaku had to penetrate Edo's larger market, and here – in a city where people did not know who their neighbours were, and who might never encounter again those they met on the streets – he was a success, too (fig. 2).

fig. 2
***The Five Sex-mad Women
(Kōshoku gonin onna)***
Book, woodblock on paper, 1686
Private collection

To curb potential excesses, the shogunate's first means of control were the sumptuary laws (see p. 27), which defined who might consume what, from dress to personal adornment to domestic furnishings. Punishments for disobedience were strict, although enforcement went through periods of laxity as well as severity, and bribery was common. Such regulations were applied to all classes, but the samurai were especially closely watched. It should be pointed out, however, that the ultimate sanction against the samurai – enforced suicide by disembowelment (*seppuku*) – is largely a modern myth and did not in fact happen.[5]

By 1617 the shogunate had decided to accept the suggestion of an enterprising Edo townsman and set up an official red-light district (*kuruwa*) in an attempt to keep sexual predators and spendthrifts off the streets; here, the sumptuary laws and class-based rigidities would be suspended. The zone was constructed near Nihon-bashi at a site called Yoshiwara ('reed fields'), but the place name was soon rewritten with the homophone 'happy fields'. In the 1640s, other cities were also required to move their sex workers and late-night entertainers into segregated areas. After a great fire in Edo in 1657, the Yoshiwara was moved out to the suburbs, making it harder to access, although also making

it less easy to police. The licensed quarters were seldom large enough to accommodate all who wished to go, and many cities developed extra-legal, though tolerated, additional places.

These quarters – emblematically the Yoshiwara, or, after 1657, the Shin ('New') Yoshiwara – formed one half of the Floating World. The other was the theatre district, where another kind of wish-fulfilment was on offer, on the kabuki stage (fig. 3). Although in Edo the Yoshiwara was relocated after the fire, the theatre district was allowed to stay in the city centre, as women were permitted to attend plays and it would not do to have them traipsing off to the suburbs. All actors were male, and while the Yoshiwara catered only for heterosexual encounters, the theatres stood in to offer male prostitution, whether for men or women. It was not thought odd that the huge numbers of unmarried Edo women (many in domestic service) sought the company of actors and other theatrical hangers-on, nor was virginity particularly expected before marriage, at least not among townswomen.

It is important to note the role that images of the Floating World (*ukiyo-e*) had in undermining civic propriety. This form of depiction came into existence about the time that Saikaku was writing. It went through many stylistic and technological

fig. 3
Hishikawa Moronobu (1618–94)
Kabuki Theatre
Six-fold screen, colour and gold-leaf on paper,
17th century
Tokyo National Museum

changes, though always it represented aspects of urban culture that the more formal schools of painting would not deign to show. Some artists had specific preferences, though most depicted both the theatre and the bordellos, actors and courtesans. Such pictures tended to be set in Edo's loveliest season, spring, with the cherry blossoming, or at the happy time of New Year, with plum blossoms. Paintings were produced for wealthier or more extravagant clients, but most images were printed. Perhaps the greatest flowering came a century later in 1765, with the commercialization of full-colour printing, first undertaken by Suzuki Harunobu, who after his death in 1770 left behind hundreds of designs as testament to the huge scale of the industry (fig. 4).

Contestation

A woodblock by the famed nineteenth-century artist Katsushika Hokusai (fig. 5) appears to be an icon of propriety, as the Tokugawa regime would have conceived it. As a print it was widely available, and was fashionable in the way that other popular images of the time were, incorporating Western perspective and the newly arrived pigment Berlin blue (or *bero*). It shows not the Floating World, but the 'fixed' world of work and rule. By this point – the 1830s – souvenir images of Edo's civic spaces had become common and were tolerated by the authorities as long as they were respectful of official hierarchies. This print is part of a series on the theme of Mount Fuji, most of which are not set in Edo itself. But Fuji was visible from the city and indeed, as the picture shows, the central area of Nihon-bashi had been laid out to incorporate its soaring peak.

At the bottom of the print, on the bridge itself, are the commoners, forced into a small strip of space. Stretching along the canal are the storehouses of the castle's official suppliers; the quiet order of the serried rows suggests plenty, but also regulation. The artist has used perspective as a way of extending this vector of shogunal power and provision. Indeed, perspective is a kind of privileged city space here: the compressed commoners do not share in it. There is a third pictorial space, also outside the perspective system: the castle. The towers should be distant and much lower down. What Hokusai seems to be saying is that society has a triple make-up: commoners (of whom he was

one), who are subservient; official merchants, whose business it is to provide necessaries for the state, for which purpose (only) they are allotted room to manoeuvre; and the regime itself, which cannot be held within any imposed logic. It is unto itself, aloft and detached, governing but ungoverned, surmounted by one thing only, Mount Fuji, the name of which – *fu ji* – puns on 'not two' (in other words, unique) and 'not death' (immortal). This is indeed how the shogunate liked to propose itself. Hokusai and his publisher were toeing the line; not everyone did so.

From the mid-eighteenth century, just about the time that the norms of the Floating World began to have repercussions throughout the city, the

fig. 4
Suzuki Harunobu (1724–70)
Parading Courtesan with Attendants
Print, woodblock on paper, late 1760s
Victoria and Albert Museum, London

shogunate was faced with significant challenges. This had been foretold in the eruption of Mount Fuji in 1707, which disfigured its perfect symmetry (discretely obscured by Hokusai). A run of bad harvests later in the century brought destitution, but also arrogant urban disregard in a classic case of the wealthy spending all the more furiously as others sank into poverty. Edo was blamed. As one social critic observed: 'When a country samurai with his good old ways comes up to Edo, in just two or three years his whole character will have transformed, with his manners becoming superficial and trivial.'[6] Fashionable trends, in other words, will overtake established patterns. The writer, Yuasa Genzō, continued: 'Urban people's customs go from bad to worse; they are like so many floating cherry blossoms.' The metaphor is telling. Unfortunate alterations, Genzō notes, affected 'newly arrived samurai, whose devotion to propriety naturally wanes; whereas they might previously have had affection for literature or military practice, they soon give these up in favour of artistic pursuits.' These 'artistic pursuits' (geiji) are regarded as showy and unreal accomplishments. Another writer, Ōta Nanpo, expressed the same sentiment:

> The money squandered was regarded as an index of a person's standing. Fans were opened just halfway and held loosely in the hand [i.e. uselessly]; no one was without his imported European pocket watch, slipped in at the fold of his costume [you cannot tell Japanese time with a European watch]. In summer and winter [sweaty and slushy seasons], it was crisp, white socks. Truly, all these fashions were hardly much help towards 'military might in the service of peace' [taiheibu].[7]

These comments were made at the same time that Hokusai was working. Several government reforms had been attempted, but had failed to stop the rise of fashion. In fact, there had been no single trajectory from early order to later disorder. The Tenka was, and always had been, like anywhere else, a place of virtue and dishonour, profligacy and restraint. But it is nevertheless true that criticisms increased over time. This catalogue celebrates 'artistic pursuits', and very fine they are, too. Yet they worried some people, all the more so as the relative wealth of the samurai dropped against that of the merchant class. The Tokugawa regime had no self-righting mechanism. When faced with problems, the shogunate could think of nothing but attempting to turn back the clock. After 250 years – a very long time – exhausted, it collapsed.

fig. 5
Katsushika Hokusai (1760–1849)
Bridge of Japan (Nihon-bashi),
from *Thirty-six Views of Mount Fuji*
Print, woodblock on paper, c. 1832
Victoria and Albert Museum, London

Dress in the Edo period: the evolution of fashion

ANNA JACKSON

Within the world of material culture, dress is one of the most expressive and significant items. How we clothe ourselves is a personal, intimate matter, yet it is simultaneously very public. Variations in cut, colour and pattern communicate information about our gender, age, status, wealth and taste, and we make assumptions about others based on what they wear. In Japan, clothing's capacity to convey meaning has long been acknowledged in literature, and the excitement aroused by new styles and designs reflected in paintings and prints. During the Edo period, there was a great flowering of the textile arts as an increased market for luxury kimono proved a catalyst for both technical developments and the emergence of a vibrant fashion culture.

The ruling military class, or samurai, were the primary consumers of sumptuous kimono. In the past their status and wealth had derived from success on the battlefield, but the peace of the Edo period denied them such opportunities to distinguish themselves. Instead the emphasis was on impressive appearances, especially when the system of alternate attendance (*sankin kōkai*; see p. 16) meant *daimyō* had to maintain a residence and lifestyle that needed to be as lavish, if not more so, than their neighbour's. The samurai were at the top of a strict social structure that served to consolidate and preserve the power of the Tokugawa dynasty. Next in the hierarchy came the farmers, who produced the most important commodity, food, then the artisans and finally the merchants, who were viewed as mere distributors of the work of others. The artisans and merchants were often identified together as *chōnin*, or townspeople.

This Confucian concept of the natural order of society became inconsistent with reality, however, as it was the merchants who most benefited from Edo-period prosperity and the increase in demand for goods and services. Samurai had a fixed income and often struggled to live within their means, becoming indebted to rich merchants from whom they were forced to borrow money. The latter were unable to use their economic position to improve their social status, so many channelled their wealth and energies towards the pursuit of pleasure and the acquisition of material luxuries. The dynamic urban culture that emerged in the Edo period was vividly recorded by the writer Ihara Saikaku (1642–93). In *Nihon Eitaigura (Japan's Treasury of the Ages)*, published in 1688, he commented on the extravagant lifestyle of the merchant class, particularly when it came to clothing:

> Fashions have changed from those of the past and have become increasingly ostentatious. In everything people have a liking for finery above their station.... In recent years, certain shrewd Kyoto people have started to lavish every manner of magnificence on men's and women's clothes and to put out design books in colour. With modish fine-figured patterns, palace-style hundred-colour prints, and bled dapple tie-dye, they go to the limit for unusual designs to suit any taste.[1]

Dress, one of the most visible of the arts, proved the perfect means by which the merchant class could proclaim its affluence and aesthetic sensibility. It was the merchants' desire for new and exciting kimono designs that provided the stimulus for increased textile production.

Kimono techniques

The weaving, dyeing and embroidery techniques for which Japan is famed reached their peak of technical sophistication during the Edo period.[2] Many methods had a long history, while others were newly developed. The sixteenth century saw the introduction from China of two fabrics that were to have an enormous impact on kimono production: *rinzu*, a monochrome figured satin silk similar to damask, normally woven with a key fret and small flower pattern (*sayagata*), although from the nineteenth century larger designs were employed; and *chirimen* (crepe), a plain weave silk with a crimped, matt appearance produced by over-twisting the weft threads.[3]

fig. 1
Baiyōken Katsunobu (fl. 1716–35)
Standing Woman
Hanging scroll, ink and colour on paper, 1700–15
Asian Art Museum, San Francisco

were also used. Some Kyoto dye houses specialized in a single colour, but most produced a spectrum of hues. The dye recipes, which allowed for the creation of numerous shades and tones from what was a fairly limited number of plant sources, were carefully guarded secrets. Designs were created with a variety of resist-dyeing techniques: selectively pre-dyeing threads prior to weaving, as in *kasuri*; binding, stitching, folding or clamping cloth prior to immersion, a technique called *shibori*; or by applying rice paste through stencils (*katazome*) or freehand (*yūzen*).[4]

In *yūzen*, one of the most important technical developments of the Edo period, a paper tube fitted with a metal tip is used to apply a thin ribbon of rice paste to the outline of a drawing on the fabric, and dyes are brushed within the paste boundaries. The paste is then washed away. This technique allowed for extremely detailed patterning and gave kimono designers almost unlimited freedom of expression. It is named after the seventeenth-century artist Miyazaki Yūzen (1654?–1736) who, already famous for his elegant fan paintings, began to design motifs for kimono. *Yūzen Patterns (Yūzen Hiinakata)*, published in 1688, explains that:

> Miyazaki Yūzen is not just a distinguished painter ... contemporary, sophisticated people praise his work. All women, from the wives and daughters of high-ranking families to maids, yearn to wear a kimono designed by Yūzen.[5]

It is not clear to what extent Yūzen was actually involved in the dyeing process. While he may have initially painted directly onto the clothing of his patrons, it is likely that he subsequently provided the kimono design, while specialist artisans created the finished garment. What this quote does imply, however, is that by the late seventeenth century a wide spectrum of Edo society would clamour for kimono created by a famous designer. The publication of the book also indicates a marketing strategy that both created and fed such a desire.

Kimono patterns

Paintings of the early Edo period reveal that at this time there were no substantial differences between the kimono worn by different sexes (see p. 17), but by the end of the seventeenth century,

Rinzu and *chirimen* provided the ground fabric for complex embroidery and dyeing techniques. Embroiderers used a myriad of colours and a range of stitches, including flat stitch (*hira-nui*), to create pattern elements such as flowers and leaves, and long and short stitches (*sashi-nui*) to define larger areas, both executed with floss (untwisted) silk to give a rich sheen. Twisted threads and knot stitches added texture, while metallic threads were used to dazzling effect. The latter, made from a silk core wrapped in paper and then with gold or silver leaf, were couched onto the fabric with tiny stitches. Embroidery was often used in conjunction with dyeing, the varied techniques creating an interesting combination of visual effects. When it was the sole decorative method, it was commonly executed on *shusu* (satin), a smooth, shimmering fabric in which long floats are created by passing the weft over or under four or more warps.

The colours used to pattern fabric, as well as the silk threads used in embroidery, came predominantly from dyes extracted from vegetable sources, although pigments derived from minerals distinctions had become more pronounced. Sleeve lengths began to vary and patterns on women's kimono became larger and bolder, the garments of younger women being especially richly decorated and brightly coloured. Prior to the Edo period, kimono design had featured continuous patterning on a ground that was divided into geometric sections, but by the early seventeenth century the fabric surface was being divided into irregular pattern areas. All forms of compartmentalization finally gave way to an approach that considered the garment as a whole, in which technique and motif, pattern and ground, were fully integrated.

By the end of the century, a fresh aesthetic had evolved that focused on dynamic and often very large, unified motifs. This can be seen in the bold kimono designs of Hishikawa Moronobu (1618–94), an artist who came from a family of Kyoto textile dyers (see p. 10). In the early eighteenth century a new style emerged, due in part to the increasing width of the obi, in which the pattern below the waist differed from that above. Later, the torso area was often left completely blank as motifs moved further down the garment. The chōnin favoured patterns concentrated around the hem, a trend that continued into the Meiji period. While these styles usually relied on subtle, small-scale patterns, the more exuberant tastes of wealthier merchants of the nineteenth century are revealed in lavishly decorated outer kimono, which have all-over designs.

The images used to decorate kimono often have complex levels of meaning and auspicious significance deriving from religious or popular beliefs. The use of particular motifs can allude to the virtues or attributes of the wearer, reflect particular emotions or relate to the season or occasion. Such symbolism was used especially on kimono worn for celebratory events, such as weddings, when it served to bestow good fortune on the wearer, wrapping them in divine benevolence and protection. Colours, too, have strong metaphorical and cultural connotations. Perhaps the most popular colour for kimono was red, derived from safflower (benibana).[6] Red connoted youthful glamour and allure, and was thus particularly suitable for the garments of young women. As beni-red fades easily, it was also a symbol of passionate but transient love.

Nature provided the richest source for kimono motifs. Elements of the natural world often had strong poetic associations, while more complex landscape scenes could refer to stories drawn from classical literature or myths. The increased

market for luxury kimono among the chōnin led to a broadening of the visual repertoire to include aspects of popular culture and visual puns. Motifs served to demonstrate the taste and discernment of the wearer, something particularly apparent in the use of characters (fig. 1). The use of calligraphy as a design motif, and the fact that this hanging scroll is mounted with kimono fabric, demonstrate the close connection that existed between the textile and other arts. The relationship between kimono design and painting, and the cultural pre-eminence of the former, is revealed in a passage from Life of a Sex-mad Man (Kōshoku ichidai otoko), one of Ihara Saikaku's most celebrated novels (see p. 16):

> The courtesan Kaoru commissioned the renowned artist Kano Yukinoku to paint a picture of flaming autumn on plain white satin. Eight court nobles were next asked to inscribe vignettes in verse, in black decorative calligraphy, on this gorgeous design. The result was a picture of breathtaking beauty, admirably suitable for a hanging scroll. But Kaoru had no idea of putting it to such trifling use. She had it made into a robe for herself.[7]

While the identity of most of those who designed kimono are not known, extant examples by Ogata Kōrin (1658–1716), Sakai Hōitsu (1761–1828)

fig. 2
Nishikawa Sukenobu (1671–1750)
Pictures of Beautiful Women
Book, woodblock on paper, 1736
Victoria and Albert Museum, London

and Matsumura Goshun (1752–1811) reveal that famous artists did engage in kimono design. Hishikawa Moronobu also designed kimono. The influence of particular schools of art, such as Rinpa, Nanga and Maruyama, and the subject matter itself – landscapes, scenes from literature, and even painting formats such as scrolls and fans – show the correlation between kimono design and painting.[8]

The straight lines of the T-shaped kimono certainly served as a kind of blank canvas, or scroll, for designers. But it is important to remember that whatever concept underlay the disposition of pattern on the garment surface, kimono are not two- but three-dimensional, and move in space with the wearer. Indeed, one can see from the art of the Edo period that donning the various layers of kimono, along with the obi and other accessories, was complex, and the question of what to wear was

a carefully considered one (fig. 2). A woman would be judged not by her physical appearance, but by her dress, as is evident in paintings and prints, where it is the detailed depiction of the kimono, not the face, that gives the viewer a sense of personality. Some works have textiles as their explicit theme (fig. 3), and there is a whole genre of screen painting from the early Edo period that has as its subject matter the representation of kimono draped over racks or screens (fig. 4). This theme derives from the practice of airing clothing, which in itself evolved into a form of interior display replicated by the painted screens. The seemingly abstract juxtaposition of garments conveys an elaborate message in much the same way as wearing particular kimono would have done. These screens are known as *tagasode*, or 'whose sleeves', a term used in classical Japanese poetry to allude to a beautiful woman who is not present.

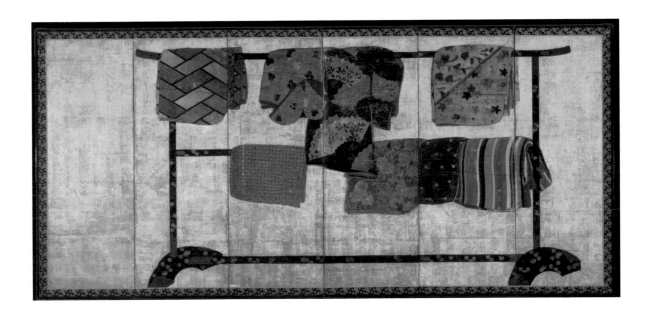

The kimono business

The textile industry played a crucial role in the economic life of Edo-period Japan. Although the capital experienced the greatest growth in population and consumption, Kyoto remained the centre of luxury production. In the early eighteenth century, Nishijin, the textile-weaving quarter of Kyoto, had an estimated 7,000 looms and provided employment for tens of thousands of artisans. A fire in 1730 destroyed over 3,000 of these looms, and resulted in the move of some weavers to provincial areas where silk spinning and weaving expanded rapidly, although much finished cloth was still sent to Kyoto for patterning. At the same time, domestic sericulture was flourishing in northern Japan and in the Kantō region around Edo, while cotton cultivation also had a major economic and social impact.[9] Many farmers began to both grow and process this very profitable plant, and by the beginning of the nineteenth century rural producers were able to compete with urban artisans and merchants in the supply of finished goods.

The simplicity of kimono construction meant that garments could be sewn together in the home. Many households, particularly in rural areas, also had their own loom, and a woman's sewing and weaving abilities were considered very important. The creation of sumptuous silk kimono required the skills of specialist artisans, however, the majority of whom were men. The business supported an

fig. 5
Okumura Masanobu (1686–1764)
Large Perspective View of the Interior of Echigo-ya in Suruga-chô
Print, woodblock on paper, c. 1745
Museum of Fine Arts, Boston

extensive network of artisans that included spinners, weavers, dyers, embroiderers, specialist thread suppliers, stencil makers and designers. At the heart of the industry were the drapery stores, the most famous of which was the Echigo-ya in Edo, founded by Mitsui Takatoshi (1622–94) in 1673. Mitsui targeted his business to the *chōnin*, realizing that this was the more lucrative end of the market. He also recognized the power of advertising, and had his logo prominently displayed on the shop's doorway curtains (*noren*), on packaging and on the umbrellas he distributed to customers when it rained (fig. 5).

While people could visit Echigo-ya to buy cloth, wealthier clients were served at home by individual merchants or specialist co-ordinators, known as *shikkai*, who would orchestrate the activities of various workshops involved in the creation of individually commissioned kimono.[10] The fashionable brocades shown in the print by Kunisada have been delivered in a box and wrapping cloth (*furoshiki*) bearing the emblem of Daimaru, a kimono store founded in Kyoto in 1717 (fig. 3). A book on the cultivation of silk, published in 1786, has as its final illustration an image of an employee of the Echigo-ya showing two women bolts of cloth and a design of a kimono to help them visualize the final garment (fig. 6). The publication of pattern books (*hinagata-bon*), were an important innovation in the area of customer choice. While individual samurai households were provided with designs hand-drawn in ink (see p. 30), woodblock-printed *hinagata-bon* served a wider *chōnin* audience.[11]

fig. 6
Shunshō Katsugawa (1726–93)
and Shigemasa Kitao (1739–1820)
The Cultivation of Silk Worms
Book, woodblock on paper, 1786
Victoria and Albert Museum, London

Various types of pattern books were published, but the most common contained illustrations of the back of a kimono with accompanying notes on colour and pattern (see p. 10). *Hinagata-bon* were read by the makers and sellers of kimono, as well as by the women who wore them, and in a world that craved the latest designs, they became indispensable. There also existed books that showed the kimono being worn, although these served more as a pleasurable diversion than as a practical tool (fig. 2).

Kimono fashion

The emergence of fashion is often seen as a uniquely European phenomenon, while the 'traditional' dress of other cultures is deemed static.[12] Yet the merchant-class desire for the latest kimono designs, the stimulus this provided to production and the subsequent commercial exploitation of consumer demand by textile makers, sellers and publishers all point to the existence in Edo-period Japan of something we would recognize today as a fashion industry.

Fashion is, by definition, transitory. As such it very much belonged within the 'floating world' (*ukiyo*) of entertainment, glamour and eroticism that developed in the urban centres of the Edo period (see pp. 16–18). This had its focus in the licensed pleasure quarters, and here fashion flourished. Courtesans needed to wear the most gorgeous clothes possible in order to attract custom, and one of the great spectacles of the Yoshiwara, the brothel district of Edo, was the procession of the highest-ranking courtesans dressed in the most sumptuous of garments (fig. 7). Despite the often tragic realities of life in the sex trade, the Yoshiwara captured public imagination. Courtesans became major figures and trendsetters, providing models of the most elegant and up-to-date styles and tastes. Those without the wealth to participate directly in the floating world were able to buy woodblock prints of the most famous beauties. The attention and detail artists lavished on the costumes of these women are a testament to the important role fashion played in the Yoshiwara and beyond. Prints of known courtesans wearing the most fashionable kimono served as wonderful publicity for brothel owners and clothing merchants alike (fig. 8).

The kabuki theatre district was also at the heart of the floating world. This was a place to see and be seen, and from the early eighteenth century it became the custom for the richest patrons to change their clothing a number of times during the day-long performances in order to show off as many outfits as possible. The leading kabuki actors were the great idols of their era, and the colours, patterns and styles they wore on and off-stage were

fig. 7
Utagawa Hiroshige II (1826–69)
Nakano Street in the Yoshiwara
Print, woodblock on paper, 1857
Victoria and Albert Museum, London

eagerly emulated (fig. 9). Actors would commission a garment in a new shade from a dye house, their appearance in which would excite their fans and be depicted in woodblock prints, which would serve to both popularize the style and help it become a trademark for the actor. The brown colour known as *rokō-cha* became a popular colour in women's dress, having been worn by Segawa Kikunojō (1741–73), who specialized in female roles (*onnagata*), while *masubana-iro*, a light blue-green, was associated with Ichikawa Danjūrō (1660–1704) and his lineage.[13] Ichikawa Ebizō (1791–1859), known as Danjūrō VII and shown in the scroll hanging behind his son in Kunisada's print, famously wore a stage costume with a design of a sickle (*kama*) and the *hiragana* syllables *wa* and *nu*, which spell the word *kamawanu*, or 'I don't care', in rebus form. This started a craze for fabrics and handkerchiefs dyed with the same witty design.

Actors and other male denizens of the pleasure quarters could be quite extravagantly dressed, as is suggested by the male client at the centre of the Yoshiwara parade (fig. 7). Here, outside the normal bounds of society, clearly defined dress codes could be ignored. On the whole, however, male dress was characterized by subdued patterns and colours, although men did often wear sumptuous undergarments. Stylish men, and women, about town were always in search of the new and exotic. Although Japan had adopted a

'closed-country' policy in the 1630s, the Dutch were permitted to trade through the port of Nagasaki and the goods they brought to Japan became part of popular culture and fashionable dress. The Echigo-ya is depicted using western perspective (a visual curiosity, rather than a better way of viewing the world) copied from European prints (fig. 5), while the courtesan Nanokoshi is shown with a clock, a novelty inspired by Dutch imports (fig. 8). Painted and printed cottons from South Asia were particularly sought after, as were European fabrics (see pp. 80–7).

The conspicuous consumption of the Edo period found its most extravagant outlet in fashion contests between the wives of the wealthiest *chōnin*. One famous story tells of a visit to Kyoto in 1680 by Edo merchant Ishikawa Rokubei and his wife, who amazed residents with her splendid costume. Not wishing her city's reputation for fine garments to be bested, the wife of Kyoto merchant Naniwa-ya Jūemon appeared in a satin kimono embroidered with the famous sites of the ancient capital. Ishikawa's wife thereupon paraded through the streets in a kimono of fine black silk with an embroidered pattern of *nandina* (flowering bamboo). Onlookers thought this no match for that of the Kyoto woman, until they noticed that the red berries of the *nandina* were made of real coral. Although the Edo woman had won the fashion stakes on this occasion, she eventually lost at the

fig. 8
Isoda Koryūsai (1735–90)
Nanokoshi from the ōgi-ya,
from the series *New Designs*
as Fresh as Young Leaves
Print, woodblock on paper, c. 1775
British Museum, London

fig. 9
Utagawa Kunisada (1786–1865)
A Gathering of Ichikawa Danjūrō VIII's
Family
Print, woodblock on paper, 1849
Victoria and Albert Museum, London

fig. 10
Utagawa Toyokuni (1769–1825)
Fireworks at Ryōgoku Bridge
Print, woodblock on paper, c. 1820–5
Victoria and Albert Museum, London

the Edo period the Shogunate periodically issued sumptuary laws that aimed to curb such excesses and ensure appropriate class display. The edicts, which restricted a variety of activities and artefacts, became increasingly detailed and culminated in the Kansei reforms of 1789 and the Tenpō reforms of 1842. Danjūrō VII fell victim to the latter and was banished from Edo for his extravagant behaviour, which is why he is not shown in person in Kunisada's print (fig. 9).

The sumptuary laws put greatest emphasis on clothing, a testament to the significance that dress had in Edo-period society. The edicts restricted the kind of fabrics, techniques and colours that could be worn and, although not consistently imposed, did usher in certain changes. *Yūzen* dyeing allowed for detailed patterning without using embroidery, and stencils were used to imitate *shibori*. More emphasis was also placed on obi, which were not restricted and may be one reason they widened so much. From the late eighteenth century, when the laws were more strictly enforced, dress styles leaned towards colours that the *chōnin* could wear without fear of prosecution, such as brown, blue and grey. Particularly popular were blue and white *kasuri* fabrics, which were woven with selectively pre-dyed yarns. The adoption of this kind of dress was not mere capitulation on the part of the urban classes, however. A new aesthetic known as *iki*, one of elegant chic, developed in which anyone with real taste turned to subtle details. Such styles stood in contrast to the extravagantly embroidered kimono worn by courtesans and by the merchant classes on special occasions, such as weddings, when a certain amount of flamboyance was tolerated.

There were other ways in which the sumptuary laws were consciously subverted. Although *beni*-red kimono were forbidden, there was no restriction on using the dye for undergarments or linings. Wearing the coveted colour in this way became increasingly popular, the fleeting glimpse of red seen at a woman's hem, sleeve edge and collar deemed far more sensuous and alluring than an overt display. In a print by Toyokuni showing crowds gathering to watch fireworks on a warm summer evening, many figures wear *kasuri* kimono, including the woman on the boat in the centre of the image (fig. 10). To attract the attention of a man sitting on top of a neighbouring vessel, she lifts the hem of her kimono to reveal her red undergarments. In the fashion-conscious world of Edo-period Japan, such seductive glamour was everything.

hands of the shogun himself. The *True Record of the Tokugawa* tells us that a year later:

> A wealthy merchant called Rokubei ... gathered with many other townsmen on the street to view the shogun's procession to Kan'ei Temple. The shogun noticed Rokubei in the crowd, displaying his wealth in the magnificent dress of the women of his household. For such extravagance inappropriate in a townsman, his houses and lands were confiscated and he was banished.[14]

This notion of appropriateness was crucial in Edo Japan. The strict ordering of the social classes was fundamental to the structure of the Tokugawa regime, and it was dangerous if status and dress became out of step. In describing the profligate behaviour of merchants, Saikaku warns that 'because they forget their proper place, extravagant women should be in fear of divine punishment.'[15] As the tale of Rokubei demonstrates, the risk of penalties was also very worldly, as throughout

opposite
Kimono for a woman (*kosode*)
Flowers and diamond pattern

Figured satin silk (rinzu); ink painting (kaki-e), stencil imitation tie-dyeing (suri-hitta) and embroidery in silk and metallic threads
Edo period, 1780–1820
170.0 × 128.0 cm
KX190

From the mid-eighteenth century, the kimono worn on formal public occasions by women of the ruling military, or samurai, elite were characterized by two particular styles. In the first of these, the entire garment was covered with an abundance of flowers, which alternated with geometric patterns such as interlocking circles (*shippōtsunagi*), curving lines (*tatewaku*), decorative swastika (*manji*), waves (*seigaiha*), clouds (*zui-un*), fret (*sayagata*) and woodgrain (*mokume*) patterns (see KX143, right, and KX150, overleaf). The most sumptuous examples were of white figured satin (*rinzu*) and featured designs that were created using ink painting, stencil imitation tie-dyeing (*suri-hitta*) and embroidery in red, purple and green silks and gold-wrapped threads. In this example, peonies, plum blossoms, irises, chrysanthemums and vine leaves have been combined with a diamond-shaped motif composed of four hollyhock leaves and a central cherry blossom.

right
Summer kimono for a woman (*katabira*)
Flowers and scrolling clouds

Plain weave ramie (asa); ink painting (kaki-e), stencil imitation tie-dyeing (suri-hitta) and embroidery in silk and metallic threads
Edo period, 1800–50
165.0 × 120.0 cm
KX143

This garment is similar in design to KX190 (opposite), although here the irises have been replaced with wisteria and the diamond pattern with one of scrolling clouds. This, however, is a *katabira*, an unlined kimono of fine ramie designed to be worn in the summer months, the cloud motif suggesting a much-needed breeze on a humid day.

left
Kimono for a woman (kosode)
Fans, bellflowers and scrolling clouds
Plain weave crepe silk (chirimen); tie-dyeing (shibori)
and embroidery in silk and metallic threads
Edo period, 1780–1820
163.0 × 126.0 cm
KX228

Whereas white, the most popular colour
for this style of kimono, creates a sense of
elegance, the striking red ground of this
example produces a more dramatic effect.
Scattered among the clouds and bellflowers
are war fans (*gunbai*), a reference to the
military heritage of the wearer. These solid,
open fans were carried in battle by high-
ranking samurai as a mark of status and
to signal troops.

opposite
Outer kimono for a young woman (uchikake)
Flowers and woodgrain pattern
Figured satin silk (rinzu); ink painting (kaki-e), stencil
imitation tie-dyeing (suri-hitta) and embroidery in silk
and metallic threads
Edo period, 1800–50
155.0 × 126.0 cm
KX150

Like many of the pieces in the Khalili
Collection, this is an *uchikake*, or outer
kimono, which would have been worn on
formal occasions without a sash (obi). There
is a fine layer of silk filaments between the
ground fabric and the red lining, with extra
padding at the hem where the lining extends
below the white decorative surface to provide
a weighted edge to the garment. The long
sleeves indicate that it would have been worn
by a young unmarried woman.

Design for a kimono
Ink on paper, 1800–50
Victoria and Albert Museum, London

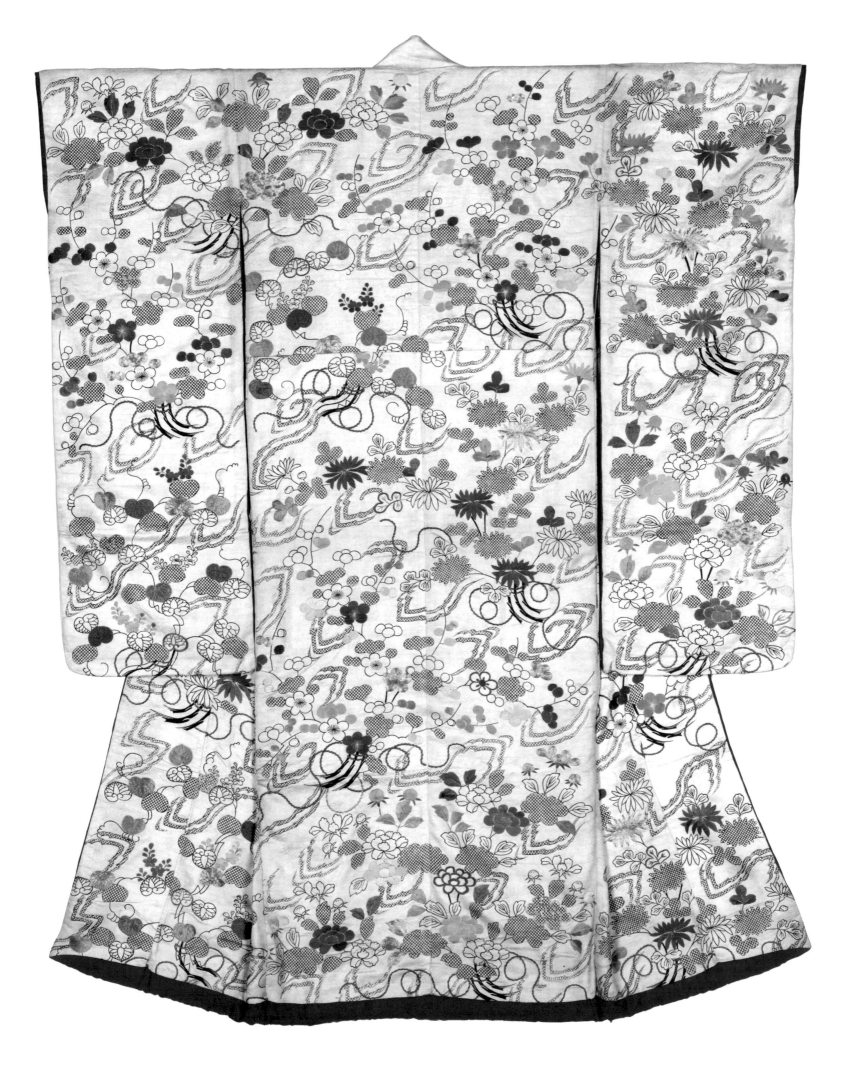

**Outer kimono for a young woman (*uchikake*)
Flowers and rolled blinds**

*Figured satin silk (rinzu); ink painting (kaki-e), stencil
imitation tie-dyeing (suri-hitta) and embroidery in silk
and metallic threads*
Edo period, 1800–50
162.5 × 126.0 cm
KX144

The court culture of the Heian period
(794–1185) was an important source of
inspiration in Edo kimono design, resulting
in patterns known as *yūsoku moyō* (imperial
dress pattern). This outer kimono for a
young samurai woman features the refined
motif of rolled palace curtains (*misu*),
executed in long stitches of glossy, untwisted
(floss) silk and finely couched gold. The
majority of the flowers are simply outlined
in ink, or stencilled to create an elegant
monochromatic contrast to the bright red
and green and opulent gold threads.

Outer kimono for a woman (uchikake)
Landscape with pavilion and carriage
Plain weave crepe silk (chirimen); freehand paste-resist
dyeing (yūzen) and embroidery in silk and metallic
threads
Edo period, 1800–50
171.0 × 126.5 cm
KX151

The second distinctive type of kimono worn
solely by women of the military elite during
the Edo period was known as *goshodoki*,
meaning 'palace court style', although the
term was not used until the late nineteenth
century (see pp. 36–45). Such garments
feature detailed landscapes of trees, flowers
and grasses, flowing water, mist, fishing nets,
thatched cottages and pavilions. Amid these
elements are motifs including carriages, fans,
hats and musical instruments, which allude
to classical literary sources such as the *Tale*

of Genji (Genji monogatari) and to particular
Nō plays.[1] Kimono with these designs would
have been worn by high-ranking samurai
women in attendance at the shogunal court
or the residence of the *daimyō*.

The fabric for *goshodoki* kimono is usually
silk crepe, although silk gauze and ramie
were used for summer garments, patterned
using the freehand paste-resist dyeing
(*yūzen*) method, combined with embroidery
in coloured silks and gold-wrapped threads.
Where the ground is dyed a dark colour, as
in this example, some undyed areas were
intentionally left unpatterned to create a
particular design effect, a technique known
as *shiroage*, or 'finishing off in white'. Here,
fine lines and dots have been skilfully used to
depict the water and mist.

This kimono has all the classic
features of a *goshodoki* design. Among a

landscape of cherry blossoms, pine trees,
chrysanthemums, grasses and fishing nets
are, in the foreground, an imperial carriage
and, moving up the garment and into the
distance, a gateway and fence, behind which
is a pavilion with its curtains partly drawn
to reveal a *koto*, a type of stringed musical
instrument. These motifs are rather generic,
making identification of a specific source
difficult, but the *koto* may suggest *Hashihime*
(*The Bridge Maiden*), the forty-fifth chapter
of the *Tale of Genji*, in which a young man,
Kaoru, catches sight of two women playing
music by moonlight in a mountain villa
in Uji.

Design for a kimono
Ink on paper, 1800–50
Victoria and Albert Museum, London

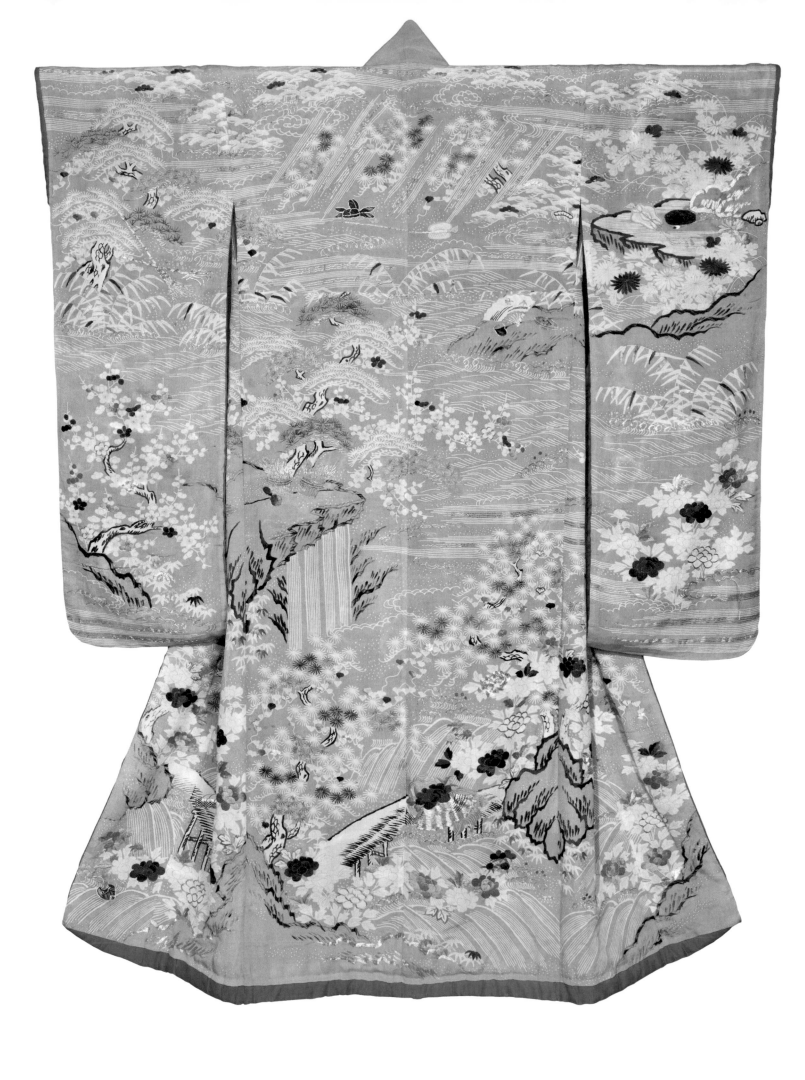

opposite
Outer kimono for a young woman (uchikake)
**Landscape with bridge and scattered court
objects**
*Plain weave crepe silk (chirimen); freehand paste-resist
dyeing (yūzen) and embroidery in silk and metallic
threads*
Edo period, 1800–50
162.0 × 126.5 cm
KX177

This *goshodoki* kimono features, on the lower
half, a rocky landscape with waterfall, bridge
and peonies and, around the shoulders,
various objects including fans, a hat,
brush, inkstone and scroll. This symbolism
suggests two Nō plays, based on famous
Chinese stories. The first, *Shakkyō (Stone
Bridge)*, tells of a monk who visits Mount
Shōryōzen, where he finds a long, narrow
bridge over a deep gorge, reputed to lead
to the Buddhist Pure Land. The highlight
of the play is a dance by *shishi* (mythical
lions), who cross the bridge and play among
the peonies. *Kikuji-do (Chrysanthemum
Youth)* is about a young man who was the
favourite of the Zhou Dynasty emperor,
Mu Wang. Forced from the court by his
rivals, he becomes a hermit and spends his
time transcribing a Buddhist *sutra*, before
achieving immortality by drinking dew from
chrysanthemums.

right
Kimono for a woman (kosode)
Landscape with pavilion and carriage
*Plain weave crepe silk (chirimen); freehand paste-resist
dyeing (yūzen), stencil imitation tie-dyeing (suri-hitta)
and embroidery in silk and metallic threads*
Edo period, 1800–50
171.0 × 127.0 cm
KX194

opposite above and right
Summer kimono for a woman (katabira)
Landscape with thatched cottage and carriage

Plain weave ramie (asa); freehand paste-resist dyeing (yūzen), stencil imitation tie-dyeing (suri-hitta) and embroidery in silk and metallic threads
Edo period, 1800–50
167.0 × 118.0 cm
KX149

The scene depicted on this garment might refer to the Nō play *Ashikari*, the 'Reed Cutter', which tells of a well-born couple who fall on hard times. The husband urges his wife to find a better life in the capital, where she obtains a good position in the home of a wealthy nobleman. She cannot forget her husband, however, and sets out to find him, only to discover he is living like a peasant and selling reeds. In a key scene, the main character dances with a straw hat, the carriage symbolizing his wife's material success and the cottage, by contrast, his poverty. The story ends happily with the couple reuniting.

When the *yūzen* technique is employed, the outline of the pattern most commonly appears white against a coloured ground (see KX151; pp. 34–5), but here it is the ground that has been left undyed, creating a feeling of freshness suitable for a summer kimono. The predominant blue colouring is created using indigo (*ai*), which would normally be applied by immersing the cloth in a dye bath. But for delicate patterning such as this, an organic pigment was created that could be brushed onto the fabric.[2]

opposite below and right
Outer kimono for a young woman (uchikake)
Landscape with carriage and fishing nets

Plain weave crepe silk (chirimen); freehand paste-resist dyeing (yūzen), stencil imitation tie-dyeing (suri-hitta) and embroidery in silk and metallic threads
Edo period, 1800–50
159.5 × 122.0 cm
KX153

The carriage, straw hat and cape on this kimono allude to the Nō play *Kayoi Komachi*, which tells the tragic story of an aristocratic general, Fukakusa-no-Shōshō, who was desperately in love with the beautiful poet Ono no Komachi. To prove his love, he came in secret every evening to sleep on her carriage platform, until, on the ninety-ninth evening, having changed out of his travel cape and straw hat and donned his court costume, he died.

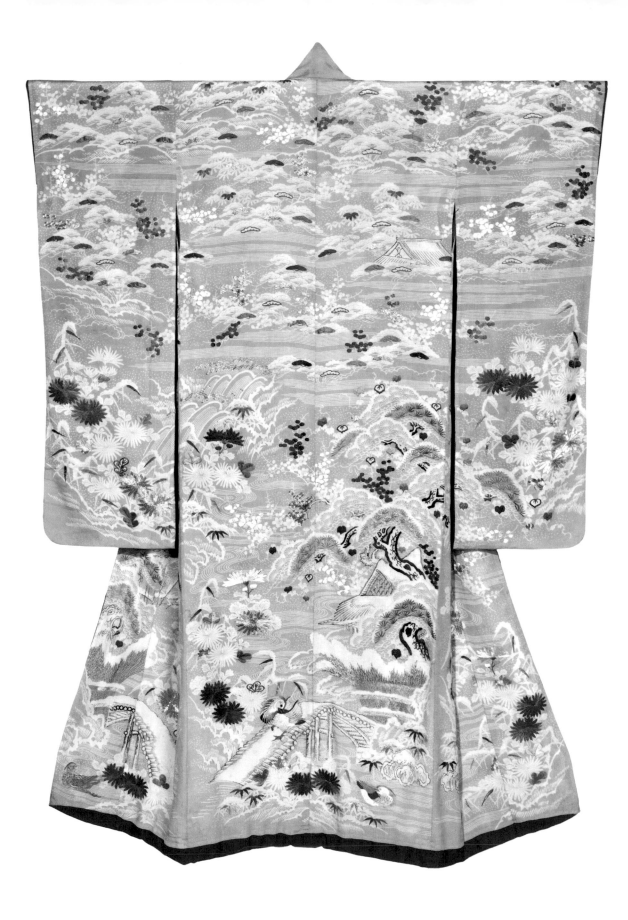

Outer kimono for a young woman (*uchikake*)
Landscape with mandarin ducks, bridge and buildings

Plain weave crepe silk (chirimen); freehand paste-resist dyeing (yūzen) and embroidery in silk and metallic threads
Edo period, 1800–50
166.0 × 121.0 cm
KX178

In this kimono for a young samurai woman, the undyed white sections of the *shiroage* design have been used to great effect to suggest a snowy landscape, the feeling of a chilly scene further emphasized by the crisp, pale blue of the ground fabric. Two pairs of ducks – symbolic of marital harmony – have been embroidered in a rich array of colours,

one on the front and the other on the back. The bridge, rustic fence, thatched building and, further up the garment, the temple roof emerging from the mist are probably standard motifs, rather than a reference to a specific place, but nevertheless bring interest and animation to the landscape.

above
Outer kimono for a young woman (uchikake)
View of Arashiyama
Plain weave crepe silk (chirimen); freehand paste-resist
dyeing (yūzen), stencil imitation tie-dyeing (suri-hitta)
and embroidery in silk and metallic threads
Edo–Meiji period, 1840–70
152.5 × 124.0 cm
KX154

The scene on this kimono is of Arashiyama,
a site of particular beauty on the western
outskirts of Kyoto. The long Toketsukyō, or
'moon-viewing bridge' over the Ōi River is
considered the perfect place from which to
view the cherry blossoms in spring and the
rich colours of autumn.

opposite
Kimono for a woman (kosode)
Landscape with thatched entrance gate
Plain weave crepe silk (chirimen); freehand paste-resist
dyeing (yūzen) and embroidery in silk and metallic
threads
Edo period, 1800–50
158.0 × 123.0 cm
KX176

This kimono and KX186 (overleaf) are also
in the *goshodoki* style worn by samurai
women, but the top sections have been
left undecorated and the densely patterned
landscape is set on a diagonal, giving extra
dynamism to the design.

Kimono for a woman (*kosode*)
Landscape with a feather cape
Plain weave crepe silk (chirimen); freehand paste-resist
dyeing (yūzen), stencil imitation tie-dyeing (suri-hitta)
and embroidery in silk and metallic threads
Edo period, 1800–50
172.0 × 129.5 cm
KX186

The feathered cape in the centre of
this design, delineated in colourful silk
embroidery, is a reference to the Nō play
Hagomoro. One spring morning, a fisherman
named Hakuryō finds a beautiful feathered
robe hanging on a pine tree. When he tries to
take it, a maiden appears and explains that
she needs it in order to return to heaven.
Taking pity on her, the fisherman gives
her the feather robe and in exchange she
performs a celestial dance.

left above
Kimono for a young woman (*furisode*)
Swallows flying over a landscape with cherry trees and wisteria
Plain weave crepe silk (chirimen); freehand paste-resist dyeing (yūzen) and embroidery in silk and metallic threads
Edo period, 1800–50
149.0 × 127.0 cm
KX210

Both of the kimono on these pages are examples of *tsuma moyō*, designs that pattern a kimono from the waist down. They feature five family crests, or *mon*, indicating that they were bestowed by the wearer's lord. This kimono has a dense design of swallows among cherry blossoms and wisteria. The motifs are suggestive of spring, with the freshness of the new season heightened by the movement of the birds and water, as well as by the bright green of the ground fabric.

left below and opposite
Unlined kimono for a young woman (*hitoe*)
Swallows flying above the shore with boat and fishing nets
Gauze weave silk (ro); freehand paste-resist dyeing (yūzen) and embroidery in silk and metallic threads
Edo–Meiji period, 1860–80
164.0 × 126.0 cm
KX187

This summer kimono is of *ro*, a type of silk that combines rows of plain weave with one where pairs of warp (vertical) threads are crossed over each other before and after the passing of the weft (horizontal) thread. This creates a fabric with a delicate open 'stripe', which has the structure characteristic of gauze but is much softer. Like KX210 (above left), the design is of swallows, here flying over a coastal landscape of pine trees, boats and fishing nets. This denotes a later season, as the birds flock to the shore before flying south in the autumn. The birds are not embroidered but rendered with delicately brushed dyes, which suggest, along with the mauve-coloured ground, that this is an early Meiji-period garment.

after Soga Shōhaku (1730–1781)
Eight Views of Ōmi

Six-fold screen, ink on paper, late 18th century
Metropolitan Museum of Art, New York

Kimono for a woman (kosode)
Eight views of Ōmi and scattered characters

Plain weave crepe silk (chirimen); freehand paste-resist dyeing (yūzen) and embroidery in silk and metallic threads
Edo period, 1740–60
163.0 × 125.0 cm
KX220

The development of *yūzen* dyeing allowed for the creation of highly detailed and delicate patterns, rendered in a wide range of colours. The technique was particularly employed in garments made for the wealthy and fashion-conscious merchant class, whose design tastes were more varied than those of the samurai or aristocracy. This *kosode*, one of

the earliest and most important in the Khalili Collection, is a testament to the great skills of the eighteenth-century textile artisans and a wonderful example of how Edo kimono functioned as a form of wearable art.

The mid-Edo period saw a boom in travel, which was reflected in kimono motifs. Landscapes and famous places (*meisho*) became popular subjects for merchant-class dress, as in this *kosode*, which has as its theme the 'Eight Views of Ōmi' (see KX142; overleaf). This subject, originally derived from Chinese painting, features celebrated sights around Lake Biwa, just northeast of Kyoto.[3] Here, these are depicted in detailed vignettes, predominantly in shades of blue

and pink: around the hem of the garment are the sails of ships returning to the old harbour at Yabase; across the centre of the back is the long bridge at Seta; and on the upper back is Ishiyama temple, built partly on supporting beams. It is said that here, on a moonlit night in 1004, Murasaki Shikibu began writing her celebrated *Tale of Genji* (*Genji monogatari*).

This particular theme is echoed in the Japanese characters on the upper part of the garment. The expressive 'brushstrokes', embroidered in orange and gold thread, form the lines of one of a series of poems on the 'Eight Views of Ōmi', composed by Konoe Masaie in 1500.

Ishiyama ya
Nio no umi teru
Tsuki kage wa
Akashi mo Suma mo
Hoka naranu kana

At Ishiyama Temple!
The moon shining
Over Little Grebe Lake
Is as wonderful as at
The bays of Suma and Akashi

Little Grebe Lake is another name for Lake Biwa, and here the poet imagines Lady Murasaki in the temple looking at the moon over the water, the very same moon that shines over Akashi, near the Inland Sea, and at Suma, near Osaka, where Prince Genji, the hero of her novel, spent time away from the capital.[4]

The use of such characters in kimono design served to demonstrate the tastes and accomplishments of the wearer, and acted as a playful way of inviting those she met to engage in word games or to 'read' something of her personality through her dress. We can do the same today, for although nothing is known of the personal history of those who originally owned the kimono now preserved in the Khalili Collection, we can deduce that the woman who wore this *kosode* was from the merchant class, was married, had the necessary leisure to visit famous sites, the wealth to employ the best kimono designers and makers, and considered herself a person of cultural discernment.

Kimono for a woman (*kosode*)
Eight views of Ōmi
*Figured twill silk (mon-aya); freehand paste-resist
dyeing (yūzen)*
Edo period, 1750–1780
138.0 × 125.0 cm
KX142

This garment features the same motif as
KX220 (previous pages), although the
overall effect is very different. Here, the
design is confined to the area below the
waist, a style known as *tsuma moyō*, which
became popular among merchant-class
women from the mid-eighteenth century.
The decoration is small and delicate in scale,
reflecting another fashion of the period, and
executed in *shiroage* (see KX151; pp. 34–5) on
a mid-blue ground with other, quite muted,
colours brushed on. The technique has
been used to skilled effect to illustrate the
climatic conditions of some of the famous
views, such as the evening rain at Karasaki
Shrine and snow on the Hira Mountains.
The ground fabric of the garment, which is
beautifully soft, is woven predominantly in
plain weave, but has roundels of dragons
in figured twill. The *kosode* was shortened,
perhaps to adapt it for wear by a younger
woman, and some of the pattern is folded
out of sight within the lining.

Isshiki Nobuhide
Fine Threads of Willow
Book, woodblock on paper, 1758
Victoria and Albert Museum, London

Summer kimono for a woman (*katabira*)
Thatched roofs and plum blossoms

Plain weave ramie (asa); freehand paste-resist dyeing
(yūzen) and embroidery in silk and metallic threads
Edo period, 1750–80
160.0 × 122.5 cm
KX225

The motifs on this supremely elegant
summer kimono form gentle, asymmetric
curves across the surface of the garment.
The undyed ramie complements the rustic
design, yet the apparent simplicity is
deceptive, for no group of flowers is depicted

nor created in the same way. The use of gold
on the pale ground also adds a touch of
unexpected opulence and creates a sensation
of glistening summer sun.

Outer kimono for a woman (uchikake)
Scattered fans and peonies

Figured satin silk (rinzu); embroidery in silk and metallic threads
Edo period, 1800–50
167.0 x 129.0 cm
KX200

The sparse, scattered motifs on this garment are suggestive of designs worn by women of the imperial court (see KX157; p. 120), but it is more likely that the kimono was commissioned by a wealthy merchant woman who aspired to aristocratic style. The fan and peony pattern alludes to the story *Shakkyō*, or *Stone Bridge* (see KX177; pp. 36–7).

opposite
Outer kimono for a woman (uchikake)
Plovers with pine trees and thatched huts

Plain weave crepe silk (chirimen); freehand paste-resist dyeing (yūzen) and embroidery in silk and metallic threads
Edo period, 1780–1820
167.0 × 125.0 cm
KX216

While the kimono worn by samurai women during the Edo period are noted for their lavish, dense designs, the garments of merchant-class women often have a more subdued beauty. The fashion for small-scale patterns, scattered sparsely over the surface to create a landscape, is evident in this example. On a soft, blue ground, tiny plovers (*chidori*) fly over a shore with pine trees and thatched cottages, while snow gently falls. The plover is an auspicious bird, because its cry, *chiyo*, is a homonym for the word meaning 'a thousand generations'.

Kimono for a woman (kosode)
Hibiscus and butterflies

Plain weave crepe silk (chirimen); freehand paste-resist dyeing (yūzen), ink painting (kaki-e) and embroidery in silk and metallic threads
Edo period, 1780–1820
159.0 × 123.5 cm
KX218

This kimono features a repeating pattern of stylized hibiscus growing against a trellis, but in each vignette, the flowers are shown in a different arrangement. The pattern was drawn on the cloth using rice paste, which protected these areas when the fabric was dyed. Parts of the design have been left plain but for fine lines that delineate the petals of the flowers and the veins of the leaves. Some of the flowers have been brushed with a delicate pink colour, while others have been embroidered in white and red or white and yellow. Some leaves have been embroidered in dark or lime green, or couched in gold-wrapped thread. Parts of the trellis are also in gold. Butterflies dance between the flowers, depicted in the same variety of techniques. The rich, plum-coloured ground, elegant design and sophisticated dyeing and embroidery suggest the wearer was a very wealthy merchant woman.

left
Kimono for a young woman (*furisode*)
Flower carts and butterflies
Plain weave crepe silk (chirimen); freehand paste-resist
dyeing (yūzen), ink painting (kaki-e) and embroidery in
silk and metallic threads
Edo period, 1800–30
163.5 × 128.0 cm
KX221

This kimono features a design of carts
carrying vases of flowers – peonies, plum
and cherry blossoms, chrysanthemums and
irises – with no two the same. The motif was
popular in the Edo period and relates to the
art of flower-arranging (*ikebana*). The handles
on the carts were originally embroidered in
black thread, which has been lost, probably
owing to the iron content of the dye, which
caused the silk fibre to disintegrate. Around
the shoulders of the garment fly embroidered
butterflies.

opposite
Kimono for young woman (*furisode*)
Reeds and gabion
Plain weave crepe silk (chirimen); freehand paste-resist
dyeing (yūzen) and embroidery in silk and metallic
threads
Edo period, 1780–1820
153.5 × 119.5 cm
KX215

Here, the *yūzen* technique has been used
to first draw the tall reeds onto the fabric,
which was then dyed to create a rich blue
ground suggestive of river waters. A few of
the reeds were then embroidered in red or
couched gold; the latter has also been used
to particular effect to delineate the gabions,
the baskets of rocks placed in the river to
control the water flow.

Outer kimono for a woman (*uchikake*)
Scenes from the *Tale of Ise*

Plain weave crepe silk (chirimen); freehand paste-resist
dyeing (yūzen)
Edo period, 1830–70
165.0 × 124.5 cm
KX198

On this kimono, the *yūzen* technique has
been used to create a scene from the *Tale
of Ise (Ise monogatari)*. One of Japan's most
famous literary works, this collection of
poems and associated texts tells of the
travels of the courtier Ariwara no Narihira
(825–80). Episode nine includes a brief scene
during which Narihira and his companions
pass Mount Fuji and pause to admire its
unseasonable covering of snow.

Toki shiranu
Yama wa Fuji no ne
Itsu tote ka
Ka no ko madara ni
Yuki no fururan

Fuji is a mountain
That knows no seasons
What time does it take this for
That it should be dappled
With fallen snow?[5]

Much of the scene is delineated by undyed
areas of fabric (*shiroage*), with touches of
blue brushed onto the pine trees and reds
onto the sails of the boats. The same pale
colours were used on the figures, whose
outlines and features appear in sketch-like
strokes. The portrayal of Narihira's horse
is particularly expressive. Rising over the
landscape, up to the shoulder, is majestic
Mount Fuji, the depiction of its snow-capped
peak reminiscent of Katsushika Hokusai's
famous series of woodblock prints from
1826–33. The garment bears five crests, or
mon, which denote the wearer's family. The
use of *mon* was originally restricted to the
aristocratic and samurai classes, but by the
1800s the commoner classes had adopted
them. This garment was probably worn by
a merchant woman.

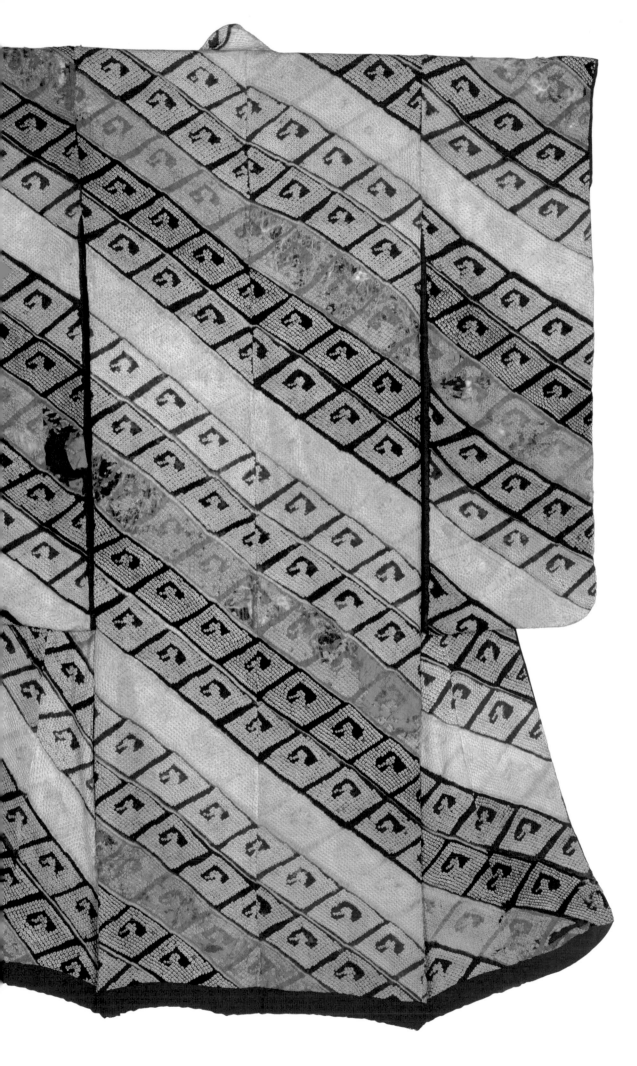

Kimono for a young woman (*furisode*)
Cranes

Figured satin silk (rinzu); tie-dyeing (shibori)
Edo period, 1800–40
164.0 × 122.0 cm
KX174

Japanese clothing culture divides formal occasions into the extraordinary (*hare*) and the ordinary (*ke*). This kimono is a very visible manifestation of the extraordinary, and would have been worn by a young woman from a wealthy merchant family on a special occasion, possibly her wedding.

The design was created using the tie-dyeing technique *kanoko shibori*, or 'fawn spot', in which small circles of fabric, closely placed in diagonal rows, are bound tightly with thread. The dye does not penetrate the bound areas. The tip of each section of cloth is left unbound, so that a tiny dot appears in the centre of each undyed circle. After the dye is dry, the binding is carefully removed. *Kanoko shibori* was very expensive and labour-intensive, and was often combined with other techniques (see KX228, p. 30, and KX229, overleaf). To have a whole garment patterned in this way was very extravagant, in terms of both cost and visual effect.

The motif of cranes is very auspicious, for these birds were believed to live for a thousand years and to inhabit Mount Horai, the land of the immortals. The cranes are depicted in a highly stylized way in repeating diamond lozenges, arranged in diagonal stripes of alternating colours. In all, this *furisode* must have looked incredibly striking when worn. Unfortunately, parts of the fabric have been lost, a result of the tannin in the brown dye, and the pattern on the sleeves does not match the body, suggesting that at some point, probably when the kimono was taken apart for cleaning, the left and right sleeves were transposed. Nevertheless, this remains one of the most sumptuous garments in the Khalili Collection.

Utagawa Kunisada (1786–1865)
The Tanabata Festival, Seventh Month,
from the series *The Five Festivals*

Print (detail), woodblock on paper, c. 1830s
Victoria and Albert Museum, London

**Kimono for a young woman (*furisode*)
Decorative partitions, cranes and clouds**

*Figured satin silk (rinzu); tie-dyeing (shibori)
Edo period, 1800–40*
165.5 × 121.0 cm
KX226

Textiles feature as the main motif on this *furisode*, hanging from stands in the form of decorative partitions (*kichō*). Their dramatic sweep fits the form of the garment in a sophisticated three-dimensional design that would have been enhanced by the movement of the wearer. A sense of perspective is evident in the cranes flying among clouds, their small scale suggesting they are soaring in a distant sky. Red was an immensely popular colour for young women's kimono, as it signified youth and passion. The dye, *benibana* (safflower), was very expensive. It took a long time to process, and about 12kg (26 lbs) of petals were required to dye a whole garment.[6] Here, it is combined with the costly *kanoko shibori* technique. This merchant daughter's kimono speaks loudly not only of glamour, but also of wealth.

Outer kimono for a young woman (*furisode*)
Pine-tree and tortoiseshell pattern
Figured satin silk (rinzu); tie-dyeing (shibori)
Edo period, 1800–40
165.0 × 124.0 cm
KX227

The arabesque curve of the pine on this kimono is reminiscent of the flowering-tree motif found on many South Asian fabrics imported into Japan by Dutch traders. It is depicted against a background of interlocking hexagons, known as *kikkō*, or tortoiseshell, which, like the auspicious creature itself, symbolize longevity. Many kimono designs demonstrate the importance of negative space in Japanese aesthetics. Here, however, the main motif and the background vie for visual attention, and it is the former that almost acts as the empty space. The pattern is created using the *kanoko shibori* technique, in striking indigo (*ai*) blue. As with the *beni* (red) example, colour was applied to the cloth by immersing it in a dye bath.

Kimono for a young woman (*furisode*)
Pine trees
Figured satin silk (rinzu); tie-dyeing (shibori) and
embroidery in silk and metallic threads
Edo period, 1840–70
157.5 × 123.0 cm
KX146

An extremely popular and auspicious motif in Japanese art, the pine tree is a symbol of longevity and endurance, and has been used here to particular bold effect. The foliage has been defined using stitch-resist tie-dyeing (*nuishime shibori*), a technique that involves outlining sections of fabric with small stitches, which are pulled tight. The cloth within the stitches is then bound to resist the colour when the fabric is dyed. Some parts of the design were further resisted using *kanoko shibori* (see KX174, p. 62) and dyed blue or green, while others were embroidered with twisted green silk or gold, couched onto the surface to create the outline of the foliage and the individual pine needles. The trunk of the tree is also couched in gold.

Kimono for a young woman (*furisode*)
Decorative partitions, fans, pine, bamboo
and plum
Figured satin silk (rinzu); tie-dyeing (shibori) and
embroidery in silk and metallic threads
Edo period, 1800–40
171.0 × 124.5 cm
KX229

The costly, labour-intensive *kanoko shibori* method was often combined with other techniques, as seen on this lavish garment. Various patterning methods were skilfully used to create the main motif, which features lengths of *shibori* fabric, hanging on stands, alternating with ones of embroidered flowers, butterflies or geometric patterns on an undyed ground. No two motifs are the same. These are surrounded by scattered fans, executed in the same techniques, and by the 'three friends of winter' (*shochikubai*): pine, bamboo and plum.

Kimono for a woman (*kosode*)
Flower sacks

Satin silk (shusu); embroidery in silk and metallic
threads
Edo–Meiji period, 1850–80
158.5 × 119.0 cm
KX189

The embroidery used to pattern this kimono
is the most sophisticated of all the examples
in the Khalili Collection. Arrangements of
flowers – hydrangeas, peonies, camellias
and chrysanthemums, and pine, bamboo
and plum – are presented in sacks tied with
long tassels, and executed in a flat stitch
(*hira-nui*), equivalent to a satin stitch in the
West, in floss (untwisted) silk, giving a rich
sheen. Twisted silk was used on some of
the stems, while in places the veins of the
leaves were couched with fine gold. For the
sacks, larger areas of the design have been
defined in long and short stitches (*sashi-nui*),
also in floss silk, overlaid with fine twisted
threads that have been couched. Threads
are generally twisted in pairs, either lightly or
tightly, depending on the required effect. In
the latter, called *katayori*, one thread is highly
twisted and then twisted again, more lightly
and in the opposite direction, with another
thread. Here, *katayori* was used to outline
certain areas of the design. The overall effect
gives the impression that the sacks are of
woven brocade, rather than embroidery.

opposite
Outer kimono for a woman (*uchikake*)
Hōō **birds and paulownia**
Plain weave silk; freehand paste-resist dyeing (yūzen), stencil imitation tie-dyeing (suri-hitta) and embroidery in silk and metallic threads
Edo period, 1800–50
157.0 × 129.0 cm
KX148

The fabric of this kimono is woven in a simple, plain weave, but the silk is very lustrous. A combination of freehand and stencil-dyeing techniques have been used to create a bold pattern of paulownia, which grows up the garment from rocks at the hem. Parts of the plant were then embroidered in silk and gold threads, and the outlines of the rocks and trunks of the plants padded with silk or cotton to add to the three-dimensional effect. Sophisticated embroidery has been employed to depict the birds flying around the shoulders of the garment, with highly twisted threads combined with gold used for their long tail feathers. These are *hōō* birds, usually translated as 'phoenix' in English, but bearing little relation to their western namesake. The female counterpart to the dragon, *hōō* are believed to appear at a time of peace and prosperity, their colourful tail feathers representing the virtues of honesty, benevolence, wisdom, fidelity and propriety. *Hōō* are often depicted with paulownia trees, the only plant, according to legend, on which the birds will alight.

left and below
Outer kimono for a young woman (*uchikake*)
Hōō **birds and paulownia**
Satin silk (shusu); embroidery in silk and metallic threads
Edo–Meiji period, 1850–80
167.0 × 127.5 cm
KX156

This garment has the same motif as KX148 (opposite), but here there is a single paulownia tree, executed almost entirely in gold-wrapped thread, which looks particularly dazzling against the dark-blue satin ground. The edges of the trunk have been padded, and various shades of gold used to create a sense of depth and shadow. The *hōō* birds are executed in a variety of colours, but look rather small against the dominating plant.

**Outer kimono for a young woman (*uchikake*)
Chrysanthemums and fences**

*Satin silk (shusu); embroidery in silk and metallic
threads*
Edo period, 1840–70
173.5 × 123.0 cm
KX145

An autumn motif of various types of
chrysanthemums growing alongside fences
is embroidered on this outer kimono in
coloured silk threads, both flat and twisted,
and couched gold. Many of the satin kimono
in the Khalili Collection are dyed a beautiful
blue. This colour is derived from indigo (*ai*),

which gets darker with repetitive dipping.
Various shades can be created, from very
pale to dark midnight blue, depending on the
desired effect. The mid-blue of this kimono
and others (KX189, pp. 66–7; KX152 and
KX155, overleaf) is called *asagi*, and is used
to represent a clear sky.

opposite
Outer kimono for a young woman (*uchikake*)
Bamboo

Satin silk (shusu); embroidery in metallic threads
Edo period, 1840–70
171.5 × 125.0 cm
KX152

The design of this outer kimono demonstrates what a dramatic effect that can be achieved with a single motif and colour. The embroidered pattern of bamboo, executed in couched gold threads, would have been carefully planned and executed, but gives an impression of spontaneity akin to an ink painting.

right
Outer kimono for a young woman (*uchikake*)
Sparrows and bamboo in the snow

Satin silk (shusu); embroidery in silk and metallic threads
Edo period, 1840–70
163.5 × 122.5 cm
KX155

This delightful and dazzling design depicts sparrows flying among bamboo, probably a reference to the story of the tongue-cut sparrow (see p. 102). The snow indicates the winter season during which the outer kimono would have been worn, but the clear blue sky and the playful birds suggest the coming of spring. The bottom part of the lining, which shows at the padded hem, is woven with chrysanthemums in red and gold.

**Outer kimono for a young woman (*uchikake*)
Bamboo**

*Satin silk (shusu); embroidery in silk threads
Edo period, 1840–70*
173.0 × 124.5 cm
KX217

Like KX152 (previous pages), the motif on this elegant outer kimono is bamboo. There are over 600 varieties of this plant in Japan, and two types are shown here, both embroidered in glossy silk thread against a white satin ground. The sweeping scene of upright bamboo, in three shades of green, contrasts with the gently bending red plants and gives the whole design a wonderful sense of movement. Bamboo is a symbol of strength and resilience, for although it bends, it never breaks.

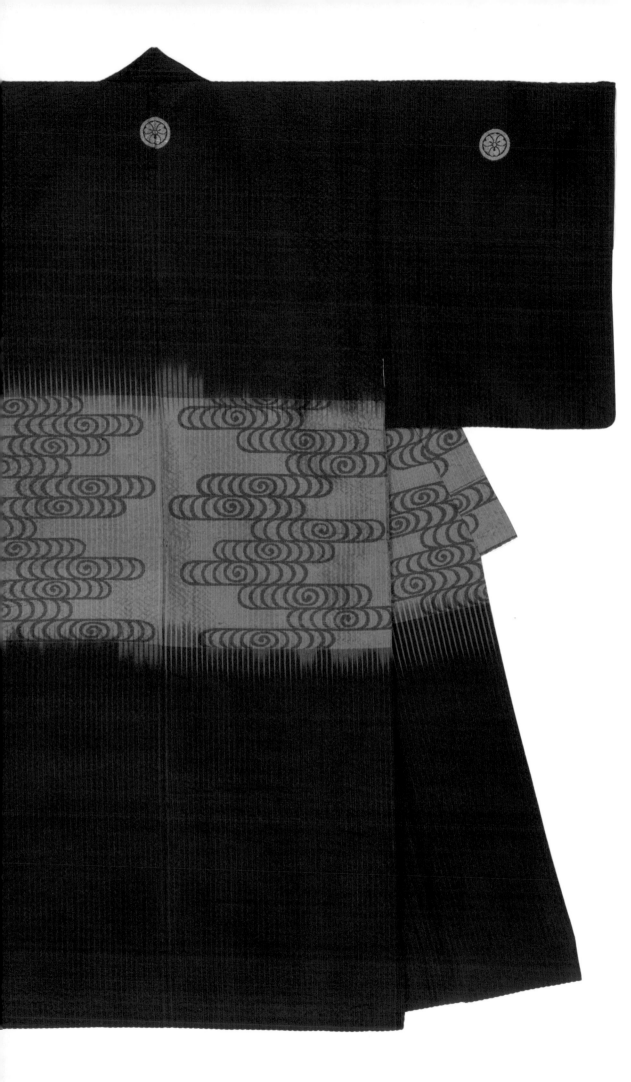

Kikugawa Eizan (1787–1867)
Samurai in noshime and kamishimo, with nagabakama (long hakama), performing the Setsubun ceremony of scattering beans to drive out demons
Print (detail), woodblock on paper, 1815–42
Victoria and Albert Museum, London

Kimono for a man (noshime)
Swirling water
Plain weave silk; hand-tied selective dyeing of warp threads (hogushi-gasuri) and supplementary wefts
Edo period 1800–50
138.0 × 136.0 cm
KX233

This type of kimono was part of the formal ensemble of samurai men during the Edo period. It would have been worn under *kamishimo*, a two-piece outfit consisting of pleated trousers (*hakama*) and a sleeveless jacket with extended shoulders (*kataginu*). The distinctive colour division of the central section is known as *koshigawari*, 'change at the waist', and was achieved by tightly binding sections of the warp threads prior to dyeing to stop the colour penetrating, a technique known as *kasuri*. Here, the swirling central pattern, and the *mon* (crests), were created with supplementary wefts. Unusually, the fabric is not smooth, but has a striped, puckered appearance, produced by alternating the tension in the warp threads.[7] Part of the *noshime* would have been visible under the *kamishimo*, the silk sheen of the former contrasting with the latter, which was usually made of bast fibres such as hemp. Such subtle aesthetics are characteristic of male dress in the Edo period.

Kimono for a man (*noshime*)
*Plain weave silk; hand-tied selective dyeing of warp
threads (hogushi-gasuri)*
Edo period, 1800–50
143.0 × 130.0 cm
KX208

Kimono for a man (*noshime*)
Checks

Plain weave silk; hand-tied selective dyeing of warp
threads (hogushi-gasuri)
Edo period, 1800–50
136.5 × 128.0 cm
KX234

The central section of this *noshime* is
patterned with an elegant check, while the
mon (crests) are those of the Tokugawa, the
ruling family of the Edo period.

Underkimono for a man (juban)
Flowers and flames; stripes

Fabric below the waist, overlap, collar and sleeve ends:
plain weave cotton; freehand resist-dyeing,
Coromandel Coast, India
Fabric above the waist: plain weave silk and cotton,
Japan
Edo period, 1800–50
135.0 × 135.5 cm
KX230

Cloth was a major item of international commerce and exchange in the early modern period. The Dutch, the only Europeans permitted to trade in Japan during the Edo period, brought Indian hand-painted and block-printed cotton textiles to the country, where they were much admired for their bright colours and exotic designs. The fabric, known in Japan as *sarasa*, was expensive and commonly cut into small pieces, to be used for fan cases and tobacco pouches or to wrap precious tea-ceremony utensils. Some complete garments do survive, however, and here such cloth has been used – along with a simple, striped fabric – to create an exuberant underkimono for a man. This kind of concealed flamboyance was an important aspect of fashionable male dress in the Edo period. What makes the garment particularly interesting is that the fabric, with its distinctive flame pattern (*kranok*), was produced on the Coromandel Coast of India in the late eighteenth or early nineteenth century, specifically for export to Thailand. This underkimono speaks of a fascinating journey, geographically and conceptually, from original producer to ultimate consumer.

Underkimono for a man (juban)
Flowers and birds

Plain weave cotton; freehand wax resist-dyeing (batik),
Java
Edo period, 1800–50
135.0 × 135.5 cm
KX235

Indian cottons were the most sought-after foreign fabrics in Japan, as they were in the West, but other kinds of cloth were occasionally imported. This very unusual underkimono is made from two types of batik, the wax-resist fabric made in Java where the Dutch East India Company had their Asian headquarters. Batik from central Java, characterized by its earthy tones, has been used for the lower part of the garment and around the collar and sleeve ends, while the upper section of the garment is of brighter coastal batik and features a design of stylized bird tail feathers.

Underkimono for a man (*juban*)
Floral arabesque

Plain weave cotton; stencilled paste-resist dyeing
(katazome)
Edo period, 1800–50
134.0 × 119.0 cm
KX231

The enormous vogue for *sarasa* textiles can be seen in a woodblock print by Utagawa Kunisada, which depicts a courtesan, the embodiment of style and fashion, writing to a lover surrounded by a great swathe of such fabric in the form of a sleeping kimono (*yogi*). From the late eighteenth century, woodblock printed manuals were published showing Indian textile designs and providing information on how to produce them using native techniques. The appetite for *sarasa* was soon being satisfied by Japanese versions of the fabric. The small-scale pattern and spotted ground of this garment suggests that it was made in Sakai, near Osaka.

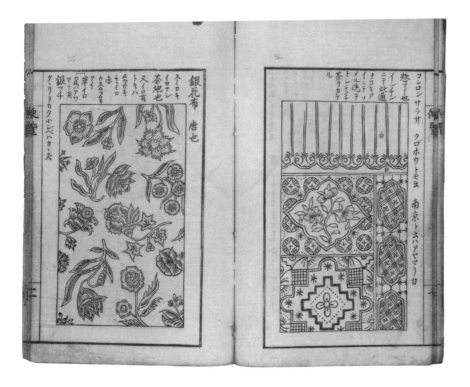

Kasumi Magozaemon Chika-ari
(fl. 1750–1800)
Sarasa Benran, vol. 1
Book, woodblock on paper, 1781
Victoria and Albert Museum, London

Utagawa Kunisada (1786–1865)
Girl Writing a Letter, from the series
A Collection of Contemporary Beauties
Print, woodblock on paper, c. 1815
Victoria and Albert Museum, London

Underkimono for a man (*juban*)
Passionflowers

Plain weave cotton; printing, Britain or France
Edo period, 1835–60
142.5 × 129.0 cm
KX232

Fabrics created in Europe also found their way to Japan. This printed cotton was produced in Britain or France in the mid-nineteenth century as a lightweight furnishing fabric. With its naturalistic flowers and bright, yellow ground, it would have seemed very exciting and exotic to Japanese eyes. As with the South and Southeast Asian fabrics, it has been used to make an underkimono for a man and would have provided a dashing touch of unconformity, known only to the wearer and a few intimates, beneath a restrained exterior. A rare commodity, the use of such fabric served as an indicator of wealth, as well as of style and taste.

left above
Unlined kimono for a young woman (*hitoe*)
Kudzu and scattered characters
*Gauze weave silk (ro); freehand paste-resist dyeing
(yūzen), stencil imitation tie-dyed (suri-hitta) and
embroidery in silk and metallic threads*
Edo period, 1800–50
161.0 × 123.5 cm
KX236

The characters on this elegant summer
kimono are from *Kimigayo*, a poem in the
tenth-century *Kokinshu* anthology of verse,
which in 1888 was adopted as the lyrics for
Japan's national anthem.

left below and opposite
Kimono for a girl
Peonies and scattered characters
*Gauze weave silk (ro); freehand paste-resist dyeing
(yūzen), stencil imitation tie-dyed (suri-hitta) and
embroidery in silk and metallic threads*
Edo period, 1800–50
111.5 × 101.5 cm
KX223

There are numerous seams on the front
of this late Edo-period girl's kimono,
revealing that it was carefully adapted from
the garment of an adult woman similar in
style to KX236 (above left). It is certainly
very sophisticated in both its design and
decoration. The fabric is *ro*, a combination of
plain and gauze weave silk, which has been
reserved and dyed a rich plum purple. Parts
of the design have been left blank but for fine
lines that delineate the petals of the flowers
and the veins of the leaves, while others have
been stencilled in imitation *shibori*. Some of
the peonies – either the whole flower or just
the outline – have been embroidered in red
silk or couched gold, with leaves and stalks
embroidered in green or gold. Scattered
across the shoulders, again in orange-red
and gold, are phrases including *tsuru kame*
(crane and turtle), *noboru Fuji* (climbing
Mount Fuji) and *kimi ga yo made matsu*
(waiting through the eras of the emperors;
in other words, forever). It may be that these
characters make up a celebratory poem, but
they are probably just auspicious expressions
and not meant to be read in a continuous
manner.[8]

above

Kimono for an infant
Cranes, bamboo and hollyhocks
Plain weave ramie (asa); freehand paste-resist dyeing
(yūzen) and embroidery in silk and metallic threads
Edo period, 1750–1800
97.5 × 78.0 cm
KX222

In the Edo period as much care and attention
was lavished on kimono for children as on
those for adults (see KX212, opposite, and
KX223, previous pages). The body of this

infant's garment is made from a single width
of fine ramie (*hitotsumi*), which has become
wonderfully soft with time. The delicate,
small-scale design, reserved in white on
the indigo-blue ground with touches of
embroidery on the birds and leaves, suggests
an eighteenth-century date. The auspicious
motifs of cranes and bamboo were designed
to bring good fortune. It is possible the
garment was worn for the child's first visit to
a Shinto shrine (see p. 142).

opposite

Kimono for a young girl
Wisteria, trellises and stream
Gauze weave silk (ro); freehand paste-resist dyeing
(yūzen), stencil imitation tie-dyeing (suri-hitta) and
embroidery in silk and metallic threads
Edo period, 1800–50
95.5 × 86.0 cm
KX212

Kimono for children echoed the styles of
garments worn by adults in their fabric and
decoration, as can be seen in this example,
which is similar to KX210 (p. 46).

Sleeping kimono (*yogi*)
Crane

Plain weave silk; embroidered in silk threads
Edo period, 1800–50
166.0 × 155.0 cm
KX183

Yogi are a form of bedding, shaped like oversized kimono and thickly wadded and quilted for warmth. Normally they are made of cotton; silk versions such as those in the Khalili Collection would probably have belonged to samurai families (see KX184; overleaf). This example has the single, auspicious motif of a crane, executed in long, flat stitches of floss (untwisted) silk, held in place by small, fine threads. The outline of the feathers has been created with twisted threads couched onto the fabric.

attributed to Sugimura Jihei (fl. 1681–1703)
Couple Under a Quilt,
from an untitled *Shunga* series

Print, woodblock on paper, mid-1680s
Private collection, USA

Sleeping kimono (yogi)

*Satin silk (shusu) and figured satin silk (rinzu);
freehand paste-resist dyeing (yūzen), tie-dyeing
(shibori), ink painting (kaki-e) and embroidery
in silk and metallic threads*
Edo period, 1780–1830
185.0 × 162.0 cm
KX184

Yogi usually feature designs and patterning
methods that are simpler than those of
kimono, but the opposite is true of this
example, which has perhaps the greatest
combination of motifs and techniques of any
piece in the Khalili Collection.

The main body is of satin silk, figured
in places with a pattern of flowering plants.
Sweeping down across the garment are
ribbons of dried abalone, known as *noshi*.
This popular motif derives from a play on
words, a homophone for *noshi*, meaning
'extend'; its use implies wishes for prolonged
happiness. The ribbons have been reserved
in white, with those left plain alternating
with those that have been hand-painted in
ink with a scrolling arabesque or a lattice
pattern. The ribbons are held together by
an ornate finial in couched gold, with some
wrapped around a large fan, hand-painted
with a crane, pine trees and plum blossoms
and edged with red silk embroidery. Below
the waist are, on the back, a box executed
in *shibori*, tied with a tassel of couched
gold, and on the front two drums, one in
shibori and couched gold, the other hand-
painted with pink camellia. The lining is of
white satin silk and the inner hem is hand-
painted with an elaborate design of floral
arrangements in three hanging containers,
which are partly embroidered in silk and
couched gold. Two of these are shaped like
boats, one with a prow of a *hōō* bird, the
other with the prow of a dragon, a reference
to the springtime lake excursion in *Kochō
(Butterflies)*, chapter 24 in the *Tale of Genji*.

The sheer extravagance of the design
suggests that this *yogi* was commissioned
for the wedding of a high-ranking samurai.
It entered the Collection with the suggested
provenance of the *daimyō* of the Nabeshima
clan, who ruled the Saga Domain on Kyūshū
in southwest Japan.

Kimono for a woman, to be worn draped over the head (katsugi)
Flowers, bamboo and sparrows, scattered fans
Plain weave ramie (asa); stencilled paste-resist dyeing (katazome) and freehand paste-resist dyeing (yūzen)
Edo–Meiji period, 1850–80
144.0 × 121.0 cm
KX171

The majority of Edo and early Meiji-period kimono in the Khalili Collection are luxurious pieces that would have been worn by the social and financial elite. But the Collection also contains a group of garments that reveal a very different kind of aesthetic. Made of ramie or cotton, and dyed predominantly with indigo, these kimono are generally associated with the less wealthy merchant classes, but their subdued elegance was a significant element in the sophisticated world of nineteenth-century fashionable dress.

This ramie garment has been dyed with four separate, small-scale patterns. The scattered fans and flowers of the lower section were drawn freehand onto the cloth using rice paste, but for the rest of the garment the paste has been applied through stencils, a technique known as *katazome*. Stencils are made from two or three sheets of mulberry (*kōzo*) paper, laminated together with persimmon juice, which, in addition to its adhesive qualities, strengthens the paper and makes it water-resistant. Various methods and tools are used to create different types of patterns, from the delicate to the bold. A stencil is placed on the cloth and rice paste is applied through it using a spatula. The stencil is then moved and carefully positioned on the next section of fabric, and the process repeated.

Here, three different stencil designs have been used, and the rice paste applied to the back of the cloth to prevent the dye bleeding into the resisted areas when the fabric was dipped into the indigo. Whole areas would then have been pasted, so that they remained a paler blue when the cloth was dyed to create the very dark colour of the lower section and the crest around the shoulders. The motif of sparrows and bamboo was created with indigo alone, but the two floral patterns use other colours, which would have been brushed on.

Stencil
Mulberry paper, c. 1800–1900
Victoria and Albert Museum, London

Nishikawa Sukenobu (1671–1750)
Woman on an Excursion, from *Ehon Tokiwa Gusa (Picture Book of the Pines)*
Book, woodblock on paper, 1731
Victoria and Albert Museum, London

Kimono for a woman, to be worn draped over the head (*katsugi*)
Floral roundels, scattered fans and flowers

Plain weave ramie (asa); freehand paste-resist dyeing (yūzen)
Edo–Meiji period, 1850–80
145.0 × 125.5 cm
KX172

Two shades of indigo were used on this garment to create a striking central section, the boldness of the design contrasting with the delicate motifs of scattered fans and flowers and floral roundels. This is an example of a *katsugi*, which would have been worn draped over the head to provide protection and an element of concealment when a woman was outside (see KX171, opposite; and KX173 and KX205, overleaf). Such garments were originally worn solely by women of the court, but by the Edo period their use had spread to the merchant classes. *Katsugi* are constructed with the neckband placed some distance below the shoulder line to create a kind of pocket for the head.

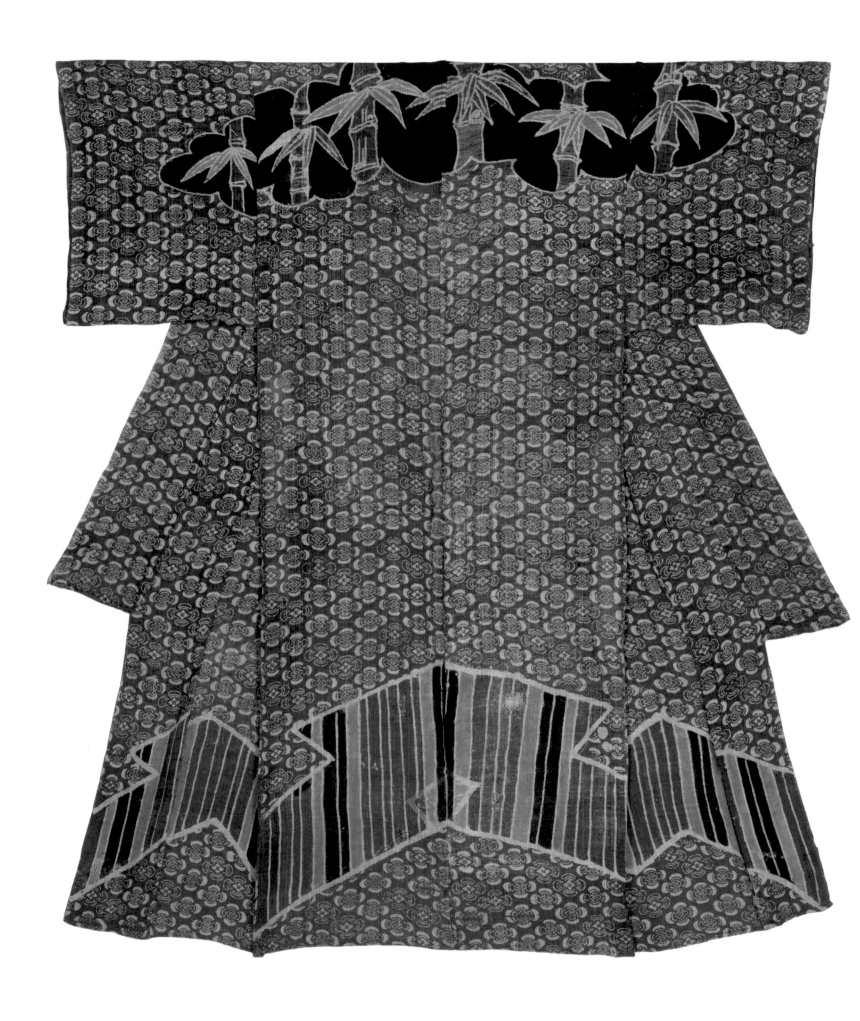

opposite

Kimono for a woman, to be worn draped over the head (*katsugi*)
Stylized flowers, stripes and bamboo

Plain weave hemp (asa); stencilled paste-resist dyeing (katazome) and freehand paste-resist dyeing (tsutsugaki)
Edo–Meiji period, 1850–80
138.0 × 120.5 cm
KX173

Here, as on a number of other examples, three distinct patterns have been employed to particular dramatic effect. Overall harmony is achieved by the use of the same colours throughout: two shades of blue from indigo, yellow from miscanthus, and green from a combination of the two. The bamboo motif, which would have sat on the head of the wearer, was created using a freehand paste-resist method, similar to *yūzen* but employing a paper tube, rather than one of cloth, with a wider nozzle, usually of bamboo. This technique – *tsutsugaki*, or tube drawing – was used to pattern cotton and bast-fibre textiles used by the commoner classes. The fabric of this garment and KX193 (below right) is hemp, which, like ramie, is a cultivated grass fibre but is not as fine or lustrous.

above right

Kimono for a woman, to be worn draped over the head (*katsugi*)
Water reeds, cranes and pine trees, crest

Plain weave ramie (asa); freehand paste-resist dyeing (yūzen)
Edo–Meiji period, 1850–80
169.0 × 126.0 cm
KX205

Cranes fly joyously among pine trees against a bright blue sky on this kimono, while reeds sway in the dark waters below. When the garment was worn, the head would have been covered with the large paulownia crest, a compositional device common in *katsugi*.

below right

Summer kimono for a woman (*katabira*)
Paulownia, hexagons and crest

Plain weave hemp (asa); stencilled paste-resist dyeing (katazome) and freehand paste-resist dyeing (tsutsugaki)
Edo–Meiji period, 1850–80
136.0 × 133.5 cm
KX193

opposite above and right
Summer kimono for a woman (katabira)
Butterflies and bamboo on a floral ground
Plain weave ramie (asa); stencilled paste resist-dyeing
(katazome) and embroidery in metallic threads
Meiji period, 1870–1900
145.0 × 125.0 cm
KX213

The dense, small-scale stencil dyeing that
decorates this kimono is known as *komon*.
It is often used on men's kimono, but the
butterflies on the garment, and the red
lining, denote that it is for a woman. Here,
the ground, not the pattern, has been pasted
and remains undyed, and the colour is not
blue but a fashionable grey. The butterflies,
pines and crests have been reserved in
white, with some edged in couched gold.
There are also splashes of flat gold threads.
The woman who wore this garment would
have appeared the epitome of understated
elegance.

opposite below and right
Water wheel and cherry blossoms
Summer kimono for a woman (yukata)
Plain weave cotton; tie-dyeing (shibori)
Meiji period, 1870–1900
133.0 × 125.0 cm
KX170

The effect of water cascading down this
kimono, driven by a giant wheel into a
dark pool where blossoms float, evokes a
cool, refreshing feeling for a hot summer's
evening. The pattern is created using the
tie-dyeing method (*shibori*), whereby small
sections of the cotton cloth are tightly bound,
before being dipped into the indigo dye bath.
The result could not be more different from
that achieved on sumptuous silk kimono that
utilize the same technique (see pp. 62–4).

left above and opposite
Summer kimono for a woman (yukata)
Swallow and bamboo
Plain weave cotton; stencil (katazome) and freehand (tsutsugaki) resist-dyeing
Meiji period, 1870–1900
138.5 × 130.0 cm
KX169

This kimono is a *yukata*, an informal cotton garment worn in the summer. The cloth is woven with undyed and indigo-blue warps, in a ratio of 6:2, to create a fine vertical stripe. It was then dyed with indigo blue using a combination of paste-resist methods: stencils for the ground and freehand for the main motifs. The bold, overall design of a single sparrow, bamboo and scissors alludes to a Japanese fairy tale about the value of friendship and the perils of avarice.

A kind and gentle old woodcutter lived with his disagreeable, greedy wife. One day he found an injured sparrow, which he took home, fed with rice and nursed back to health. His wife resented the care her husband lavished on the bird and one day, catching the sparrow eating starch, she cut out its tongue and sent it flying back to the mountains. The old man went searching for the bird and, with the help of other sparrows, found his way to the bamboo grove where it lived. His feathered friend gave him food, while the other birds sang and danced for him. Upon his departure, the sparrow offered the old man the choice of two baskets: one large and heavy, the other small and light. Not wishing to be greedy, the woodcutter chose the latter and when he got home was amazed to find it full of treasure.

His wife, annoyed that he had not chosen the bigger basket, went herself in search of the sparrow she had harmed. She was greeted kindly by the birds and given the large basket. Eager for the wealth she assumed it contained, the woman opened the basket on the way home only to discover it was full of monsters and ghosts. So surprised and scared was she that she tumbled to her death.

left below
Summer kimono for a woman (yukata)
Fish among waves
Plain weave cotton; stencil (katazome) and freehand (tsutsugaki) resist-dyeing
Meiji period, 1870–1900
131.0 × 124.5 cm
KX168

II

MEIJI

1868
—
1912

The Meiji era: the ambiguities of modernization

CHRISTINE M. E. GUTH

Marking a dramatic rupture with the feudal political system that had been in place under the Tokugawa shoguns for over 250 years, the rule of Mutsuhito, known posthumously as Emperor Meiji (1852–1912), is commonly recognized as the beginning of Japanese modernity.[1] After the changes in political leadership in 1868, Edo, renamed Tokyo, 'eastern capital', became the seat of government, and the young emperor moved from Kyoto into the castle formerly occupied by the shoguns and redesignated the Imperial Palace. The new government of the Meiji Restoration (*Meiji ishin*) mobilized all its efforts towards building a modern, industrialized and militarily powerful nation-state, a mission expressed in slogans such as 'civilization and enlightenment' (*bunmei kaika*) and 'rich country, strong military' (*fukoku kyōhei*).

But the reality proved to be far more complex and ambiguous than these tidy dates, displacements and nation-building efforts would suggest. Institutional and technological changes did not erase earlier, deeply entrenched world views, practices and values, many of which persisted in the newly legitimating guise of tradition. Indeed, the term *ishin*, used to refer to the 'restoration' of direct imperial rule, derives from Confucianism.[2] Rather than identifying clearly demarcated spheres of tradition and modernity, however, this essay seeks to bring a more multi-stranded approach to thinking about the complicated processes of negotiation through which Japanese modernity was formed.

Modernizing strategies

Nomenclature can be misleading, and the restoration of imperial rule was more image than reality. Responsibility for the new administration was entrusted primarily to members of the former samurai elite, who were already experienced in such affairs. Departments devoted to industry, foreign trade and the like speak to the new imperatives facing the fledgling government. The Imperial Household Ministry was especially powerful, and as part of its strategy to promote worship of the

fig. 1
Yōshū Chikanobu (1838–1912)
Portrait of the Meiji Emperor
Print, woodblock on paper, c. 1887–1900
British Museum, London

Emperor, organized elaborate ceremonies and commissioned photographs, paintings and other visual documentation to record these events.[3] Such propaganda, widely circulated domestically and internationally in the form of inexpensive woodblock prints, commonly featured the Emperor dressed in European military uniform to help project an image of this still inexperienced young man as a powerful modern leader and policy-maker (fig. 1). The emergence of imperial portraiture was a new development in the Meiji era; until this time, the emperor was never seen in public. The Empress was also depicted in photographs and in woodblocks. While the former often show her in an ancient style of court dress, in popular prints she is dressed in the latest European fashions, modelling such activities as the use of a sewing machine, associated with the womanly arts and technological progress (see p. 115). This duality reflects broader uncertainties about women's roles in modern Japan.

Under the influence of enlightenment ideology, and following the government's pledge to seek 'wisdom throughout the world', new institutions, including public schools and universities, museums and parks, were formed. An army and navy were equipped, at huge cost, chiefly through the purchase of modern arms and ships from Europe. International commerce and trade in commodities such as silk and tea helped to underwrite the expense of this new infrastructure. Earlier, a vibrant growing domestic economy had led many craftsmen to develop some standardization and economies of scale, but the demands of the overseas market were larger, more varied and complicated by unfamiliarity with foreign consumer tastes.[4] The government actively promoted and subsidized the modernization of crafts production, much of it intended to bring in foreign exchange.

Schools of art and design were established in cities including Tokyo, Kyoto and Kanazawa to provide technical instruction in machine-based production methods for the manufacture of ceramics, metalwork, lacquer and woodwork. The prospectus of the Kanazawa Kōgyō Gakkō, founded in 1887 by Notomi Kaijirō, announced:

Today's industry of this country is practised mainly by hand without the help of machinery. As industry develops and wages rise, however, it is natural and a matter of course to use machines in industry. Therefore, we teach how to use machines to produce various things and call the teaching unit for it Mechanical Woodwork Division.[5]

World Expositions in Vienna, Paris, Philadelphia, Chicago and elsewhere became major venues for the display and sale of the goods produced in such schools (fig. 2). Even as it fulfilled economic objectives, participation in these expositions also became a public-relations vehicle for Japan's self-representation as an 'artistic nation', a form of soft power that served to offset the increasingly militaristic image that developed in the wake of Japan's victory over Russia in 1905.

In an era dominated by European and American colonialism, the formation and mobilization of a well-equipped and trained military force capable of protecting the nation and extending its reach abroad was another of the new government's objectives. Following the model of European powers, Japan began aggressively asserting territorial authority beyond the archipelago in the Sino-Japanese war of 1894–5, with patriotic propaganda for this 'much-recorded war' appearing on everything from combs and toys to towels and clothing.[6]

In its aftermath, China ceded Taiwan, the Pescadores Islands and the Liaodong Peninsula to Japan. The reparation funds paid by China were put towards the purchase of the modern armed ships that would help secure the naval victory against the Russians a decade later (fig. 3). Having gained a foothold on the continent, Japan went on to add the southern half of Sakhalin Island and, in 1910, Korea. The redefinition of portions of China as colonies radically altered Japan's relationship with continental culture and with its own past, as well as with the West. Previously deemed to be of little global geo-political concern, Japan's spectacular naval triumph left western leaders fearful of this new Asian power with imperialist aspirations.

Ambiguous modernities

The impact of modernization was extremely uneven and more conspicuous in the metropolitan centres of Tokyo, Kyoto and Osaka than in rural areas. Travel conditions and communications improved following the gradual opening of railway lines, regular postal deliveries and telegraphs, but even by

fig. 2
Japanese display at the Centennial Exhibition, Philadelphia
Photograph, albumen print, 1876
Free Library of Philadelphia

fig. 3
**Japanese Squadron Outside
the Harbour of Port Arthur**
*Print (detail), woodblock on paper, 1904
Victoria and Albert Museum, London*

travelling and studying abroad. The Iwakura Embassy, a two-year journey in 1871–3 that took members of the new government and their assistants across Europe and the United States, was in fact an extended study tour to learn about western legal, military, diplomatic and scientific matters.[10] Solo travel by artists, many of them aspiring to study in Paris, began later in the period. For many Japanese, travel abroad was an unsettling experience that brought home an awareness of their insignificant place in the larger world. Following his sojourn abroad, Takamura Kōtarō, the privileged son of a professor at the Tokyo School of the Arts, and a leader of those artists seeking to break from the world of their fathers through the adoption of modernist idioms, penned a poignant poem likening himself to a tiny netsuke.

> Cheekbones protruding, thick lips,
>   eyes triangular,
> With a face like a netsuke carved
>   by the master Sangorō
>   Blank, as if stripped of his soul
>   Not knowing himself, fidgety
> Life-cheap
> Vainglorious
> Small and frigid, incredibly smug
> Monkey-like, flying squirrel-like,
>   mud-skipper-like,
> Minnow-like, gargoyle-like,
>   chip-from-a-cup-like
> Japanese.[11]

the end of the Meiji era many parts of the country still lacked reliable services. For the 'imperfectly civilized' indigenous Ainu inhabitants of the northern island of Hokkaidō, standards of living changed slowly despite enforced assimilation into the new nation-state through dress, hairstyles, language and other measures.[7] By contrast, the Treaty Ports of Yokohama, Nagasaki, Kobe and Hakodate became dynamic 'contact zones' through the interaction between local and foreign residents.[8]

It was in and from such settings that new hybrid cultural forms and practices, such as photography, first arose and were disseminated. Port cities also welcomed tourists, whose numbers grew dramatically with the development of regular shipping routes and the popularization of round-the-world tours. Photographers catered to the tastes of these tourists by offering albums of 'views and types', which contributed to the spread of enduring stereotypes of Japan (fig. 4).[9] Paradoxically, the new technology of mechanical reproduction, rather than helping to locate Japan in a universalizing discourse of modernization, was instrumental in fostering an image of the country as timeless and unchanging.

Even as newly founded institutions were heavily staffed by foreign teachers in subjects ranging from engineering and medicine to music, Japanese with the means to do so also began

fig. 4
**Felice Beato (1832–1909)
Japanese Supper**
*Photograph, albumen print, 1868
Victoria and Albert Museum, London*

fig. 5
Utagawa Yoshitora (fl. 1850–80)
*Imported Silk-Reeling Machine
in Tsukiji, Tokyo*
Print, woodblock on paper, 1872
Metropolitan Museum of Art, New York

Life in the Meiji era was strongly inflected by deeply entrenched ideas about class and gender. The government bureaucracy was dominated by members of the former samurai class, especially those from Chōshū, Satsuma and Tosa, who had been early leaders of the faction that had helped to overthrow the Tokugawa rulers. Despite the abolition of the feudal system and official encouragement of mercantile activity, prejudice against those of merchant-class background persisted. The 'good wife, wise mother' (*ryōsai kenbo*) became the feminine ideal, but like many other virtues celebrated in word and image, this derived in part from Neo-Confucian teachings inculcated in Tokugawa times through texts such as *Onna Daigaku (Great Learning for Women)*. The 'good wife, wise mother' ideal in the Meiji era differed from its earlier counterpart, however, by being 'inseparable from such issues as the formation of the modern citizen-state and the formation of the "modern family".'[12]

Although education, marriage and family were extolled, the forces unleashed by industrialization also made other demands on Japan's female citizenry. Women had long been involved in silk cultivation and hand-spinning, but recognition of textiles as a key source of export revenue made increased output a major government objective. The new industrialized silk and cotton spinning mills set up in various parts of the country relied heavily on female workers. In 1872, for instance, a large silk mill was built at Tomioka, in Gunma prefecture, under the direction of a French engineer who earlier had supervised construction of the first modern ironworks near Yokohama. It was designed to train four hundred young women from across the country in modern machine-reeled silk production (fig. 5), but there were few volunteers. Many of the first recruits came from prosperous farming families already involved in silk production and former samurai families 'who were the most likely to identify with the government's call to go for the sake of the nation', but also needed to find new sources of income.[13]

The experience of time

The often contradictory realities of the Meiji era come into particularly sharp focus when considering the experience of time, one of the most fundamental facets of daily life. The adoption in 1868 of the era name 'Meiji', or 'bright rule', was a continuation of the traditional practice of assigning a new era name every time an emperor ascended the throne. In the fifth year of the rule of Mutsuhito, however, the Gregorian calendar (*seiki*) was introduced, making that year the equivalent of 1873. Replacing the old lunar calendar also advanced by a full month the date when festivals were celebrated. When the first day of the first month (January) was officially designated New Year, other festivals were obliged to follow suit, often resulting in a disturbing month-long gap between traditional seasonal signifiers and the actual event. This had implications for kimono fashions, in which design motifs and colours were carefully coordinated with the seasons.

These new temporal systems also co-existed with the traditional Chinese sexagenary cycle and the twelve animals of the zodiac associated with it. Garments, as well as other forms of material culture, featuring rats, horses, dragons and so on, continued to be produced in the years identified with those animals. The marking of time also changed from a twelve-hour day, with each hour identified by an animal, to a twenty-four-hour one, with each hour divided into sixty minutes.

The introduction of the western calendar and clock time went hand in hand with another ideologically driven method of marking historical time, in the form of the *kōki*, a chronology that began with the ascension in 660 BC of the first emperor Jimmu. According to this system, Mutsuhito was the 122nd in an unbroken imperial line descended from the sun-goddess Amaterasu. This new historicism found expression in forms ranging from positivist scholarship following western models and archaeological excavations, to didactic paintings and prints featuring mythical heroes and heroines, both in traditional woodblock and newer lithographic form (fig. 6).[14] The institutionalization of *kōki* (it was only abolished following World War II) was one of many signs of the strong emphasis on (re-)writing national history in keeping with a new awareness of linear, evolutionary time.

Modern times demanded modern personal time-keeping, as well, and watches and clocks became fashionable accessories for men and forms of household decoration. Their ubiquity in the popular visual culture of the era speaks both to their significance as cultural markers and to the anxiety and tension they provoked (fig. 7). Despite their adoption, the perceived failure to adhere to the demands of clock time was a common trope

in European critiques of Japan. While the demands of an industrializing economy undermined the previously customary patterns of task-orientated work mingled with social intercourse, the top-down discipline of time in factories had little impact on the farmers who constituted the majority of the population. The rhythms of their lives continued to be dictated primarily by the agricultural cycle. Planting, rotating and harvesting crops all required thinking about time abstractly in terms of duration, order and interchange of tasks, but in relation to man-days per unit of land, rather than clock time.[15] Negotiation with these multiple and conflicting protocols was one of many ways in which men and women across Japan constructed their daily lives simultaneously and variously in keeping with practices of Chinese, local and European origins.

Sartorial choice

Dress was another conspicuous area in which a kind of 'code-switching' was required on a daily basis.[16] The kimono remained the dominant form of dress for women, and while some men adopted western dress in their professional lives, they generally wore kimono in the home. For most women, sartorial choices were bound up with the everyday drudgery of hand-sewing. A married woman's domestic duties had for centuries involved making and remaking clothing for herself and her family, and this changed little in the Meiji era. This was a practical necessity since every time a kimono was washed, it had to be disassembled into its seven basic components, laid flat on boards to air-dry, and then re-stitched

fig. 6
Tsukioka Yoshitoshi (1839–92)
Empress Jingu Leading the Invasion of Korea
Print, woodblock on paper, 1879
British Museum, London

fig. 7
Kobayashi Kiyochika (1847–1915)
Time-keeping
Print, woodblock on paper, 1886
British Museum, London

before being worn again. Family economies could also be dependent on a wife's skills as a seamstress. The diary for 1910 of Nakano Makiko, the wife of a Kyoto pharmacist, testifies to the contribution her labour made to the family business: not only did she sew clothing for her extended family, but she also stitched the hand towels intended as gifts for business associates and clients at the New Year.[17]

Home sewing assumed considerable moral and social weight. The recollections of Ushigome Chie offer clear expression of this public justification of sewing:

> In the provinces, until that time [1910–20s], the idea remained widespread that skill in sewing determined a person's value as a woman. I was bad at sewing and calligraphy as a child, and was scolded at home: 'You're not a girl.' This was not simply a judgement on skill in sewing, but a view of education that believed morality was nurtured through mastery of the techniques of what one might call the Way of Sewing.[18]

By her reference to the 'Way of Sewing', Ushigome implies that this activity assumed a ritual dimension akin to that of other professions or activities to which the honorific word 'way' (*michi*, or *dō*) was commonly appended, such as *judō*, *chadō* (the way of tea) or *shodō* (the way of writing).

The Singer sewing machine, introduced to Japan via the Treaty Ports in the 1860s, was promoted by the government as part of its campaign to construct the modern ideal of a good wife and

wise mother in the service of family, nation and empire (fig. 8).[19] This did not take into account, however, the fact that the purchase of such a machine was beyond the means of most families or that machine-stitching, while well suited to western tailored suits and dresses, was impractical for the making of kimono, still the daily wear of the majority of women. Nor did it acknowledge the way this technology altered familiar processes and undermined the value of the needles with which women had lived intimately for most of their lives. As the sewing machine became equated with western modernity, its use became implicated in nativist debates about Japanese identity. The view that, for a Japanese woman, sewing is far more than a household skill was both product and producer of this discourse.

The impact of western modernization in Meiji-era Japan is undeniable, but was more variously inflected than is often assumed. There was no single experience of modernity, no set of agreed values and styles. Many existing ideas and institutions were 'reinvented', making a present by imagining and fabricating connections with the past. By the same token, the fact that many of the era's transformations were identified with 'westernization' contributed to a growing preoccupation with maintaining a distinctive Japanese cultural identity. It is impossible to map a coherent narrative of the culture of an epoch made up of so many disparate, fragmentary and contradictory parts, but it is precisely these tensions that testify to the degree to which Japanese men and women of all classes were active agents in the formation of Japanese modernity.

fig. 8
Adachi Ginkō (fl. 1874–97)
Ladies Sewing
Print, woodblock on paper, 1887
Museum of Fine Arts, Boston

Dress in the Meiji period: change and continuity

ANNA JACKSON

Much of our comprehension and categorization of the clothing we and others wear is fairly unconscious, but when a society experiences a period of enormous change, the significance and meaning of dress demands more attention. This is certainly true of the Meiji period. As Japan sought to define a new national identity, the question of what to wear became central to the transformations of political, social and cultural life.

The intrusion of western powers into Japan threw native culture into high relief, with the result that many things came to be distinguished as either *yō* ('western'), or *wa* ('Japanese'). Dress styles emerged as one of the most visible markers of difference and the terms *yōfuku* and *wafuku* (*fuku* meaning clothing) were coined. It was also in the Meiji period that the word 'kimono', or 'the thing worn', gained broad currency. As Japan sought to define itself in relation to the West during the late nineteenth and early twentieth centuries, the kimono took on an increasingly symbolic, as well as literal, meaning.

Western dress in Japan

Western clothing had the most dramatic and immediate effect on the imperial court. Clothing reform was proclaimed by the Emperor Meiji in September 1871:

> The national polity is firm, but manners and customs should be adaptable. We greatly regret that the uniform of our court has been established following the Chinese custom, and it has become exceedingly effeminate in style and character.... The Emperor Jimmu, who founded Japan, and the Empress Jingu, who conquered Korea, were not attired in the present style. We should no longer appear before the people in these effeminate styles. We have therefore decided to reform dress regulations entirely.[1]

With this statement the Emperor distanced his court from Japan's now weakened continental neighbour, implied that he was a firm ruler and, most importantly, established a connection between western dress and that worn by heroic figures from the country's mythical history. The suggestion that the court's adoption of European clothing was somehow more 'Japanese' created continuity with the past and made the transformations of the present a little less daunting. Within a few years of the restoration, courtiers had abandoned the high lacquered caps and wide-sleeved robes they had worn for centuries in favour of formal western clothing. This was not a mimicking of the West, but a way of projecting a new power structure that signified the desire to be treated equally in the cultural and political arenas. The Emperor first appeared publicly in western dress in 1872, and was subsequently always depicted in European-style uniform (p. 106). Interestingly, a print of Empress Jingu from 1879 depicts her in a costume that suggests a western ensemble (p. 110).

There was no sudden or wholesale acceptance of western dress, but as the government sought to transform Japan into a modern nation under the slogan 'civilization and enlightenment' (*bunmei kaika*), items of European apparel became useful symbols of allegiance to the state cause. Men started to wear leather shoes, bowler hats, capes and umbrellas with kimono, creating a curious and eclectic mix of *yōfuku* and *wafuku* styles (fig. 1). Adopting foreign accessories was much easier, and cheaper, than wearing an entire outfit. There was also, inevitably, a lack of understanding about how all the items of western dress went together. One often repeated story tells of an official dressed in silk hat, dress coat and shirt but no trousers, because he had not realized they were an essential part of the outfit.[2]

In 1860, the social reformer Fukuzawa Yukichi accompanied Japan's first delegation abroad, travelling to Europe and the United States. Members of the delegation wore traditional Japanese dress, which caused much curiosity in the West and helped to brand them, Fukuzawa feared,

fig. 1
Utagawa Kuniteru (1808–76)
View of Nihon-bashi in Tokyo
Print, woodblock on paper, 1870
Victoria and Albert Museum, London

fig. 2
Fukuzawa Yukichi (1835–1901)
Western Clothing, Food and Homes
Book (three volumes), woodblock on paper, 1867
Keiō University Library, Tokyo

as exotic and picturesque, rather than as a nation to be taken seriously. Travelling again to Europe in 1862 and America in 1867, Fukuzawa became an expert on all matters western. His first book, *Conditions of the West (Seiyō jijō)* was published in 1866 and *Western Clothing, Food and Homes (Seiyō ishokujū)* in 1867, on the eve of the Meiji restoration. The latter, which included illustrations and a phrasebook, advised readers on how to eat, dress and even urinate in western style (fig. 2).[3]

Personal grooming was also affected by changes to dress as men abandoned the shaved head and topknot in favour of cropped hair to better express their modern attitude. It was said that if you tapped a head sporting a topknot it would ring to the sound of the old order, but tap a cropped head and it would sing out 'civilization and enlightenment'.[4] In emulation of the Emperor, men grew beards and moustaches. Women's dress styles also changed, although at first not so radically. Women began

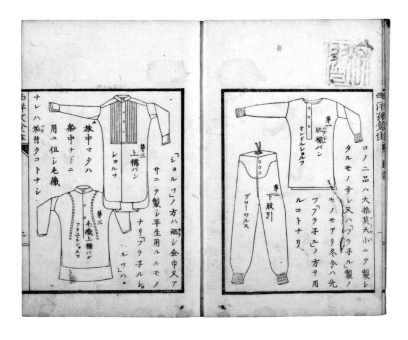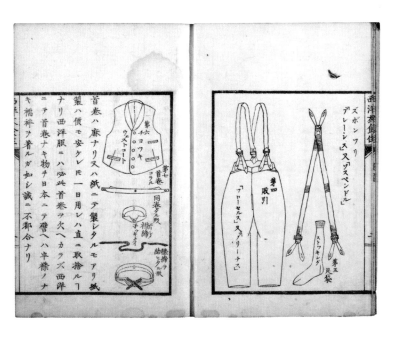

to wear *hakama* (wide, pleated trousers) and *haori* (kimono jackets), items previously reserved for men, along with leather shoes and silk umbrellas, a look that was particularly associated with female teachers and students. A few women also cut their hair, but this was considered almost indecent. A more popular style (*sokugami*) was one that swept the hair up, coiling it up at the crown of the head. The most startling cosmetic change was that married women stopped blackening their teeth.

The mid-Meiji period was a high point of westernization, often called the Rokumeikan ('Deer Cry Pavilion') era, named after the building designed by British architect Josiah Condor and erected in Tokyo. Here, the Japanese elite would entertain foreign dignitaries in order to demonstrate how the country had left its feudal past behind and was now a modern nation. Japanese men appeared in western-style regalia, while their wives and daughters appeared in corseted gowns and danced with foreign guests. Wearing tightly fitted, revealing clothes and mixing, let alone dancing, with men was not something women of the elite had been brought up to do, and for many it cannot have been a comfortable experience, physically or psychologically.

Japanese women in western dress often provoked scorn from westerners and their own countrymen, but some had their admirers. Nagako, the wife of Nabeshima Naohiro, drew admiring comments from Pierre Loti, the author of the novel *Madame Chrysanthème*, when he attended a ball at the Rokumeikan in 1885. Nabeshima Naohiro (1846–1912), the last *daimyō* of Saga, studied in England for eight years in the 1870s and was then appointed Japanese envoy to Rome, where he was stationed with his wife from 1881–2. Lady Nabeshima was thus more acquainted than most with the manners and dress of Europe. Her western-style dress is fashioned from kimono fabric of the kind worn by women of her samurai class (fig. 4).

Western fashion for women was boosted in 1886 when Empress Haruko appeared in European dress.[5] In January the following year the newspaper *Chōya Shimbun* published a statement by the Empress, which advised Japanese women to adopt western styles but to use Japanese materials. Invoking a link with the past, as her husband had done earlier, the Empress noted that at the time of Emperor Shōmu, in the eighth century, women had worn an upper garment and a skirt, and only later did the lower part get

fig. 3
Gown made for Empress Haruko
Satin silk and velvet, embroidered with silk and metallic threads, c. 1888–9
Bunka Gakuen Costume Museum, Tokyo

fig. 4
Gown of kimono fabric made for Lady Nabeshima
Silk with resist-dyeing and embroidery, c. 1881
Nabeshima Hokokai, Saga

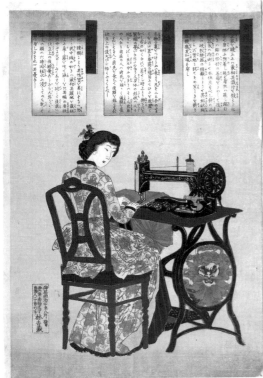

fig. 5
Yōshū Chikanobu (1838–1912)
Court Ladies Sewing Western Clothing
Print, woodblock on paper, 1887
Metropolitan Museum of Art, New York

abandoned as the upper part of the ensemble – the kimono – lengthened. She continued:

> Now when we regard women's western clothing, we note that it consists of an upper garment and a skirt, and thus accords with our ancient system of dress. Not only is it suitable for the performance of ceremony, it also allows for freedom of movement. It is thus entirely appropriate that we adopt western tailoring. As we bend our efforts to this reform, however, we must take care to use only domestically produced materials. If we do so, we will aid manufacturing techniques, advance art and assist business.[6]

One of the few of the Empress's garments to have survived is an elaborate dress and train (fig. 3), richly embroidered with Japanese chrysanthemums.

The Emperor and Empress were publicly visible in a way never known before and how they dressed commanded greater attention. They were the subject of numerous woodblock prints, the master of the genre being Yōshū Chikanobu.[7] One of his most striking images shows the Empress in an elegant bustle gown, which gives her tall form an exaggerated S-curve (fig. 5). The imperial figure, small and dainty in real life, has taken on not merely the clothing, but also the physique of a western woman in a way that is totally antithetical to Japanese concepts of dress and the body. Haruko is accompanied by her son and flanked by two women, one cutting cloth and the other operating the latest western import, the sewing machine. The panels above give instructions on how to measure the body and to cut and sew the new western styles.

The kimono in the West

Just as the Empress was encouraging her fellow countrywomen to adopt western dress, fashionable women in Europe and America were donning kimono. The 'opening' of Japan aroused enormous interest, and the subsequent flood of goods that reached foreign shores led to a craze for all things Japanese that was satisfied by an increasing number of dealers and shops specializing in Asian merchandise. Japanese textiles transformed the domestic interior and by 1888, according to an article in the British magazine *The Woman's World*, 'there is now hardly a drawing-room in which the influences of Japanese art are not felt.

fig. 6
John Atkinson Grimshaw (1836–93)
Spring
Oil on canvas, 1875
Private collection

Walls are draped and tables covered with the rich brocade of the Land of the Dragonfly.'[8] Women also wore kimono in the style of a dressing gown, as can be seen in *Spring*, by John Atkinson Grimshaw (fig. 6). Here, surrounded by Asian textiles and ceramics, a woman is shown loosely clad in a dyed and embroidered white kimono. Geographically and culturally transformed, a garment created for a high-ranking samurai woman has become part of an aestheticized space where it evokes the novelty and exoticism of Japan.[9]

In late nineteenth-century Europe and America, the kimono could represent a number of things. It signified something artistic, fashionable, exotic and, at times, non-conformist. In the aesthetic interior it could denote a woman's social confinement, while hinting at the supposed eroticism of the East. It could also be liberating, offering a new form of dress unrestricted by tight corsets. Japan itself was seen as a medieval society and often viewed with idealistic longing by those doubtful about certain aspects of life in the industrial West. Its people were believed to be innately artistic and to live in harmony with nature, while respecting the ties of social deference. Such perceived traits were admired, but never without a firm conviction of western superiority.[10]

This picturesque image of the East was, however, increasingly out of step with the realities of Meiji-period Japan. As those with artistic flair were enjoying dressing up in kimono in Europe and America, the Japanese elite were donning western clothing. While wearing Japanese dress in the West suggested a wish to escape, momentarily, from modernity, the adoption of western dress in Japan signified a drive for modernity and a permanent recognition of equality. Such changes to Japanese dress codes rather alarmed Europeans. The kimono served as a potent sign of Japanese tradition, and to adopt western clothing was to shatter the romantic image of Japan.[11] What is certain is that in both Japan and the West the ability of dress to challenge notions of political power, social identity and cultural difference was clearly understood.

The kimono in Japan

Although western dress styles were adopted by the most elite sections of society, the vast majority of Japanese women continued to wear kimono. The garments of the early Meiji period were the stylistic descendants of the late Edo era, and reflected contrasting tastes for conservative colours and small-scale motifs around the hem, as well as lavish and densely patterned designs. In 1862 *daimyō* wives and their ladies-in-waiting were allowed to return to their domains, which had a great impact on the makers and purveyors of kimono in the capital. Unsold stock, sometimes taken apart or cut up, became popular among the townspeople in the late Edo and early Meiji periods.[12] Many such garments were exported to the West, which explains the prevalence for this type of kimono in European and American paintings of the period.

As the Meiji period progressed, dress styles began to strongly diverge along lines of place and gender. By the 1880s, full western garb had been adopted in the public arena by men who considered themselves part of the new political order. Even in rural areas, where changes were less dramatic, farmers would have a western suit, called a *seiburo* (from 'Savile Row'), for smart occasions. Most men would, however, change into kimono when they were in the privacy of their own homes. There were practical reasons for this: western clothing was considered appropriate for a workplace furnished with desks and chairs, while Japanese dress suited the living arrangements of a domestic space. This double sartorial life served to reinforce the binary oppositions that increasingly defined Japanese identity: between public and private, and what was foreign and what was Japanese. Significantly, it served to equate westernization with modernity and identified men as agents of progress, while women, who predominantly occupied the

domestic sphere and continued to wear kimono, came to embody traditional Japanese values.

In the 1890s there was something of a kimono renaissance, which was part of a broader resurgent nationalism born of increased disillusionment with the supposed benefits of western-inspired civilization and enlightenment. As national pride surged with victory in the Sino-Japanese War of 1895, new bolder, brighter kimono styles emerged along with a fashion for layered sets and interesting linings (see p. 129). While in earlier periods there had been a large gulf between everyday wear and formal wear, a new type of kimono known as *hōmongi*, literally 'visiting wear', developed. The Empress continued to wear western dress, but for most women the influence was now expressed more subtly in the boxy *taiko* obi style, worn low like a bustle, and in the use of accessories such as coats and handbags. The artist Chikanobu reverted to creating images of bygone eras and kimono-clad women, although the colour and patterning of the garments he depicted reflected Meiji style and taste (fig. 7).

Developments in Meiji-period kimono were bound up with changes in textile technology. Interestingly, Japan's textile industry was one of the first to modernize, and silk production became the nation's most valuable export, with factories established in and around Tokyo (see p. 109).

fig. 7
Yōshū Chikanobu (1838–1912)
Pictures of Ladies' Etiquette
Print, woodblock on paper, c. 1893
Art Gallery of New South Wales, Sydney

Luxury silk weaving in Kyoto was dealt a heavy blow, however, when the imperial capital was moved to Tokyo in 1869, thus depriving the city of its longest-standing patron. Kyoto recovered by embracing the new, rather than rejecting it. In 1872 Kyoto's mayor Makimura Masanao dispatched three students to Lyon to learn about European textiles techniques, and the following year a delegation was sent to the Exposition in Vienna with a similar purpose. The jacquard loom and other apparatus brought back to Japan revolutionized weaving practises, and a Weaving House (*Ori Koba*) was established in 1874 as a training centre for Kyoto artisans.

The introduction of chemical dyes also had a profound impact on textile production. The world's first aniline dye was created in 1856 by British inventor William Henry Perkins, and 'Perkins Purple', introduced to Japan as early as 1859, took the world by storm. Previously purple had been obtained from the root of the gromwell plant, *murasaki*, and large quantities were required for even a small amount of dye. Aniline purple was much cheaper, more readily available and produced a brighter colour. Previously restricted to members of the imperial court and high-ranking samurai, now anyone could clothe themselves in a colour that suggested luxury and nobility. With the assistance of experts from Germany and Holland, a Department of Chemistry (*Seimi Kyoku*) was established in Kyoto in 1870 to undertake research into new dyes; five years later, the *Somedono*, or Dyeing Palace, was created to teach craftsmen the necessary skills. The new dyes, used for prints and textiles, were viewed as the 'colours of progress'.[13] A political cartoon of 1879 depicted one prospective customer of a dye shop exclaiming: 'In my heart I don't want to be dyed, but if I don't get to be a popular colour how will I succeed?'[14] Despite the rapid introduction of western innovations, it took over ten years for new weaving and dyeing techniques to be assimilated and for technical problems, such as early issues of colourfastness, to be overcome.[15]

What is interesting is the way in which Japanese weavers and dyers, rather than adopting western methods wholesale, adapted them to suit native production methods and the creation of Japanese, rather than western-style, textiles and dress. Around 1879 the Kyoto dyer Hirose Jisuke (1822–90) perfected a method of mixing chemical dyes with rice paste that could be applied directly through stencils. This 'print-paste' (*utsushinori*) method was used to speed up freehand *yūzen*

resist-dyeing. The new technique (*kata-yūzen*) enabled pictorial designs to be produced in multiples. Using such new techniques, silk kimono fabric was produced in greater quantities and for lower prices than ever before. Many women could afford to buy silk kimono for the first time and, with the end of the Tokugawa-era sumptuary laws, were no longer forbidden from wearing them. The technical advances also afforded textile designers greater opportunities to create exciting new patterns to suit modern tastes.

Continuing the tradition established in the Edo period, leading artists of the day such as Kishi

fig. 8
Design for a kimono
Painted silk, c. 1880–1900
Victoria and Albert Museum, London

fig. 9
Kimono department, Mitsukoshi
Photograph, silver gelatin print, 1911
National Diet Library, Tokyo

Chikudō (1826–97), Kōno Bairei (1844–95) and Takeuchi Seihō (1864–1942) were hired by Kyoto kimono companies such as Chisō. In contrast to the printed *hinagata-bon* of the Edo period, designs were individually painted and embellished onto thick paper (fig. 8 and see p. 144). In the late Meiji period, Chisō began to hire graduates from the recently established design departments of art schools and *nihonga* (Japanese-style painting) gave way to a fresher approach that echoed western Art Nouveau styles. The concept of an artist working exclusively to create designs was new to Japan, and the word coined to describe this – *zuan* (design) – carried connotations of the modern and exciting.

Companies such as Chisō and Marubeni supplied kimono to the new department stores that had evolved from the Edo-period drapery stores. In 1904 Echigo-ya became Mitsukoshi; Daimaru was transformed in 1908; Matsuzakaya, founded in 1611, in 1910; and by 1907, Takashimaya, which began life as a purveyor of second-hand

kimono in 1831, had also converted its shops into department stores. These establishments, which sold Japanese and western-style clothing, as well as other merchandise, were modelled on European and American examples and on methods of display utilized at the international expositions. Mitsukoshi led the way, creating a new brand identity with in-house publications and was the first to have western-style display cases, transforming shopping into a visual, rather than a purely commercial, activity (fig. 9). In 1905, echoing Japan's euphoria following its defeat of Russia, the store launched a kimono range inspired by the flashy styles of the Genroku period (1688–1704). By using the latest methods of textile production to evoke the celebrated patterns of the past, and by updating the clever marketing and selling strategies of founder Mitsui Takatoshi, Mitsukoshi promoted a style that was both traditional and modern and set the tone for the dramatic kimono designs of the early twentieth century.

left
Kimono for a woman (*kosode*)
Paulownia, peach tree and flower vine
Figured crepe silk (mon-chirimen); embroidery in silk
and metallic threads
Edo–Meiji period, 1880–1900
148.0 × 132.5 cm
KX157

The scattered motifs that decorate this
kimono are typical of the traditional styles
worn by the imperial aristocracy. The bright
colours, however, reveal that women of the
court could also embrace the possibilities
offered by the newly imported chemical dyes.

opposite
Kimono for a woman (*kosode*)
Flowers on rafts
Plain weave crepe silk (chirimen); embroidery in silk
and metallic threads
Meiji period, 1880–1900
147.0 × 127.0 cm
KX158

This kimono is decorated with flowers on
rafts, a motif associated with the samurai
class, but the design composition is
aristocratic, so it is difficult to be certain
about who wore it. Such hybridity is a mark
of many late Edo and early Meiji garments.
The bright-purple ground was created with
the new, popular aniline dye.

opposite
Unlined kimono for a woman (*hitoe*)
Swallows with willows and wild pinks
Plain weave silk; embroidery in silk and metallic
threads
Meiji period, 1870–1900
168.0 × 124.5 cm
KX159

One style of kimono typically worn by women
of the imperial court featured vignettes of
trees and flowers that together made up a
landscape. Unlike the dense patterns and
bird's-eye view seen on garments for the
military elite (pp. 34–45), aristocratic dress
favoured a sparser arrangement of motifs,
which are shown in a more intimate aspect.
On this unlined summer kimono, wild pinks
grow among rocks at the water's edge, while
above, swallows fly among willow trees and
clouds. The fabric has the open structure
characteristic of gauze, but the warps are
not crossed.

left and below
Outer kimono for a woman (*uchikake*)
Fans with vignettes and flowers
Satin silk (shusu); embroidery in silk and metallic
threads
Edo–Meiji period, 1850–80
179.0 × 122.0 cm
KX201

Nineteenth-century kimono often feature
designs that are concentrated around the
hem, a style known as *suso moyō* (patterned
hem). The luxurious feel of this outer
garment has been achieved by the large
expanse of shiny satin silk, dyed a dramatic
midnight blue. This is balanced by the
small-scale embroidered design of scattered
fans, outlined in couched gold and featuring
flowers, animals, landscapes and figures.
The elderly couple with the brush and rake
are Jo and Uba. According to legend, they
enjoyed a long and happy life together; after
their deaths, their spirits occupied the pine
trees on the island where they had lived. On
moonlit nights, they returned in human form
to clear the forest floor: Jo raked in the good,
and Uba swept out the bad.

Kimono for a woman (kosode)
Landscape with pine trees, plum, bamboo,
cranes and turtle along the shoreline
Plain weave silk; freehand paste-resist dyeing (yūzen),
ink painting (kaki-e) and embroidery in silk and
metallic threads
Meiji period, 1880–1900
133.5 × 123.0 cm
K27

This kimono bears some of the key
characteristics of Meiji-period kimono.
Around the hem are delicate, detailed
landscapes, created using a combination of
paste-resist dyeing and ink painting, with
tiny touches of embroidery on the blossoms
of the plum and crests of the cranes. A
simplified version of the design continues
onto the lining. Another important feature
is the delicate shading technique, which
creates the transition from the pale ground
of the lower section to the dark colour above,
a dyeing method known as *akebono bokashi*.
The rich purple dye is synthetic and was very
popular in Japan, as elsewhere in the world.

Kimono for a woman (kosode)
Landscape with thatched huts and pine trees
Plain weave pongee silk (tsumugi); freehand paste-
resist dyeing (yūzen), ink painting (kaki-e) and
embroidery in silk threads
Meiji period, 1860–80
150.5 × 121.0 cm
K134

This is one of the most understated kimono
in the Khalili Collection. The back of the
garment has always been the main focus
of kimono design, but here it is completely
plain. The natural quality and texture of
the *tsumugi* silk, dyed a soft blue, is the
main feature, while a small-scale landscape
motif of thatched huts among pine trees
is confined to the lower hem of the front
section and overlap, both on the exterior
and interior. While seemingly modest and
unassuming, this kimono suggests a woman
of refined taste.

**Layered kimono set for a woman (*kasane*)
Landscape with pine trees, plum, bamboo,
cranes and thatched buildings along the
shoreline**

*Outer kimono: broken twill silk (kawari-aya); freehand
paste-resist dyeing (yūzen), ink painting (kaki-e) and
embroidery in silk and metallic threads. Inner kimono:
broken twill silk (kawari-aya); freehand paste-resist
dyeing (yūzen), ink painting (kaki-e): plain weave silk;
block-clamp resist-dyeing (itajime)*
Meiji period, 1880–1900
*147.5 × 128.0 cm (outer kimono); 149.0 × 127.0 cm
(inner kimono)*
K101

One notable fashion trend of the Meiji
period was the emergence of the two-layered
kimono set, which featured outer and inner
garments of the same design. Here, the inner
garment (*dōnuki*) has a simplified version of
the patterning of the outer kimono on the
hem, sleeve openings and collar, while the
main body is of a light, plain weave silk, dyed
bright red using a clamping resist-dyeing
technique (*itajime*). Not designed to be seen,
the fabric was mass-produced and cheaper
than that used for the main parts of the
ensemble, but was nevertheless considered
very modern and stylish.

left
Outer kimono for a woman (*uchikake*)
Cranes and pine trees at the water's edge
Broken twill silk (kawari-aya); freehand paste-resist dyeing (yūzen), ink painting (kaki-e) and embroidery in silk and metallic threads
Meiji period, 1880–1900
164.0 × 129.0 cm
KX162

Here, the delicate, painterly design around the hem – again of cranes and pine trees on a pale ground – contrasts with the formal black above. The birds flying above the trees disrupt the harsh division and lend movement to the design, while the irregular twill weave, which creates a diamond lattice pattern, gives texture to the fabric.

opposite
Outer kimono for a woman (*uchikake*)
Cranes and pine trees at the water's edge
Figured satin silk (rinzu): freehand paste resist-dyeing (yūzen), ink painting (kaki-e) and embroidery in silk and metallic threads
Meiji period, 1880–1900
162.0 × 127.0 cm
KX164

Like other Meiji kimono in the Khalili Collection (see K27, p. 126; K101, previous pages; and KX162, above), this garment features a design around the hem of cranes among pines trees at the shore, repeated on the inside, and the use of colour gradation. Yet the bolder depiction of the motif, the lustrous figured silk fabric and the cool, pistachio green of the main body create a very different effect. Below the pine trees, bamboo leaves are scattered, but at first glance the third 'friend of winter' – plum – is missing. This is not the case, however, as by artful contrivance the silk fabric is patterned with plum blossoms. Small blossoms, created by resist-dyeing, also appear around the crests on the front of the garment.

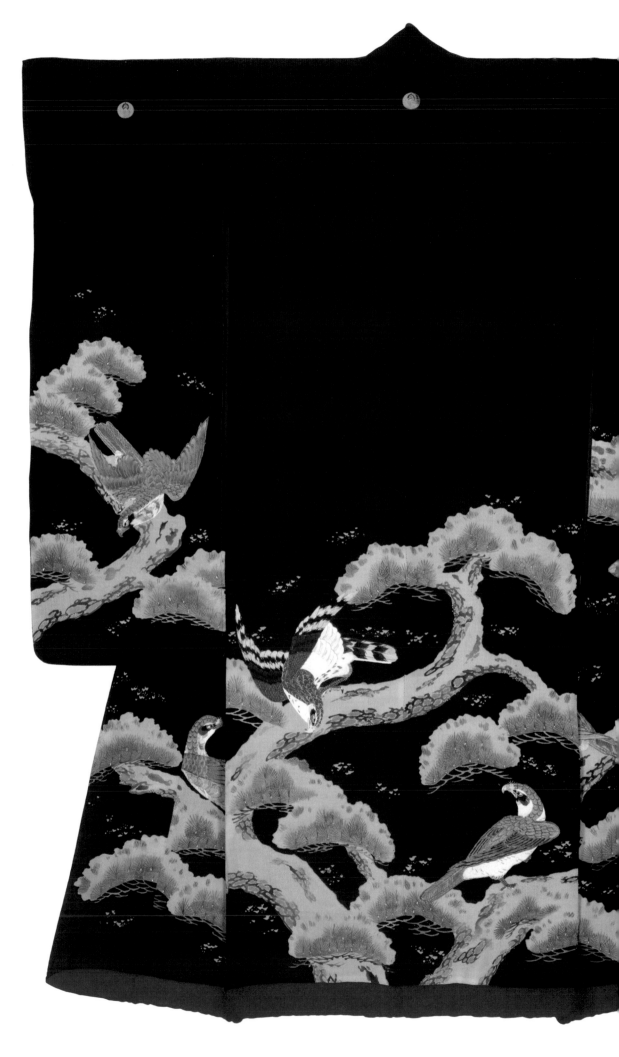

opposite

Outer kimono for a young woman (*uchikake*)
Hawks, blossoms and decorative partitions

Plain weave silk; freehand paste-resist dyeing (yūzen)
and embroidery in silk and metallic threads
Meiji period, 1880–1900
155.0 × 123.0 cm
KX195

Like KX161 (right), this kimono has hawking
as its theme. The rather fierce-looking birds
embroidered on the black ground on the
upper part of the garment contrast with
the delicate and intricately dyed pattern on
the lower section, where the hawks perch
on stands of floating fabrics surrounded
by cherry blossoms. The silk cloth has a
basic, plain weave structure, but the wefts
are much thicker than the warps, creating
a rippled effect.

right

Outer kimono for a young woman (*uchikake*)
Hawks and pine trees

Plain weave crepe silk (chirimen); freehand paste-resist
dyeing (yūzen), ink painting (kaki-e) and embroidery in
silk and metallic threads
Meiji period, 1870–1900
151.0 × 125.0 cm
KX161

The relationship between painting and textile
design is very clear on this outer kimono,
which depicts hawks on a pine tree, a motif
found on painted screens and scrolls created
for the ruling military class during the Edo
period. Hunting with hawks was a popular
pastime, symbolizing the status and warrior
spirit of the samurai. It may seem odd to
find such a masculine motif on a kimono
for a young woman, but perhaps after the
abolition of the samurai class in 1876 such
symbolism became even more important for
families of such lineage. Hawks were also
used as an auspicious symbol, because of
the association with sharpness of mind.

**Kimono for a young woman (*furisode*)
Decorative partitions, fans, boxes and
flowers**

*Plain weave silk; freehand paste-resist dyeing (yūzen)
and embroidery in silk and metallic threads*
Meiji period, 1880–1900
161.0 × 127.5 cm
KX188

This elegant kimono epitomizes the great
skill of *yūzen* dyers in the Meiji period.
Rather appropriately, it celebrates the beauty
of textiles through its decoration, which
features lengths of fabric hanging on stands
and gently fluttering in the breeze. This motif
is based on the decorative partitions (*kichō*)
first used in aristocratic homes during the
Heian period. Each of the fabric lengths are
different, some featuring elaborate designs
and all in a combination of delicate colours.
They are surrounded by flowers and elegant,
courtly accoutrements such as fans and the
boxes used for the shell-matching game (see
K92; pp. 168–9). The garment is dyed using
the fashionable method *akebono bokashi*
('dawn gradation'); the effects of daybreak
can certainly be seen here, as the soft, grey
clouds melt into a cool, blue sky.

opposite and right above
Underkimono for a woman (*dōnuki*)
Patchwork of fabrics with flowers, birds and animals
Plain weave crepe silk (chirimen); tie-dyeing (shibori), stencil dyeing (katazome) and freehand paste-resist dying (yūzen)
Meiji period, 1890–1910
145.0 × 125.0 cm
KX203

A *dōnuki* is an undergarment constructed from pieces of more than one fabric (see K101; pp. 128–9). In the late Meiji period, there was a fashion for creating patchwork inner kimono from fragments of other fabrics. The two such garments in the Khalili Collection illustrate the skill needed to create a harmonious balance from a disparate selection of fabrics, and the rich visual effect that can be achieved when this is done successfully. This example is more subdued in appearance and features predominantly stencil-dyed fabrics and a large central section, tie-dyed on a plum-coloured ground. KX204 (below right) is bolder and uses bright red and purple tie-dyed cloth and, around the hem and shoulders, fragments of fabric patterned with freehand paste-resist dyeing (*yūzen*), stencil imitation tie-dyeing (*suri-hitta*) and embroidery that was once part of an Edo-period kimono designed for a samurai woman.

right below
Underkimono for a woman (*dōnuki*)
Patchwork of fabrics with flowers, birds and animals
Plain weave crepe silk (chirimen) and plain weave cotton; tie-dyeing (shibori), freehand paste-resist dyeing (yūzen), stencil imitation tie-dyeing (suri-hitta), stencil dyeing (katazome) and embroidery in silk and metallic threads
Meiji period, 1890–1910
140.0 × 121.5 cm
KX204

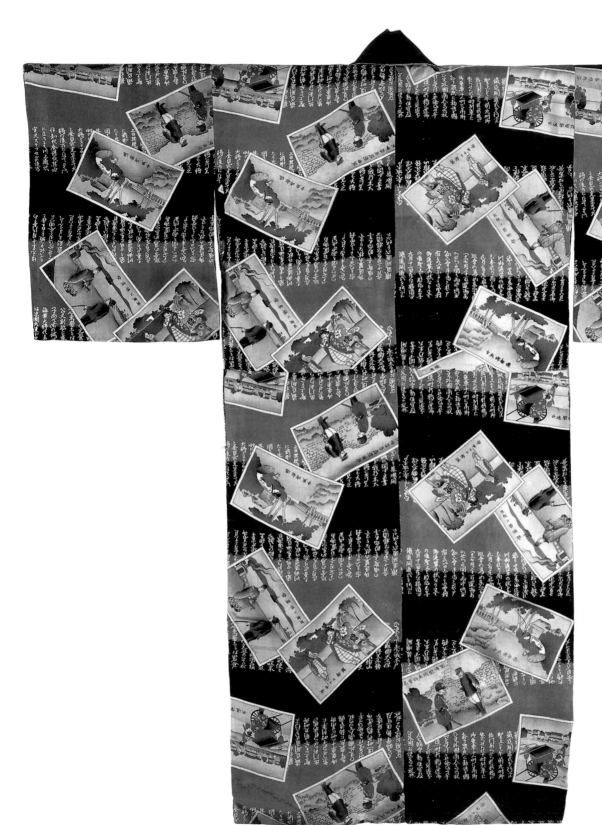

Underkimono for a man (juban)
Achievements of the Meiji period

Plain weave silk; stencil-printing on fabric surface
(kata-yūzen)
Meiji period, 1905
130.5 × 130.5 cm
K74

In the twentieth century, men's underkimono
bore increasingly graphic images. This
early example features inscribed postcards
celebrating achievements of the Meiji period:
the departure of the Iwakura diplomatic
mission to America and Europe in 1871; the
ceremonial opening in 1872 of Shinbashi
station, the terminus of Japan's first railway;
the thirtieth anniversary of the transfer of
the capital to Tokyo from Kyoto in 1898; and
the opening of Ryojun Port after the Battle
of Port Arthur in 1904. The text behind the
postcards reads as a diary entry describing
the events of the day.

Underkimono for a man (*juban*)
Vignettes of travellers
Plain weave silk; freehand paste-resist dyeing (yūzen)
Meiji period, 1880–1910
126.0 × 130.0 cm
KX207

During the Meiji period, kimono for men
bore only very small-scale patterns or were
completely plain. The underkimono worn by
men, however, were often highly decorative.
This lively example features figures of
performers, dancers, travellers, workers and
samurai, accompanied by haiku poems. It
is possible that all the scenes relate to a
particular Shinto festival.

Underkimono for a man (*juban*)
Nō masks
Plain weave pongee silk (tsumugi); stencil-printed on
fabric surface (kata-yūzen)
Meiji period, 1890–1910
116.0 × 155.5 cm
K71

This man's underkimono features a variety of
motifs, most conspicuously Nō masks of an
elderly man and woman.

Hasegawa Mitsunobu (fl. 1730–70)
First Shrine Visit, from
Moral Lessons for Girls
Book, woodblock on paper, 1730–60
Victoria and Albert Museum, London

Kimono and vest for an infant boy
Cranes and pine trees; crane, turtle and pine tree

Plain weave hemp (asa); freehand paste-resist dyeing (yūzen) and ink painting (kaki-e)
Edo–Meiji period, 1850–80
99.5 × 81.5 cm (kimono); 100 × 79.5 cm (underkimono); 42.0 × 32.0 cm (vest)
KX167

This kimono was probably worn by, or more accurately, draped on, a baby boy for his first visit to a shrine, which takes place about a month after birth. During this important Shinto rite (*miyamairi*), parents and grandparents express their gratitude to the deities and a priest prays for the child's health and happiness. The *koshigawari* ('change at waist') design features a central area decorated with cranes among pine trees, auspicious motifs carrying wishes that the child should have a long life. The body of the kimono is constructed from a single width of fabric. As it was believed that a garment with no back seam would invite evil spirits, decorative stitching known as *semamori* (back protection) has been used. On boys' kimono, these stitches were of the same size and placed up the centre back and then, usually, at an angle to the left, while on those for girls long and short stitches alternated and were angled to the right. Such conventions were not always followed, however, and on this garment the stitches are of regular size, but the angled section comes down on the right of the centre line. The stitching also appears on the vest, which is decorated with a crane, tortoise and pine tree. The ensemble includes an undyed underkimono.

Design for a kimono
Dyed and embroidered silk, c. 1880–1900
Victoria and Albert Museum, London

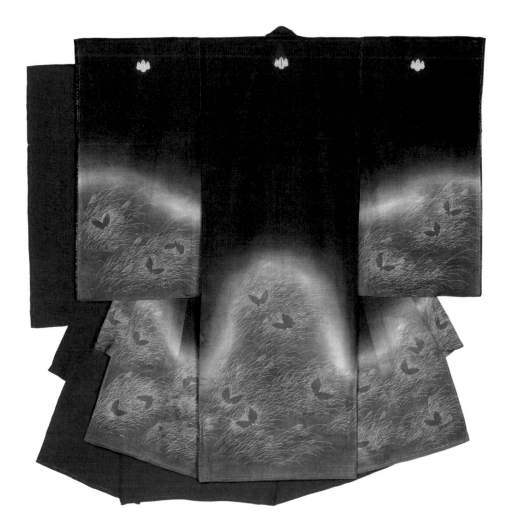

Kimono and underkimono for an infant girl
Butterflies and grasses
Kimono: gauze weave silk (ro); freehand paste-resist dyeing (yūzen) and embroidery in metallic threads; underkimono: gauze weave silk (ro)
Meiji period, 1880–1900
96.0 × 89.5 cm (kimono); 95.5 × 89.0 cm (underkimono)
KX219

The care and expense bestowed on children's clothes in the Meiji period are revealed by this two-layered kimono set (*kasane*). Probably worn by an infant girl for her first shrine visit, the outer garment bears *semamori* protective stitching at the back, with the alternating short and long stitches distinctive to girls' garments. The fabric is of *ro*, a type of silk gauze in which rows of plain weave alternate with one in which adjacent warps are crossed. The *yūzen* technique has been used to create a design of wind-blown grasses, over which butterflies flutter. Some of the grasses have been picked out in fine gold-wrapped thread, couched onto the surface of the cloth, with splashes of flat gold embroidered into the fabric in places. *Akebono bokashi* dyeing has been used to shade the grey into the dark blue above, giving a sense of early dawn. The red inner kimono would have shimmered under the blue, adding to the effect. This is a very sophisticated ensemble for such a young child, and echoes the styles worn by adult women.

Kimono for an infant girl
Plovers and flowers

Figured satin silk (rinzu); freehand paste-resist dyeing
(yūzen) and ink painting (kaki-e)
Meiji period, 1880–1900
93.0 × 83.0 cm
KX166

During the Meiji period, children's kimono reflected the fashions of adult garments in their decorative styles and techniques. Here, a ground of figured satin, patterned with maple leaves and water, has been shaded with pink and fashionable purple dye, and bears a painterly design of delicate flowers and birds. As in many of the children's garments in the Khalili Collection, the sashes on the front have been sewn on with decorative stitches (*kazari-nui*), here in the shape of *noshi*, folded paper ornaments derived from an auspicious bundle of dried abalone (see KX184; pp. 94–5).

Kimono for a young girl
Musical instruments, fans, screens of fabric, bamboo blinds and chrysanthemums
Figured satin silk (rinzu); freehand paste-resist dyeing (yūzen)
Meiji period, 1890–1910
104.0 × 105.0 cm
K91

This graceful garment is adorned with such courtly motifs as *koto* (a stringed instrument), fans, decorative partitions of fluttering fabrics and bamboo blinds, all glimpsed through lilac clouds, which form the main ground colour. Long sashes have been sewn onto the front collar and large,

red decorative ties onto the front sleeves. The latter are attached with stitches that pass through to the back of the sleeve, rendering the garment impossible to wear. It is possible these were added after the garment was worn by a child for a special occasion, and carefully kept as a prized possession.

opposite
Pair of kimono for a young girl
Flower roundels

Figured satin silk (rinzu); freehand paste-resist dyeing (yūzen)
Meiji period, 1880–1910
124.0 × 115.5 cm
KX206

Floral roundels are a traditional motif, but on this pair of kimono for a young girl they have been rendered in a very painterly, realistic manner. The two garments are made from the same *rinzu* silk and are virtually (but not completely) identical in terms of motif, but the different colours of the grounds – one a dramatic dark blue, the other a vibrant yellow – gives each a distinct appearance.

right above
Kimono for a young girl
Cherry blossom roundels

Plain weave pongee silk (tsumugi); tie-dyeing (shibori)
Edo–Meiji period, 1850–80
114.5 × 120.0 cm
K70

This bright-red kimono for a young girl features cherry blossoms executed in *shibori*. It is less formal than other examples in the Khalili Collection. The ties would have been used to safely secure the garment around an active child's body.

right below
Kimono for a girl
Sparrows and cherry blossoms

Plain weave crepe silk (chirimen); freehand paste-resist dyeing (yūzen) and embroidery in silk and metallic threads
Meiji period, 1870–90
132.0 × 119.0 cm
KX163

This girl's kimono has a charming and playful image of sparrows among cherry blossoms, against a soft, blue sky. The continuous composition and the flight of the birds give the design movement, while the embroidery on some of the birds and flowers adds lustre.

III
TAISHŌ
AND
EARLY
SHŌWA

1912
—
1950

Delirious Japan: politics, culture and art in the Taishō and early Shōwa periods

KENDALL H. BROWN

To the close observer, each historical epoch is unique in its contours and vivid in its intensity. This caveat noted, in Japan's long history the epoch constituted by the Taishō era (1912–26) and first two decades of the Shōwa (1926–89) may only be rivalled in drama by the Momoyama (1573–1603). The thirty-three years from 1912 to 1945 saw dynamic growth and devastating destruction. In the span of a single generation, the Japanese experienced relative social liberalism emanating from cosmopolitan cities, fervent nationalism fostered in part by rural famine, and, finally, foreign occupation that brought American military control.

Despite the exhilarating changes of the Meiji period, at the succession of Emperor Taishō in 1912 the great majority of Japanese still lived in villages, tilled the soil or tended family businesses, and took direction from an authoritarian government rooted in imperial divinity. When Taishō's son, the Emperor Shōwa (1901–89), renounced his divine status in 1946 at the behest of General Douglas MacArthur, the majority of Japan's citizens found inspiration in the cinema, worked in industry, and lived in cities. American bombs reduced those cities to ash and rubble in the final year of the war. For the second time in a generation, the great capital Tokyo lay shattered, with over 100,000 residents incinerated by maelstroms of flame.

In the previous three decades, Japanese culture blazed with passions that boldly reconceived national identity, spatially and temporally. The spaces of Taishō and early Shōwa were often conceived around imagined polarities of progressive metropolis and timeless countryside, pure home islands and diluted colonial periphery. In the most feverish dreams, these expanding territories might even include the foreign nations against which Japan measured itself. Chronologically, the Japanese looked with equal enthusiasm to the future and to the past, so that bestselling books included ruminations on Japan's brooding ancient temples and its brilliant future at the apex of a new world order. Dates could either be rendered in the western

calendar, the years of the current imperial reign or, with growing popularity, in the year since the Japanese empire's ostensible founding by Emperor Jimmu (see p. 110). Thus, 1940 – a banner year with a great international exposition (fig. 1) and the 12th Olympiad planned for Tokyo – was rendered year 2600. Some intellectuals even postulated contemporary Japan as constituting a 'world historical moment', in which such dualities as East and West, tradition and modernity, spiritualism and materialism, would be overcome as the nation finally became a 'Japan for the world'.

During the heady years of increasing imperial conquest, culminating in the Greater East Asia War (*Daitōa sensō*, now called World War II), many of these dreams briefly became realities. Japanese urban planners, architects and tradesmen working under quasi-governmental organizations and corporations created grand cities: in Tokyo, rebuilt and expanded after the devastating earthquake of

fig. 1
Nakayama Yoshitaka (1888–1969)
Japanese International Exposition
Postcard, 1940
Museum of Fine Arts, Boston

1923; in Taihoku (Taipei) and Keijō (Seoul), the capitals of Japan's colonies in Taiwan and Chōsen (Korea); and in Hsinking, capital of the puppet state of Manchukuo (Manchuria). Military and business leaders crafted – and executed – plans for the conquest of all Asia and the creation of a Greater East Asia Co-Prosperity Sphere. This grand project was to be realized through the perspirations of a unified imperial body politic (*kokutai*) and the inspiration of an unbroken imperial house (*tennōsei*) that embodied a divine past and embraced an international future. The twin deliria of urban cosmopolitanism and nativist militarism were paralleled in politics by deep tensions between individual liberty and authoritarian order. And, in the realm of material culture, there was unprecedented growth of the discrete but linked spheres of elite and mass cultures. Artists might aim to win prizes in the national art salon, and perhaps be named an Imperial Court Artist (*teishitsu gigei'in*), even as their work was reviewed in mass-circulation newspapers, reproduced in postcards and re-created in prints or textile designs for middle-class consumers.

Politics and policy

In the 1910s and 1920s, industrial revolution and westernization resulted in the expansion of the vote among male citizens (in 1925), establishment of new 'popular' political parties (including a Communist Party from 1922), and the creation of labour unions to advocate for the armies of skilled, semi-skilled and unskilled male and female industrial workers in large cities and provincial towns. To the old Meiji political and business oligarchy was added a new business class of self-made men and a burgeoning middle class of managers, bureaucrats and other professional men. These social and institutional changes, together with an embrace of western fashion and entertainment in 'mass culture' (*taishū bunka*) and the European avant-garde in elite culture led to the broad notion of 'Taishō democracy'.

Yet this ostensible ascent of western-style liberalism was matched by unrest and repression. Assassinations of political leaders by extremists on the left and right marked the entire period and signalled the intense insecurity of the era. Rice riots roiled Japanese cities in 1918, and violence against Koreans (who had protested Japan's colonial rule), socialists, radical labour leaders and other dissidents took place in the confusion just after the Great Kantō Earthquake in 1923 (fig. 2). In the face of transgressive acts and subversive movements, the Peace Preservation Law of 1925 sought to impose order by widening police power. From that year, new laws and coercive directives sought to quiet or silence dangerous thoughts, organizations and individuals, and to encourage proper thought and action. Proactively, Japan's participation in national and international competitions in culture (like expositions) and sports (including the Olympics) fostered national pride and inculcated a sense of both Japan's connection to the world and its unique place within it. By the late 1930s, most Japanese belonged to some regional or national association defined by locality, profession, or even affinity.

This metastasizing nationalism led to new economic investment and military intervention in Asia, building on the colonization of Taiwan and Korea and fed by China's political fracturing after the fall of the Qing dynasty in 1911. In the face of tension between unilateralist-military and multilateralist-diplomatic approaches to foreign policy in Asia, in 1931 Japan's Kwantung Army staged a sham uprising in Manchuria, the 'suppression' of which led to the creation of the puppet state Manchukuo the following year. Japan's departure from the League of Nations in 1934 was followed by greater expansion in northern China and the South Pacific. In response to negotiations with western powers, intended to moderate the Army's colonial ambitions, cliques of ultra-right young officers agitated for greater action and direct imperial rule. Although a coup in 1936 failed, a

fig. 2
Actual Conditions of the Catastrophe in Tokyo, Miwa-machi, after the Great Kantō Earthquake and Fire
Postcard, 1923

東京市内三輪町附近の惨状　　關東地方大地震實況

year later the so-called 'China Incident' launched a full-scale second Sino-Japanese war in 1937, often termed the 'Holy War' (*seisen*) at the time.

Brewing conflict in Europe and resulting opportunities for imperial expansion in Asia and the Pacific, together with fractious political in-fighting in Tokyo, resulted in the dissolution of political parties, the creation of the Imperial Rule Assistance Association, a National Spiritual Mobilization campaign and steps to realize a New Order in East Asia. The Tripartite Pact of 1940 with Germany and Italy, and a non-aggression treaty with the Soviet Union in 1941, led to advances into Indo-China. Stating that subsequent American trade sanctions and embargoes threatened its empire, Japan made war on the Allied powers on 8 December 1941.

Japan's defeat of the Americans in the Philippines, the British in Hong Kong and the Malay Peninsula, and the Dutch in Indonesia heralded the creation of the Greater East Asian Co-Prosperity Sphere. Railway officials drafted plans for a transportation network connecting Tokyo with Singapore, renamed Shōnan (Radiant South). Architects planned imposing war shrines and cultural centres across the empire, and museum officials even imagined a string of regional museums under the auspices of Tokyo. Military defeats, however, beginning with the navy's disaster at Midway and the army's loss of Guadalcanal in 1942, meant the practical end of such grandiose plans. Despite such realities and the existence of anti-luxury campaigns, throughout the war painters, sculptors and craft artists created works to memorialize efforts on the battle and home fronts and express the burning vitality of Japanese culture.

Society and ways of living

Japanese society between the wars was increasingly defined by a dual economic structure comprised, on the one hand, of traditional agriculture and small business and, on the other, of the modern financial-industrial combines (*zaibatsu*). While the former provided labour and, in the 1920s and '30s, economic distress, the latter contributed to Japan's foreign expansion and its urban affluence. Cities rapidly expanded into suburbs. These metropolises were traversed by buses, trolleys and, in Tokyo from 1927, Asia's first subway line (fig. 3). Although the latter only ran a few

fig. 3
Sugiura Hisui (1876–1965)
The Only Subway Line in Asia
Poster, lithograph, 1927
National Museum of Modern Art, Tokyo

kilometres from Ueno to Asakusa, it was a symbol of technological progress and urban sophistication. Interurban trains connected cities, and a network of private and national rail lines reached into the countryside. Tourism grew with transportation to bring urbanites to beach and mountain resorts, as well as to venerable sites of cultural patrimony that provided the diverse spaces of modern leisure.

These structures of work and consumption created shopping and entertainment districts that replaced the old 'downtown' neighbourhoods (*shitamachi*) comprised of small businesses and attached residences. Hubs around railway stations served salaried workers commuting from suburban developments of hybrid 'culture houses' (*bunka jūtaku*). These workers, epitomized by the 'salary man', resonated to the call for a 'cultured life' (*bunkateki seikatsu*) authorized by government studies, proselytized in popular periodicals and fulfilled in the richly constituted department stores (see p. 163). These fashionable emporia sold up-to-date, or *haikara* ('high-collar'), goods, together with the potent promises of self-improvement and status fulfilment.

This society was intensely literate and highly visual. The publishing industry boomed, with about half of the households subscribing to newspapers, and top-selling magazines reaching the one-million-sales mark by 1930. Magazines, calibrated for distinct demographics, included news, lifestyle features, editorials and serialized novels, as well as photographs, drawings, and even woodblock or lithographic frontispieces (*kuchi-e*). Books also proliferated, whether cheap novels, translations of European philosophy or 'collected works' (*zenshū*). These boxed sets suggested that topics such as 'classic literature' or Japanese garden history could be fully understood and conveniently possessed.

The seeming certainty about the past was balanced by the dynamic ambiguity of the present. Radio broadcasts brought news and music to half a million Japanese households by 1928, but radio was no match for film. Movie theatres introduced foreign and domestic film stars to Japanese viewers, and through them fresh fashions, ideas and attitudes. They also introduced popular songs that inculcated western cosmopolitanism and Japanese nationalism. Music enthusiasts bought songbooks (fig. 4), and heard music at concert halls (with orchestras), live revues (with bands, comedians and chorus lines), and dance halls (with live music or records, and taxi dancers). Competitive sporting events offered 'healthy' entertainment relative to the bohemian atmosphere of cafés, with their café waitresses (*jokyū*). In many ways, these demi-mondaines were the modern equivalent of the nineteenth-century geisha, and provoked condemnation from progressives and conservatives.

fig. 4
Saitō Kazō (1887–1955)
In Praise of Women
Songbook cover, lithograph, 1930
Robert Levenson collection, Florida

Whereas the countryside was viewed as the locus of traditional culture and stable gender roles, often imagined in the form of the 'pure' country girl, the city was the home of her modern counterpart, the *moga*. Whether an icon of social subversion or merely of bourgeois rebellion, the *moga*'s penchant for drinking, smoking and wearing western clothing engendered great debate. When she did wear kimono, the bright patterns were equally daring. The gender shifts and ambiguities of the *moga* and *mobo* (modern boy) in the context of the modern city epitomized a perceived rift between timeless domestic virtues and the giddy pace and dubious morals of modern life.

These easy oppositions emphasize the disorientation of an era marked by physical and cultural dislocation. Yet such divisions were often modified through small but telling acts of cultural hybridism. More broadly, political groups and mass-culture frequently provided a means of connecting realms theorized as in opposition. For instance, although the café waitress might stand as a symbol of a hedonistic age defined by such terms as *eroguro nansensu* ('erotic-grotesque-nonsense'), in the early 1930s there were attempts to organize waitresses as union members; by the decade's end, they formed one phalanx in the patriotic National Defense Women's Association. And while nationalist Japan is sometimes presented as a fascistic monolith, the government often relied on coercion, rather than edict. In 1940, when campaigns to stamp out foreign culture and luxury resulted in pressure to banish the permanent wave, the national association of beauty parlours agreed only to change the hairstyle's name from *paamanento* to the Chinese characters reading *denpatsu*, or 'electric hair'.

The worlds of art

The bifurcation of culture into 'East' and 'West', 'tradition' and 'modernity', provided a fundamental structure for the performing and visual arts inherited from the Meiji era. Yet the binaries embedded into categories such as *yōga* (western-style painting) and *nihonga* (Japanese-style painting) also spurred attempts to find common ground by discovering or adding elements from one mode to its polarity. Despite such attempts, the embrace of western academia and emphasis on promoting national character often hardened into orthodoxy in the 'fine arts' of painting, sculpture and architecture.

From the early Taishō period, however, young artists chafed against such strictures, calling for innovative styles and fresh spirit. Encouraged by Europe's modern movements (Art Nouveau, Expressionism, Futurism, Cubism and Surrealism, in painting as well as related styles in architecture and design) and a reassessment of Japanese styles (literati painting, or *bunjinga*, decorative Rimpa, ink painting and equivalents in other fields), artists and designers sought creative and spiritual fulfilment. Many hoped to integrate art with creativity, daily life and society to remedy the perceived hollowness of Meiji culture. This search for a universal artistic language was frequently realized more in the rhetoric of artistic manifestos than in the art produced. In some cases, cultural traditions were already so mixed that even attempts at cultural purity were untenable. Thus, the architect Itō Chūta (1867–1954), who had studied Gothic cathedrals and Buddhist temples, created self-consciously pan-Asian designs in poured concrete that also evoked elements of Art Nouveau and Art Deco (fig. 5).

While the recently termed approaches of neo-traditionalism and aesthetic nationalism defined one pole of theory and practice, there was also an assumption of internationalism in many arts. Although it was expected that western-style artists and architects would study in Europe and America, even *nihonga* painters and artists working in 'traditional crafts' took study trips abroad. No longer simply striving to acquire the techniques that would allow them to match Westerners, Japanese increasingly found native styles integrated into European modernism and that European study led to a 'return to Japan' (*nihon kaiki*). Other Japanese artists had distinguished careers abroad – painter Fujita Tsuguji (1886–1968), graphic designer Satomi Munetsugu (1904–96) and lacquer artist Sugawara Seizō (d. 1940) all worked successfully in Paris in the 1920s and '30s.

This centrifugal action was nearly matched by a flow of foreign artists into Japan. Artists from Taiwan, Korea, China and Manchuria studied at the increasing number of Japanese schools of art and design, while Europeans and Americans also came to Japan, no longer searching for teaching opportunities or exotic inspiration, but fuelled by a desire to work in a complex and compelling modern society. Westerners made a particularly strong contribution to architecture in Japan. American architects Frank Lloyd Wright and Antonin Raymond spurred distinct approaches to

Japanese modernism. In other fields, too, foreigners forged close ties with Japanese artists. British studio potter Bernard Leach worked closely with Hamada Shōji (1894–1978) and *mingei* (folk-craft) theorist Yanagi Sōetsu (1889–1961), while French-born, Japan-based Paul Jacoulet was the best known of a half-dozen foreign print artists. Interior designer Charlotte Perriand worked briefly in Japan in 1940, invited by the Industrial Arts Institute of the Ministry of Commerce and Industry. Such transnational intercourse was common among commercial manufacturers. The Noritake Company successfully mass-produced ceramics for markets in America and Japan by employing American, European and Japanese designers in New York, who fed patterns to the Japanese production studios.

When surveying the fine and applied art of the Taishō and early Shōwa eras, one has the impression of significant growth in production. Increases in population, education and discretionary income created significant art-viewing and buying audiences in Japan's burgeoning cities. There was also a dynamic foreign market for some kinds of art, including works from the *shin hanga* (new print) movement, sold primarily in the United States from the 1920s and spurred by the entrepreneurial artist Yoshida Hiroshi (1876–1950). In addition to more domestic buyers, there were also more venues for selling art (through independent and department-store galleries), displaying it (in the juried national

fig. 5
Itō Chūta (1867–1954)
Tsukiji Hongwan-ji
Tokyo, 1935

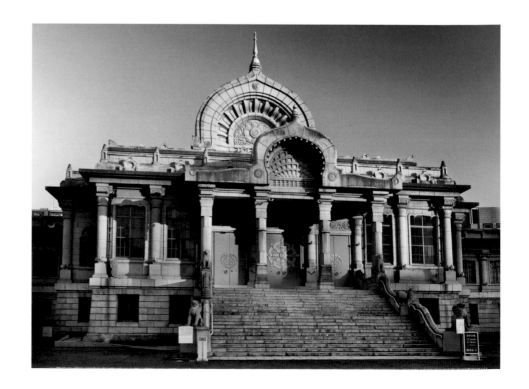

fig. 6
Teiten Exhibition, Tokyo
Photograph, silver gelatin print, 1927
Mount Holyoke College, Massachusetts

fig. 7
Ashikaga Honmeisen
Poster featuring the actress
Tanaka Kinuyo
Poster, lithograph, 1932
Kyoto Institute of Technology Museum
and Archives

salon organized by the Ministry of Education (fig. 6), metropolitan art galleries and private exhibits sponsored by artists' associations) and publishing it (in newspaper reviews, art magazines and exhibition catalogues). There were also more artists, trained both in private atelier (*juku*) and educated in formal schools of art and design. This art education infrastructure – including art classes in primary schools and in specialized secondary schools such as the Women's Art School (*Joshi bijutsu gakkō*) – provided many artists with a day job that allowed more creative work. Commercial outlets, including the burgeoning fields of illustration, graphic design and art direction for movies, also provided gainful employment for the struggling artist.

Arguably, art was best integrated into the fabric of daily life and society through fashion – in actual textile designs, in the ways that women could compose or curate their own appearance and in the images used to market fashion. Many of these stylish posters were created by leading painters of women (*bijin*) and featured noted actresses of the day (fig. 7; see also p. 173). Some artists worked on the side as textile designers, and a few had their contemporary paintings of young women printed on kimono, so that art, quite literally, became fashion. Through fashion, women – and, to a much lesser degree, men – could negotiate composite and shifting identities that referenced Japan's past, the Euro-American present or sought to link them in complex ways.

In many ways the war seemed to end an era in larger culture and in fashion. By 1942, many women had given up precious silk kimono for *monpe* (the loose trousers of field workers), and rationing of silk and cotton led to the use of coarse hybrids of wool mixed with 'staple fibre' (*sufu*), made from wood pulp. Yet after 1940, when government anti-luxury campaigns spelled the end of high-grade silk, popular and populist *meisen* (machine-spun pongee silk) rolled off the looms throughout the war. *Meisen* continued to decorate the bodies of Japanese women during the post-war epochs of Occupation and the Economic Miracle that followed. While it is tempting to see the war as ending one chapter in Japanese political and cultural history, kimono fashions reveal that many of the tensions that defined pre-war and wartime Japan continued in similar or modified form. Indeed, following only the history of *meisen* from 1930 to 1960 would disclose some of the intriguing contours and intricate patterns of a trans-war culture.

Dress in the Taishō and early Shōwa periods: traditions transformed

ANNA JACKSON

The years of the Taishō and early Shōwa periods were truly transformative ones. As the Japanese examined their past and looked to their future, the present offered a myriad of ever-shifting possibilities. Issues of national, social and cultural identity, constantly re-evaluated, were clearly articulated through the fashions of the day. Dress itself became a significant focus for the debates that surrounded notions of tradition and modernity, of the native and the foreign.[1]

New techniques

The dazzling kimono designs of Taishō and early Shōwa Japan have their foundations in the technical innovations of the Meiji era. Vibrant colours are their most striking aspect, with chemical dyes being used with particular skill by artisans employing the *yūzen* technique. The most formal garments, which bear five crests across the shoulders, usually have a black ground that acts as an intense foil to radiantly coloured motifs.[2] It was just such a kimono, decorated with fans and flowers, that Shimojima Sachiko wore for her wedding day in 1934 (fig. 1). Sachiko was of samurai descent, while her husband, Shimojima Saburō, came from a family of wealthy oil merchants; their union was of a kind that would have been unthinkable in the nineteenth century. The kimono was made to order by Shirokiya, one of Tokyo's leading department stores.[3]

Semi-formal kimono have similarly opulent designs, but often on a brightly coloured ground of figured silk. While it is the dyes used in early twentieth-century kimono that make the most obvious visual impact, advanced weaving techniques also introduced new looks and textures to fabrics. Threads of different thickness were used; crepe was woven with varying twists to the warps and wefts or figured with patterns; and supplementary wefts were added to create luxurious effects. *Ro* gauze, in which rows of plain weave alternate with one in which the adjacent warps are crossed over each other, became

popular for delicate summer garments, while gauze-like effects were also created in plain weave fabrics.

Many of these new fabrics were used for informal kimono, which, although not as costly as formal garments, would still have required a level of expenditure beyond the means of most women. The *kata-yūzen* technique (see p. 118) allowed for the production of multiple garments, and was therefore less pricey, but it was the development of *meisen* that brought modern kimono fashions within the reach of many women for the first time. *Meisen* is connected not so much with the traditional silk-weaving area of Kyoto, but with towns around Tokyo, in particular Isesaki. Weavers from this area traditionally employed thick silk thread derived from double or deformed cocoons. With the advent of mechanized spinning and weaving in the late nineteenth century, it became possible to produce a more lustrous and fine fabric

fig. 1
Wedding of Shimojima Sachiko
Photograph, silver gelatin print, 1934
Victoria and Albert Museum, London

fig. 2
Kageyama Kôyô (1907–81)
One Hundred Views of Tokyo:
Pola Negri-style moga in Ginza
Photograph, silver gelatin print, 1929
Kageyama Tomohiro collection

that was still hard-wearing. *Meisen* was patterned using a technique developed in Isesaki in 1909 by Shiraiishi Kai. Known as *hogushiori* ('unravel and weave'), this capitalized on the *utsushinori* paste-dye invention. Patterns were printed directly on warp threads, held in place by temporary wefts. The latter were then unravelled and discarded and true wefts woven in. This was a speeding up of the traditional *kasuri* technique, but one that retained the blurred outline characteristic of the hand-tying method. Sharper patterns became possible when the means to print on both warp and weft were developed.

This new technique was used to create highly distinctive designs, which often utilized dramatically enlarged traditional motifs. *Meisen* was thus a fairly inexpensive, durable yet attractive fabric, patterned using a relatively quick method and bright chemical dyes to bold effect on what was essentially an informal, everyday garment. Other production centres adopted the technique and in the interwar years almost half the output of silk kimono was *meisen*. In Isesaki in 1930, despite the depression, 1,200 weavers and dyers working on 3,500 power looms produced 4.5 million tan (54 million metres, or about 177 million feet).[4]

Modern women

The Taishō period was one of economic prosperity and urban growth, particularly in Tokyo. People moved to the suburbs, commuting on expanding railway networks to new types of office and factory jobs. Women entered the workforce in large numbers for the first time, employed as typists, bank clerks, bus conductors and shop assistants. These workers were the consumers of a new mass urban culture that centred around the cinema, department store, café and dance hall. Culture itself became a commodity, seen in the use of the adjective *bunkateki* (cultural), for many accoutrements of everyday life. The main 'cultural' space was the Ginza, the most fashionable district of the capital. The home of the biggest department stores and the smartest cafés, it was a site of consumption and spectacle encapsulated in the phrase *gimbura*, or 'wandering the Ginza'. This was the world of the 'modern boy' and 'modern girl', popularly abbreviated to *mobo* and *moga*, who enthusiastically participated in all aspects of contemporary culture. *Modanizumu*, or 'modernism', became the catchword of the

period, and the latest trends in western art, literature and fashion were eagerly followed.

In the Meiji period, it had been a very select group of the elite who had worn western dress, but in the Taishō period it was generally not the politically and financially powerful who sought to embody modernity through their choice of western clothing. The wearing of European styles was not an expression of political authority, but of emancipation and freedom (fig. 2). Unlike the Victorian dress styles encountered during the Meiji period, western fashions of the 1920s seemed more appropriate to Japanese changes in lifestyle and made more aesthetic sense given that, in the early twentieth century, Asian dress had greatly influenced European and American fashion designers. This was seen particularly in Paris, where designers abandoned tightly corseted, highly structured styles in favour of less tailored layers of fabric that wrapped or draped the body. Thus western fashion favoured a flat-chested, slim, straight look that was not unfamiliar to Japanese women.

The confident mood of the Taishō period was shattered on 1 September 1923 when an earthquake struck the Tokyo and Yokohama area, killing 60,000 people in the capital alone. The disaster had a direct impact on Japanese dress as, on a practical level, people tended to replace the clothing lost in the devastation with western garments. The physical reconstruction of Tokyo also effected the sartorial, as newly erected buildings created an even greater awareness of notions of *modanizumu*. These western-style spaces, which included, for the first time, domestic interiors, better suited western dress styles for women, as well as men.[5] After 1923 the number of cafés in Tokyo rose dramatically. The café was viewed as the quintessential space of modernity, a site that symbolized freedom, youth and the future. Famous places such as Café Maru and Ginza Palace proclaimed their glamorous modernity through the use of bright neon lights and surfaces of stainless steel, aluminium and glass.

What distinguished such establishments from their European counterparts was the role of the waitress, for the Japanese café was a sexualized space. In some respects, work as a café waitress liberated women from traditional social and economic restraints, but circumstances often pushed them into prostitution. It was certainly the lure of the erotic that drew male customers to the cafés. They were a major site of *eroguro nansensu*, 'erotic-grotesque-nonsense', the term used to describe the Japanese equivalent of the 'flapper' age. The café waitress, and her sisters in the bars and dance halls, embodied the image of the *moga*, a focus not only of fascination, but also of anxiety about the modern. Reactionaries called for a return to past values, while the experiences of the eroticized and victimized 'modern girl' were the subject of social critique, fiction and films.[6]

As Japan grappled with a new cultural identity, it was women – their role in society and the clothes they wore – that lay at the heart of the debate. It was accepted that men worked in the new economy and their wearing of western dress caused no concern, but the westernization of women, who had come to embody essential Japanese values, was problematic. The *moga*, conspicuous in the leisure spaces of the city in her short dress and bobbed hair, was the antithesis of the 'good wife and mother' (*ryōsai kenbo*) championed in official ideology, who wore kimono, occupied the home and guarded traditional morality. But rather than reflecting the lives lived by real women, both these images of womanhood were hybrid social constructions.[7] Similarly, issues of dress failed to fall neatly into two conflicting camps. The archetypal *moga* is Naomi, the female protagonist in the 1924 novel *Chijin no ai (A Fool's Love)* by Tanizaki Jun'ichirō (1886–1965), yet she spends her lover's money not on western dress, but on kimono and Japanese-style

shoes, which she wears to jazz clubs and parties. Western-clad *moga* were also hard to find on the streets of Tokyo. In 1925 the ethnographers Kon Wajirō and Yoshida Ken'ichi surveyed the clothing of 1,180 people walking through the Ginza. Of these, 67 per cent of men wore western clothing, but only 1 per cent of women did so. For women living in interwar Japan, elements of the foreign did not exist in opposition to the native, but were assimilated into it as part of a complex personal identity. When it came to fashionable dress, the new kimono styles offered them a rich middle ground between the two dominant ideologies, one where the supposed radical subversion of the modern girl was deflected and the orthodox styles of the traditional Japanese woman were infused with contemporary vitality (fig. 3).

Modern style

A simple way that a kimono-clad woman could embrace the new was through hair and make-up, with the permanent wave becoming a symbol of modern femininity after curling machines were introduced to Japan in the early 1920s (fig. 4). By 1934 the country was manufacturing its own machines, lowering the costs and increasing the popularity of the latest hairstyles. The latest looks could be acquired with a visit to the beauty parlour. The most prominent were those of the cosmetics

fig. 3
Kageyama Kōyō (1907–81)
Young Women in Summer Kimono Heading for Ginza
Photograph, silver gelatin print, 1930
Kageyama Tomohiro collection

fig. 4
Kobayakawa Kiyoshi (1889–1948)
Staircase, December*, from the series *Pictures of the Months
Hanging scroll, ink and colours on paper, 1935
Robert Levenson collection

fig. 6
Sugiura Hisui (1876–1965)
*Opening of the Mitsukoshi Department
Store, 10 April 1930*
Poster, lithograph, 1930
National Museum of Modern Art, Tokyo

fig. 5
Kanenori Suwa (1897–1932)
*Ginza Scene, from Shiseido's
Lady's Pocketbook*
Book, lithograph, 1927
Shiseido Corporate Museum, Kakegawa

company Shiseido, which, through its salons, products and magazines promoted a stylish lifestyle that appealed directly to the sophisticated, urban woman. Fukuhara Shinzō (1883–1948) took over as head of the company from his father in 1915, and the following year established the Shiseido Design Department to create a coherent approach to advertising and packaging. In the late 1920s and '30s, company designers made a lyrical Art Deco style the core of Shiseido's corporate image (fig. 5). This double-page image comes from a publication that featured articles on lifestyles and art, and shows two women strolling in the Ginza

outside the Shiseido parlour: one is dressed in kimono with a western fringed scarf, and the other is wearing European fashions with a chic cloche hat.

This combination of dress styles can also be seen in the striking posters of the Mitsukoshi Department Store (fig. 6), which established its own design department in 1909, with Sugiura Hisui, one of the Japanese pioneers of modern graphic design, as its chief designer. Stores such as Mitsukoshi were part of the modern spectacle of the city, drawing large crowds with their exciting displays of merchandise. After the earthquake, a mass clientele was further encouraged when customers were allowed to wear their street shoes inside stores, rather than having to leave them at the door in the traditional manner.[8] Department stores played an important role in promoting not only western fashion, but also new kimono designs through design competitions, seasonal exhibitions, catalogues and advertising. They collaborated with textile manufacturers to commission artists to create compelling images of fashionable women, often using actual celebrities to promote the latest kimono (see pp. 159 and 173).

The cut of kimono remained the same, but the designs bore an unmistakable modern flavour aimed at creating a dynamic visual statement for the chic city dweller. The kimono, sold ready-made and at affordable prices, were suitable vehicles for rapidly changing fashions. Many of the dynamic patterns that decorated them reveal the important influence that Art Nouveau and Art Deco had on early twentieth-century Japanese textile design. It is no surprise that western art and design should have had such an impact. This was not a case of mere artistic emulation, however, but one of stylistic synthesis. The evolution of Art Nouveau and Art Deco in Europe and America owed much to the inspiration provided by the arts of East Asia, and it was this cultural affinity that gave the styles such special resonance in Japan.⁹ In a poster from 1914 for the latest kimono fashions, Sugiura depicts a woman in a butterfly kimono holding Mitsukoshi's magazine and surrounded by Seccessionist-style furniture (fig. 7); the combination of simplified floral forms and scrolling arabesques so redolent of the Art Nouveau style was a particular feature of many early twentieth-century kimono patterns.¹⁰

By the 1920s the Art Deco style, which epitomized the glamour, luxury and hedonism of the era, had taken the world by storm. In its use of simplified pictorial space, dramatic lines, bold, flat colours, and geometric and stylized natural forms, Art Deco was a successor to Art Nouveau. Kimono motifs evolved to reflect the exuberance of the new style: colour combinations became brighter, flowers were bolder, streams and waves transformed into whirlpools, and abstract motifs danced across the surface to the rhythms of the Jazz Age. Art Deco placed emphasis on sumptuous surfaces and striking effects, making it a style ideally suited to the talents of kimono designers. With its concentration on surface decoration, the style is characterized by the use of simplified and flattened pictorial space, in which the relationship between pattern and ground, so central to Japanese aesthetics, becomes central. The whirlpool and large dot motifs that look so radical also have a long heritage, and are found, for example, in the late seventeenth-century designs of Hishikawa. Kimono designers were thus able to harness elements of contemporary western styles in the creation of a modern mode of expression that fused them with Japanese elements.

An enormous range of kimono patterns were available to the modern woman, ranging from those imbued with romantic nostalgia for Japan's lyrical past to those that embraced the country's fast-moving future. A page from a 1920s design book demonstrates, as do the actual garments of the period, how long-popular motifs such as cranes or pine trees could be rendered in a variety of ways, from the conventional to the stylized (fig. 9). Such books also reveal that the same kimono company was simultaneously producing both figurative and abstract designs. Others consciously looked to the West for inspiration. Okada Kirojiro, a director of the Kyoto kimono company Marubeni, collected textile samples from across Europe in 1923–5 and swatches of the French examples, considered the best, were compiled in book form to provide inspiration (fig. 10).

fig. 7
Sugiura Hisui (1876–1965)
Mitsukoshi Kimono Department
Poster, lithograph, 1914
Advertising Museum, Tokyo

fig. 8
Itō Shinsui (1898–1972)
Hand Mirror
Print, woodblock on paper, 1954
Freer and Sackler Galleries,
Smithsonian Institution,
Washington, DC

fig. 9
Designs for kimono
Pages from an album by the company
Suwa Ei
Ink and colour on paper, c. 1924
Khalili Collections

fig. 10
French fabric samples
Album, printed silk mounted on paper, c. 1923–5
Khalili Collections

While some of her sisters might be shocking conformist members of society with their 'flapper' fashions, the woman clad in the latest kimono styles showed that she had not abandoned traditional Japanese values. But dressed in boldly patterned and brightly coloured garments, she demonstrated that she was no reactionary either, but a modern, glamorous, fashionable woman (fig. 8).

Kimono fashions for men

Male clothing is so often overlooked in any discussion of fashion and Japanese dress. In the Taishō and early Shōwa period, what men wore was not an issue; they had adopted western clothes in the Meiji period and continued to wear them. While tradition was perceived as the natural preserve of women, modernity was certainly for men and it was thus 'natural' that they would wear western dress. Some men did wear Japanese clothing, however. Male dress continued to be characterized by sober colours and subtle patterning, yet such garments could hide rather fabulous interiors that spoke more of individuality than the restrained exterior might suggest. The tradition of using vibrant designs on undergarments or linings has its roots in the Edo period, a taste that continued into the early twentieth century when linings for *haori* (jackets) and *juban* (underkimono) often bore painterly images that related to popular stories or were inspired by modern life. In the 1930s, motifs such as aeroplanes and skyscrapers, symbols of Japan's progress and modernity, became increasingly popular.

Garments for young boys were also often patterned with highly graphic propaganda images. A belief in the literal, as well as the figurative, power of images is revealed in such garments. These designs not only commemorated great achievement, bravery and loyalty to the nation, but were also a reflection of parental hopes and the conviction that wrapping the child in such auspicious imagery would bring about a magical transference of similar attributes. In the late 1930s, as Japan expanded aggressively on the continent, motifs became more nationalistic. On adult garments for men, the imagery was still not on public display, being confined to underkimono and jacket linings, but the fact that the Japanese did not wear such sentiments on their (outer) sleeves does not reflect a lack of patriotic fervour. Indeed, in many ways it meant that they aligned themselves to the nation's goals on an even more intimate level.[11]

Whether for women or men, what all the remarkable kimono of this period reveal is that so-called 'traditional' culture was not a static remnant of the past, struggling to find meaning in a modern world. It was a vital and vibrant element that evolved to suit and express changing circumstances. Despite the seemingly polarized debates of Taishō and early Shōwa Japan, 'tradition' and 'modernity' were not fixed concepts: they were constructs subject to constant modification. As the country negotiated a position that could be at once Japanese and modern, sartorial expression was of central significance.

Kimono for a young woman (*furisode*)
Boat filled with flowers on swirling water,
pine tree, plum blossoms and maples

Plain weave crepe silk (chirimen); freehand paste-resist
dyeing (yūzen) and embroidery in silk and metallic
threads with applied gold and silver (surihaku)
Meiji–Taishō period, 1910–26
161.5 × 128.0 cm
K106

The striking contrast between the delicate,
small-scale patterning of late nineteenth-
century kimono and the bold, colourful
designs of early twentieth-century garments
is exemplified by this extravagant example.
The motif of a pine tree at the shore with
other plants and flowers is a familiar one,
but the way in which it is depicted is very
different. The tree grows up the back of
the garment in an asymmetrical sweep, its
branches, together with plum blossoms and
maple leaves, cascading down again from
the shoulders onto the back and front. The
two boats, richly laden with flowers, float
from the front of the kimono to the back,
giving a sense of movement that is greatly
heightened by the swirling blue waters. This,
in turn, contrasts with the mellow, golden
yellow of the centre ground, which then
darkens into black around the shoulders.
The sense of distance or depth created on
earlier examples has here been rejected in
favour of one of immediacy, in which the
landscape seems almost to break out of the
confines of the cloth. This kimono reveals
the enormous skill with which textile artists
of the early twentieth century who used the
yūzen technique exploited chemical dyes
to produce designs that were precise and
detailed yet dramatic and exciting. Here,
lustrous silk embroidery has also been used
to highlight the petals of some of the flowers,
while others have been edged with couched
gold or with fine gold and silver leaf, adhered
directly onto the fabric.

Like many formal kimono of the Taishō period, this example is decorated with traditional auspicious motifs rendered in a flamboyant manner. While most utilize *yūzen* dyeing, the design of this garment was created using tie-dyeing techniques combined with embroidery. The golden clouds are reminiscent of the compositional device used on painted screens of the Edo period.

This highly decorative kimono has as its subject the shell-matching game, *kai-awase*, an elegant pastime that dates back to the Heian period. The game was one of memory and was normally played with 360 pairs of clam shells, the interior of the two halves of each were painted with a matching scene, often drawn from classical literature, or lines from a poem. Since the objective of the game was to perfectly match the two halves, *kai-awase* came to symbolize marriage. The hexagonal boxes (*kai-oke*) used to store the shells were often included in bridal trousseau and were a popular motif on kimono for young women. In this *furisode*, each box has been patterned differently, with the orange tassels tying two of them executed in embroidery to give a more three-dimensional effect. Only one shell can been seen, on the lower left, but there is another, hidden on the inside hem of the garment.

This is an example of the semi-formal
kimono style that emerged in the late Meiji
period known as *hōmongi*, or 'visiting wear'.
Roundels of flowers are scattered over the
purple-plum ground, which is woven with a
pattern of scrolling paulownia. Over the right
shoulder is a medicine ball (*kusadama*), its
long tassels hanging elegantly down almost
the full length of the back. These bundles of
fragrant herbs and flowers were traditionally
hung inside to ward off evil and sickness.

This kimono is decorated with views of
Matsushima, Miyajima and Amanohashidate,
Japan's three most celebrated sights (*Nihon
Sankei*) as identified by the Confucian scholar
Hayashi Gahō in 1643. Matsushima is a
group of small, wooded islands in a bay near
Sendai in northeast Japan; depicted here is
Godaido, a Buddhist pavilion accessed by a
short wooden bridge. The island of Miyajima,
also known as Itsukushima, near Hiroshima,
is famous for the vermilion gate, or *tori*, of
its shrine, which seems to float on the water
at high tide. Amanohasidate is a pine-clad
sand spit near Kyoto. These landscapes are
depicted only around the hem of the garment
and mostly on the front. On the back is a
glimpse of deer and pines, below the expanse
of silk crepe woven with a pattern of scrolling
peonies and dyed a striking teal colour.

Kitano Tsunetomi (1880–1947)
*Opening of the Minami Tenma Cho store
of Takashimaya*
Poster, lithograph, 1916
Takashimaya Historical Museum

**Kimono for a young woman (*furisode*)
Poem slips**

*Plain weave silk; freehand paste-resist dyeing (yūzen)
with applied gold (surihaku)*
Meiji–Taishō period, 1900–20
153.5 × 129.0 cm
KX160

Formal kimono from the first decades of
the twentieth century are distinguished
by patterns that are positioned below the
waist and concentrated on the front, with
only minimal decoration on the back, which
tapers to a completely plain area at the
centre hem (see K26, previous pages; K78,
overleaf; K133, pp. 76–7; and K103,
p. 177). Many of the examples in the Khalili
Collection are five-crested black garments,
denoting that they are highly formal
garments, and the motifs are executed
predominantly in freehand paste-resist
dyeing (*yūzen*) and bright colours. The
design on this *furisode* is of poem slips. Each
strip of paper, decorated with images of
flowers and trees or with the lines of a poem,
reveals the artistic skill of the dyer. Some
are further enhanced with gold adhered
directly to the surface. On the lower left,
easily missed on first glance, is a graceful
butterfly, fluttering towards the peonies. The
fabric is woven, in both warp and weft, with
four thick threads alternating with two fine
ones, giving a textured, chequered effect.
A kimono with similar motifs was depicted
by the artist Kitano Tsunetomi who, in 1916,
was commissioned by Takashimaya to create
a poster to advertise the opening of one of
their new stores. The model, Wakamatsu,
was a Kyoto *maiko* (apprentice geisha).

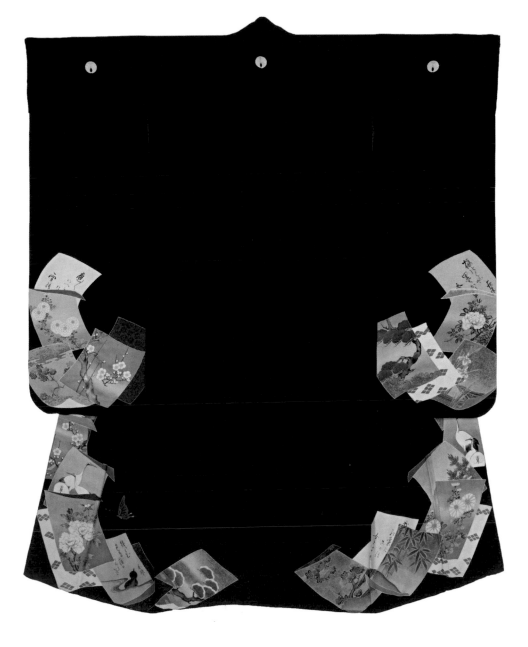

Design for a kimono
From an album of designs by the company Suwa Ei
Ink and colour on paper, c. 1924
Khalili Collections

Kimono for a woman (*kosode*)
Fans and flowers, Prince Genji and carriage
Plain weave crepe silk (chirimen); freehand paste-resist dyeing (yūzen) and embroidery in silk threads
Taishō–Shōwa period, 1920–30
158.0 × 124.0 cm
K78

Here, four large fans are placed among maples and chrysanthemums. On one of these is depicted Prince Genji, from the famous eleventh-century tale, together with an imperial carriage. This motif harks back to the *goshodoki* designs of the Edo period, although executed in the characteristic bold, bright styles of the Taishō and early Shōwa era.

opposite

Unlined kimono for a woman (*hitoe*)
Treasure ship in swirling water, gabions and
flowers

Gauze weave silk (ro); freehand paste-resist dyeing
(yūzen) and embroidery in silk and metallic threads
Taishō–Shōwa period, 1920–30
149.0 × 126.0 cm
K133

The formality of this unlined, summer
kimono is offset by the delicate gauze fabric
and the bright, fresh colours of the pattern,
which features the auspicious motif of a
treasure ship (*takarabune*).

right

Kimono for a woman (*kosode*)
Cranes

Plain weave crepe silk (chirimen); freehand paste-resist
dyeing (yūzen) and embroidery in silk and metallic
threads with applied gold (surihaku)
Taishō–Shōwa period, c. 1920–30
157.5 × 126.0 cm
K103

The contrast between colourful pattern
and black ground that characterizes formal
kimono from the Taishō and early Shōwa
period is employed to dramatic effect
in this garment. A great flock of cranes,
representing the thousand birds that bring
extra good fortune, rise from the rocky shore
at the hem to golden clouds at the front
waist. Their strong colours and elegant,
outstretched wings are augmented with
embroidery and applied gold. As in many
of the kimono, the design continues on the
inside, but here only features soft waves and
clouds, suggesting a calm emptiness after
the cranes have flown away.

This flamboyant garment is a wedding
kimono. It is completely covered with
cranes, woven into the fabric, dyed in bright
colours and applied in gold leaf. Cranes are
perhaps the most popular of all Japanese
motifs; symbols of longevity and good
fortune, they are said to live for a thousand
years and inhabit Mount Horai, the land of
the immortals. These mythical attributes,
combined with the fact that cranes mate for
life, make these elegant birds the perfect
motif for wedding kimono. The use of
impressed gold or silver (*surihaku*) dates
back to the Muromachi period, but became
a particular feature of Taishō and early
Shōwa-era garments. Here, rice paste has
been applied to the fabric through a stencil;
when this became partially dry, gold or silver
foil would be pressed over the pasted areas.
This kimono also has a striking lining of
orange silk dyed with pines and clouds.

This very lavish kimono with the auspicious
motif of cranes, pine, bamboo and plum
was worn by a bride on her wedding day. A
combination of techniques has been used to
great effect. The bold, red *rinzu* silk, woven
with a pattern of curving lines (*tatewaku*),
phoenix roundels and flowers in a diamond
lozenge, provides a sumptuous ground for
the sophisticated *yūzen* dyeing of the cranes,
tree branches, plum blossoms and, at the
bottom in fresh green, bamboo. The birds'
feathers and head crests are embroidered
in glossy silk and the pines are rendered in
embroidered and applied gold.

Kimono for a woman
Vertical stripes
Plain weave pongee silk (tsumugi)
Taishō period, 1912–20
142.0 × 124.0 cm
K4

From the Edo to the Shōwa era, the most common form of kimono patterning was the stripe. Despite the simplicity of the technique, in which different coloured warp threads are used in specific combinations, the variations of design are almost endless. Here, the wefts are in purple-blue and the warps in the same colour to produce the thick stripes, or in yellow, blue, cream and red to create the thin stripes. In the Taishō period, striped kimono were often worn by women working in restaurants or department stores, or as casual wear.

Kimono for a woman
Vertical stripes
Machine-spun plain weave pongee silk (meisen)
Taishō–Shōwa period, 1920–40
146.0 × 122.0 cm
K90

Unlined kimono for a woman (*hitoe*)
Crosses

*Plain weave pongee silk (tsumugi); hand-tied selective
dyeing of warp and weft threads (heiyō-gasuri)*
Taishō period, 1912–26
140.0 × 124.0 cm
K121

Kimono for a woman
Key fret

*Machine-spun plain weave pongee silk (meisen);
hand-tied selective dyeing of warp and weft threads
(heiyō-gasuri)*
Shōwa period, 1930–50
145.0 × 124.0 cm
K44

Kimono woven with selectively pre-dyed
yarns (*kasuri*) were often decorated with
interconnected swastika (*manji*) or key fret
(*sayagata*) patterns. Traditional hand-tying
methods have been used in this Shōwa-
period kimono, but the enlargement of the
motif creates a modern geometric pattern on
the opulent purple ground.

Kimono for a woman
Crosses

Machine-spun plain weave pongee silk (meisen); hand-tied selective dyeing of warp threads (hogushi-gasuri)
Shōwa period, 1930–50
145.5 × 128.0 cm
K24

As in K44 (p. 181) and K29 (below left), here the hand-tied *kasuri* technique has been combined with strong colours and a dramatically enlarged traditional geometric pattern to create a sophisticated modern look. The fabric has a fine horizontal stripe and a ribbed texture, created by using two thicker threads after every ten wefts.

Kimono for a woman
Wood lattice

Plain weave crepe silk (omeshi chirimen); hand-tied selective dyeing of warp threads (hogushi-gasuri)
Shōwa period, 1930–50
149.0 × 128.0 cm
K29

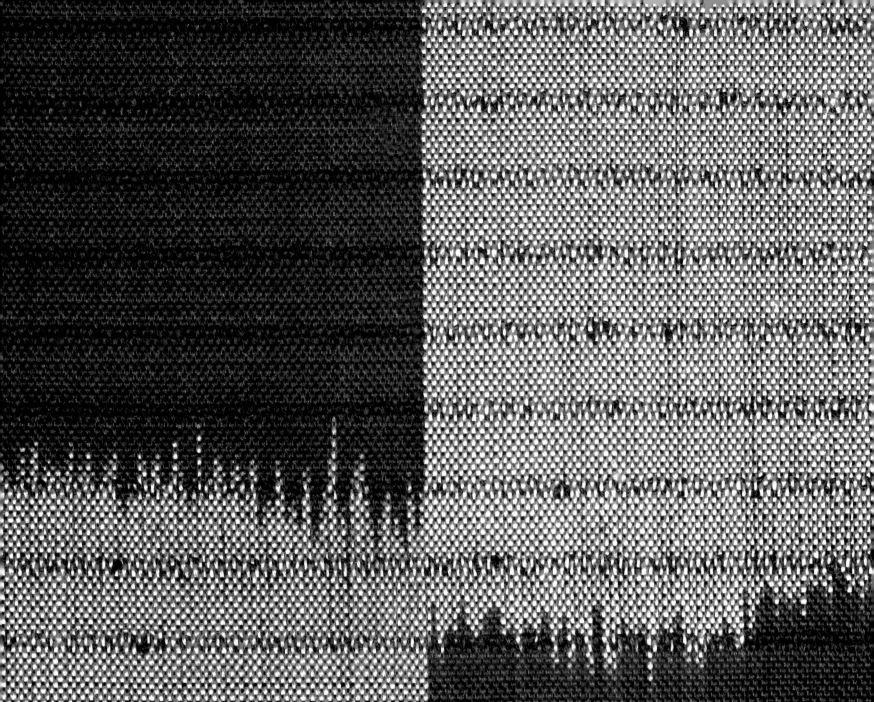

During the Heian period, the wheels of
carriages were placed in water when not
in use to prevent them drying out and
cracking. This practice came to be used
as a decorative motif, part of an extensive
imagery that romanticized courtly culture
(*yūsoku moyō*). Here, the wheels have been
placed in diagonal bands to create a modern,
geometric look. This kimono demonstrates
how new fabrics, including a thick silk crepe
known as *omeshi*, were combined with
innovative techniques to create different
effects. Only limited colours – black and
three shades of purple – were used to focus
attention on the pattern form and the texture
of the cloth.

One of the most popular motifs in Taishō
and early Shōwa-period kimono is the arrow
feather, which has military associations
and symbolizes the power to destroy evil.
In typical Taishō style, the motif has here
been enlarged to bold effect. In other
examples (see pp. 186–93), it is abstracted
to its simplest form, and then employed
in a variety of colours and thicknesses,
sometimes in combination with vertical
stripes. This creates patterns in which the
arrows zip up and down the garments in
dramatic visual rhythms.

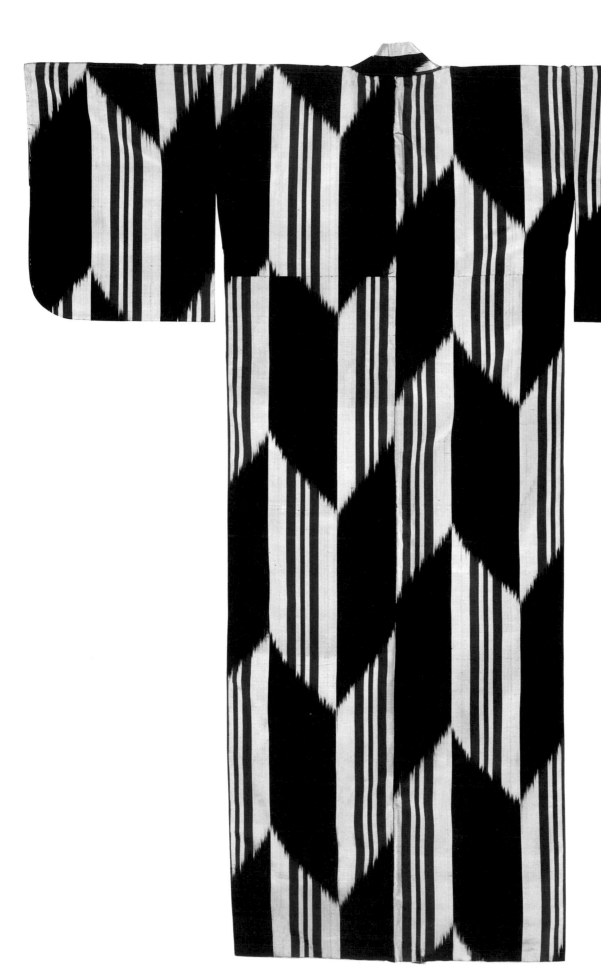

left
Kimono for a woman
Arrow feathers
Machine-spun plain weave pongee silk (meisen); hand-tied selective dyeing of warp threads (hogushi-gasuri)
Taishō–Shōwa period, 1920–30
151.0 × 126.0 cm
K65

opposite
Kimono for a woman
Arrow feathers
Plain weave pongee silk (tsumugi); hand-tied selective dyeing of warp threads (hogushi-gasuri)
Taishō period, 1912–26
148.5 × 122.0 cm
K25

Unlined kimono for a woman (*hitoe*)
Arrow feathers on a vertical stripe
Plain weave crepe silk (chirimen) and vertical silver
thread; hand-tied selective dyeing of warp threads
(hogushi-gasuri)
Taishō–Shōwa period, 1920–40
148.5 × 121.0 cm
K2

**Unlined kimono for a woman (*hitoe*)
Hollyhock leaves and arrow feathers**

Plain weave crepe silk with supplementary wefts; hand-tied selective dyeing of warp threads (hogushi-gasuni)
Taishō–Shōwa period, 1920–30

145.0 × 124.0 cm

K122

This summer kimono is very sophisticated in both pattern and fabric. The narrow feathers and stripes create a sense of vigorous motion, while the hollyhock leaves floating delicately across the garment suggest more languid movement. In the striped sections, the pattern has been produced by selectively dyeing the warp threads prior to weaving. The blue weft threads are highly twisted and in the plain blue areas, the warp is also twisted. The leaves were created with supplementary weft threads of silver, turquoise blue silk or silver combined with green silk.

Kimono for a woman
Key fret, arrow feathers and vertical stripes
Figured crepe silk (mon-chirimen); stencil-printing of warp threads (hogushi-gasuri)
Shōwa period, 1930–40
146.0 × 122.5 cm
K135

This kimono is decorated with the key fret motif (*sayagata*), predominantly in green and black. By picking out sections in red and white, however, the textile artisan has skilfully combined this pattern with that of arrow feathers (*yabane*). The design was produced by stencil-printing the warp threads prior to weaving. A fine yellow vertical stripe runs through the centre of the arrows, while a fine black vertical stripe runs across the whole garment, making what is an energetic and powerful pattern seem far more subtle. The fabric is a satin weave silk, which is weft-faced in the black stripe and warp-faced otherwise, but woven with a lightly twisted weft. This creates a lustrous fabric that also has texture. At first sight this garment does not appear to be the most dramatic in the Khalili Collection, but the complex yet understated design and the sophisticated weaving and patterning of the fabric make it one of the most interesting.

Unlined kimono for a woman (*hitoe*)
Morning glories on chequered pattern and
vertical stripes
Figured crepe silk (mon-chirimen); stencil-printing of
warp threads (hogushi-gasuri)
Shōwa period, 1930–40
145.5 × 121.0 cm
K126

This kimono has the identical weaving and
patterning technique as K135 (previous
pages), suggesting that they were produced
in the same workshop. The design of
morning glory on a chequered ground
creates a much softer effect, however, and
the fine black vertical stripes evoke a sense
of summer rain.

opposite

Unlined kimono for a woman (*hitoe*)
Morning glories

Gauze weave silk (ro); stencil-printing on fabric surface
(kata-yūzen)
Shōwa period, 1930–40
140.0 × 124.0 cm
K130

Like K126 (previous pages), this kimono
is decorated with morning glories, but in
appearance it is completely different. The
fabric is *ro*, a type of silk gauze in which
rows of plain weave alternate with one where
adjacent warps cross over each other, with
the pattern created by stencil-printing onto
the surface of the cloth. The bright colours
are strongly contrasting, but the arabesque
arrangement of the flowers and the fine
fabric give the design delicacy. Morning
glories (*asagao*) are a favourite summer
flower, their brilliant but brief appearance
captured on many kimono designs from the
Edo period onwards.

right above

Kimono for a woman
Camellias and fret pattern

Machine-spun plain weave pongee silk (meisen);
stencil-printing of warp threads (hogushi-gasuri)
Taishō–Shōwa period, 1920–30
141.0 × 126.0 cm
K56

right below

Kimono for a woman
Camellias

Plain weave pongee silk (tsumugi); stencil-printing of
weft threads (yokoso-gasuri)
Taishō period, 1912–26
141.5 × 124.0 cm
K3

Camellias are another popular decoration on
women's kimono. The examples on these
pages and overleaf illustrate how one motif
can be represented in numerous different
ways and how the stencil-printing technique
allowed for the creation of painterly effects.

right above
Kimono for a woman
Lilies
Plain weave pongee silk (tsumugi); stencil-printing of weft threads (yokoso-gasuri)
Taishō period, 1912–26
141.5 × 125.0 cm
K35

In this fresh, lively design, the bright pink, blue, yellow and silver-grey of the flowers creates a dramatic contrast to the black ground. The spots of colour suggest morning dew.

right below
Kimono for a woman
Flowers
Machine-spun plain weave pongee silk (meisen); stencil-printing of warp and weft threads (heiyō-gasuri)
Shōwa period, 1930–40
151.0 × 129.0 cm
K115

The visual impact of most Taishō and early Shōwa kimono rests on the use of large and dramatic motifs, but this garment is adorned with a dense pattern of scattered small flowers that resemble those on Indian chintz fabrics, known in Japan as *sarasa* and imported by Dutch traders in the Edo period (see pp. 80–1, 84–5). Here, the colours have been limited to the striking contrast of black against an orange-red ground.

opposite
Kimono for a woman
Camellias
Machine-spun plain weave pongee silk (meisen); stencil-printing of warp threads (hogushi-gasuri)
Taishō–Shōwa period, 1920–40
141.0 × 124.0 cm
K64

Unlined kimono for a woman (*hitoe*)
Irises
Plain weave pongee silk (tsumugi); stencil-printing of warp threads (hogushi-gasuri)
Taishō period, 1912–26
136.0 × 122.0 cm
K42

Kimono are constructed from pieces of fabric that drape from hem to hem, and to and from the lower sleeve edge, without a seam at the shoulder. Where stencils are used to form a repetitive design, the pattern will appear upside down on parts of the garment, either the back or, more usually, the front.[1] In the early twentieth century, this inevitable reversal of the pattern direction was used to create an interesting rhythm to the design, as seen here, where the irises on the back are facing down on the right sleeve, up on right body, down on left body and up on left sleeve. The flowers have been depicted in a realistic way, with pink highlights and shading achieved through the stencil-dyeing of the warp threads.

**Kimono for a woman
Chrysanthemums**

*Machine-spun plain weave pongee silk (meisen);
stencil-printing of warp and weft threads (heiyō-gasuri)*
Taishō period, 1912–26
137.0 × 124.0 cm
K53

This garment epitomizes stylish, informal dress of the Taishō period. Made of *meisen* silk and patterned by stencil-printing both the warp and weft thread prior to weaving, it takes as its design motif one of the most beloved of Japanese flowers – the autumn-blooming chrysanthemum – and renders it so large and in such bright colours that it seems about to escape the boundaries of the kimono surface.

Charles Rennie Mackintosh (1868–1928)
Rose and Teardrop
Textile design, pencil, watercolour and gouache on
paper, 1915–23
Hunterian Museum and Art Gallery, Glasgow

left
Kimono for a woman
Roses and lattice
Machine-spun plain weave pongee silk (meisen);
stencil-printing of warp threads (hogushi-gasuri)
Taishō–Shōwa period, 1915–30
142.5 × 124.0 cm
K34

In the early twentieth century, European
art movements exerted much influence
in Japan. The rose-and-lattice pattern of
this kimono echoes the designs of Charles
Rennie Mackintosh and the artists of the
Glasgow School. As with many of the most
visually striking garments of the era in the
Khalili Collection, the success of the design
derives from the visual unity of composition
and colour. The asymmetric yet balanced
disposition of the motifs across the fabric
surface is made more arresting by the skilful
use of a limited range of colours. The intense
pink of the ground is offset by the pale
pink and yellow of the roses and the green
framework of the lattice pattern, suggestive
perhaps of a rose thorn. The pink roses are
outlined in the green of the lattice and have
a leaf in the pink colour of the ground, while
the yellow flowers are outlined in the pink of
the ground and have a leaf in the colour of
the lattice. That this is all achieved through
the stencil-dyeing of the warp threads prior
to weaving is testament to the enormous
talents of kimono designers and makers in
the Taishō and early Shōwa period.

opposite
Kimono for a woman
Roses
Plain weave pongee silk (tsumugi); stencil-printing of
weft threads (yokoso-gasuri)
Taishō period, 1912–26
147.0 × 126.0 cm
K55

Red and blue roses tumble down the lush
green surface of this kimono. While certain
varieties of roses are native to East Asia, this
flower is an unmistakably western motif. The
characteristic blurriness of the stencil-printed
kasuri technique has been emphasized and
used to create shading around the leaves
and petals.

right
Kimono for a woman
Floral bouquets
Machine-spun plain weave pongee silk (meisen);
stencil-printing of warp and weft threads (heiyō-gasuri);
Shōwa period, 1930–40
149.0 × 126.0 cm
K88

The floral motifs so popular on Japanese kimono of all periods are portrayed in endless variations. Here, informal bouquets are depicted in a naturalistic manner, revealing the influence of western styles of representation.

opposite
Summer kimono for a woman (*katabira*)
Irises, bridge and willow trees
Plain weave ramie (asa); freehand paste-resist dyeing
(yūzen), stencil imitation tie-dyeing (suri-hitta), hand-
painting, and embroidery in silk and metallic threads
Taishō–Shōwa period, 1920–30
153.0 × 118.0 cm
K38

While western-style motifs became increasingly prevalent in Taishō and early Shōwa kimono design, many garments echoed styles of the past. Indeed, nostalgia was a key element of Taishō culture, as can be seen in this lyrical garment, in which sweeping willows line the bank of a river with irises and a wooden bridge. The design alludes to the famous chapter in the *Tale of Ise* (see KX215; pp. 58–9), when the Heian courtier Ariwara no Narihira and his companions arrive at the eight-fold bridge (*yatsuhashi*), in the iris marshes of Mikawa province. He composes a poem suggestive of the sense of loss he feels at having departed from the capital, beginning each line with a syllable from the word 'iris' (*kakitsubata*):

Karagoromo
Kitsutsu narenishi
Tsuma shi areba
Harubaru kinuru
Tabi o shi zo omou

I have a beloved wife,
Familiar as the skirt
Of a well-worn robe,
And so this distant journeying
Fills my heart with grief[2]

**Summer kimono for a woman (*katabira*)
Autumn flowers and grasses**
*Plain weave ramie (asa); stencil-printing on the fabric
surface (kata-yūzen)*
Taishō period, 1912–26
144.5 × 118.0 cm
K37

Like K38 (previous pages), this summer
kimono recalls earlier styles in its elegant use
of areas left undyed, a technique known as
shiroage (see KX151; pp. 34–5). Cloudforms
with autumn grasses and flowers,
suggestive of the cooler season to come, are
surrounded by a dense pattern of bamboo,
irises and blossoms.

left above
Kimono for a woman
Peonies and bush clovers
Plain weave crepe silk (chirimen); tie-dying (shibori)
Taishō period, 1912–26
142.5 × 126.0 cm
K136

left below
Kimono for a woman
Hemp leaves
Figured crepe silk (mon-chirimen); tie-dyeing (shibori)
Taishō–Shōwa period, 1920–40
143.0 × 125.0 cm
K50

The continued use of traditional patterning methods is seen in both of these kimono, which were dyed using the tie-dyeing, or *shibori*, technique (see KX174; p. 62). The hemp-leaf (*asa no ha*) motif – derived from the hexagonal shape of the leaf and abstracted to form a continuous, interconnected pattern – has been popular for centuries in Japan. Large hemp-leaf patterns were extremely fashionable in the Taishō and early Shōwa period. Here, the motif has been dyed an extremely striking purple.

opposite
Summer kimono for a woman (*katabira*)
Pinks on a chequerboard ground
Plain weave ramie (asa); stencilled paste-resist dyed (katazome)
Taishō–Shōwa period, 1920–40
144.0 × 126.0 cm
K54

This garment also reveals how established materials and techniques remained popular in the Taishō and early Shōwa period. Fine hand-spun ramie has been dyed using the rice-paste stencilling technique, *katazome* (see KX171; p. 96) with a design of small wild pinks arranged in diagonals on a chequerboard of alternating blocks of fine horizontal lines. Only one colour has been used, the very popular purple, but in a pale shade befitting the delicate patterning of this extremely elegant summer kimono.

Kimono for a woman
Pine needles
Broken twill silk (kawari-aya); stencil-printing of warp
threads (hogushi-gasuri)
Shōwa period, 1930–40
158.0 × 131.0 cm
K124

The pine tree is one of the most ubiquitous
motifs in Japan. Here, this symbol of
longevity and endurance is not depicted in
its normal form, but reduced to an almost
abstract scattering of large pine needles.
The design is rendered more striking by the
limited colour range; the weft is very dark
purple, while the warp is a purple and white.
The fabric is twill, a type of weave in which
the weft passes over or under two or more
warps, each passage of the weft starting to
the right or left of the previous one to create
a diagonal movement across the fabric.
The weave direction has been periodically
reversed to create a lozenge or diamond
shape. A red stamp on the interior sleeve
end is presumably the mark of the workshop
that made this sophisticated fabric, but
unfortunately, it is unreadable.

opposite
Kimono for a woman
Bamboo
Plain weave pongee silk (tsumugi); stencil-printing of
weft threads (yokoso-gasuri)
Taishō period, 1920–6
152.0 × 128.0 cm
K18

Bamboo, symbolic of resilience, is an
enduringly popular motif in Japan (see
KX152, pp. 72–3; and KX217, pp. 74–5).
The tall, vertical appearance of the plant is
normally emphasized to visual effect, but in
this design an unusual and dynamic diagonal
pattern was created, the impact of the design
heightened by the limited but effective range
of colours used.

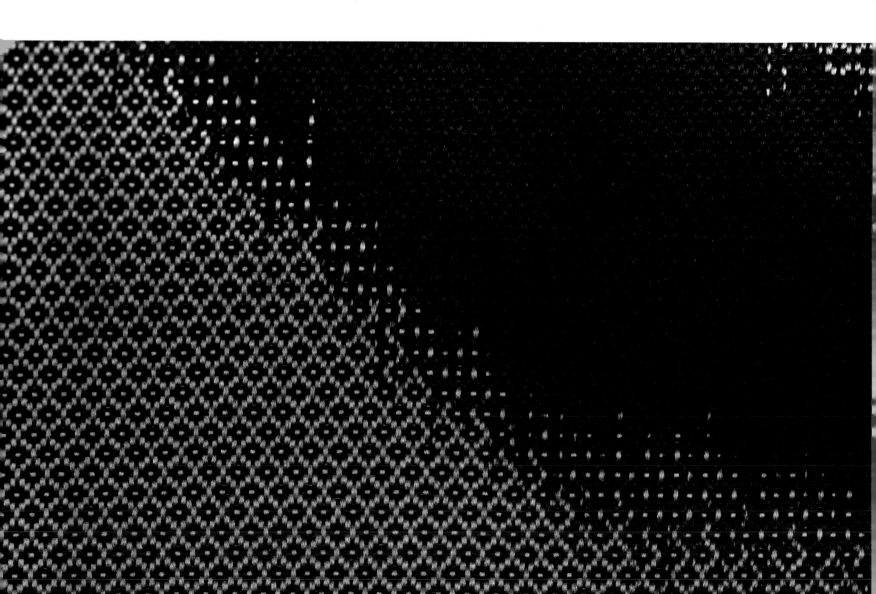

**Unlined kimono for a woman (*hitoe*)
Bamboo**
*Figured crepe silk and rayon (mon-chirimen); stencil-
printing on fabric surface (kata-yūzen)
Taishō–Shōwa period, 1920–40
136.0 × 121.0 cm
K58*

In this kimono, the powerful vertical form
of bamboo, in cream against a red ground,
provides a backdrop and counterbalance to
the diagonal spread of large yellow and blue
leaves. The design is stencil-printed onto the
surface of the rather unusual fabric. Possibly
a mix of silk and rayon, it has an open weave,
in which both warps and wefts are twisted,
leaving the feel but not the structure of
gauze. In places the wefts float in twos and
threes, creating a barely discernible pattern
of waves.

A kimono design in the Khalili Collection
has a similar design of bamboo, while
the alternating colours are suggestive of
other garments from the period (see K127,
opposite, and K36, overleaf).

Design for a kimono
*Ink and colour on paper, c. 1930
Khalili Collections*

Unlined kimono for a woman (*hitoe*)
Bush clovers and vertical bands
Machine-spun plain weave pongee silk (meisen);
stencil-printing of warp threads (hogushi-gasuri)
Taishō–Shōwa period, 1920–30
148.0 × 125.0 cm
K127

This kimono has an elegant colour
combination, with turquoise-blue flowers,
set against a silver-grey ground, alternating
with a column in which the silver-grey
becomes the pattern of the flowers against a
dark-blue ground. The bush clover (*hagi*), a
favoured motif of poets, as well as of kimono
designers, is associated with autumn.

Unlined kimono for a woman (*hitoe*)
Dragonflies on vertical bands
Gauze weave silk (ro); stencil-printing of warp and weft
threads (heiyō-gasuri)
Taishō period, 1912–26
132.6 × 120.0 cm
K36

The dragonfly (*tombo*) is one of the oldest
motifs in Japan, and despite its delicate form
has rather powerful connotations. In classical
Japanese the insect is called *akizu*, which has
associations with the mythical first emperor
Jimmu, who, looking down onto the country
from the top of a mountain, called it *akizushima*,
or 'dragonfly island'. In medieval times, the
dragonfly was known as the victory insect (*kachi
mushi*) and used as a motif on samurai armour.
Thus dragonflies are symbolic of patriotism
and valour. In kimono, small dragonflies are
sometimes shown darting over water, but it is
only in the bold designs of the Taishō period
that they assume decorative prominence.

   This garment demonstrates what
sophisticated effects can be achieved using
only two colours. The motif alternates in colour
with the vertical bands, adding to the sense of
movement created by the diagonal flight of the
insects, which change direction on each panel
of cloth. The dark-blue hue, the circular devices
and the delicate stripe of the gauze weave
fabric combine to suggest dragonflies flying low
over gently rippling water. In style and subject,
this kimono is perfect for a late summer's day.

above

Unlined kimono for a woman (*hitoe*)
Swallows flying over water

Gauze weave silk (ro); stencil-printing on fabric surface
(kata-yūzen)
Taishō period, 1912–26
133.0 × 129.0 cm
K41

There is a wonderful sense of movement
in this kimono, as swallows sweep over a
curving stream. The motif is a traditional
Japanese one, but the style suggests the
influence of European Art Nouveau. The use
of yellow against white and black is very
effective, and while the birds are simply
delineated, tiny differences in the eyes and
open or closed beaks give them character.

opposite

Unlined kimono for a woman (*hitoe*)
Swallows

Plain weave silk; stencil-printing of weft threads
(yokoso-gasuri)
Taishō–Shōwa period, 1920–30
141.0 × 121.0 cm
K120

Swallows provide the design motif for a
number of summer kimono in the Khalili
Collection (see K129, pp. 224–9). Here, they
are rendered in subtle shades of green and
golden brown on a dark-red ground. The
fabric has the feeling of gauze, although in
fact it is plain weave with the warps in pairs
and a slight gap in between.

Kimono for a woman *(hōmongi)*
Sparrows and bamboo
*Plain weave crepe silk (chirimen) with supplementary
wefts; discharge dyeing*
Shōwa period, 1930–40
150.0 × 125.0 cm
K79

This semi-formal kimono is a very refined
garment. Sparrows flying among bamboo
are a popular motif for kimono (see KX155;
p. 73) and are usually depicted in a cheerful,
lively manner, even when they allude to a
story with a strong moral (KX169; pp. 102–3).
By contrast, here the subject is executed in a
manner that is understated yet opulent. The
silk is a weft-faced, plain weave crepe, which
has a ribbed effect and is patterned with
discharge dyeing and supplementary threads
of white silk, gold and silver.

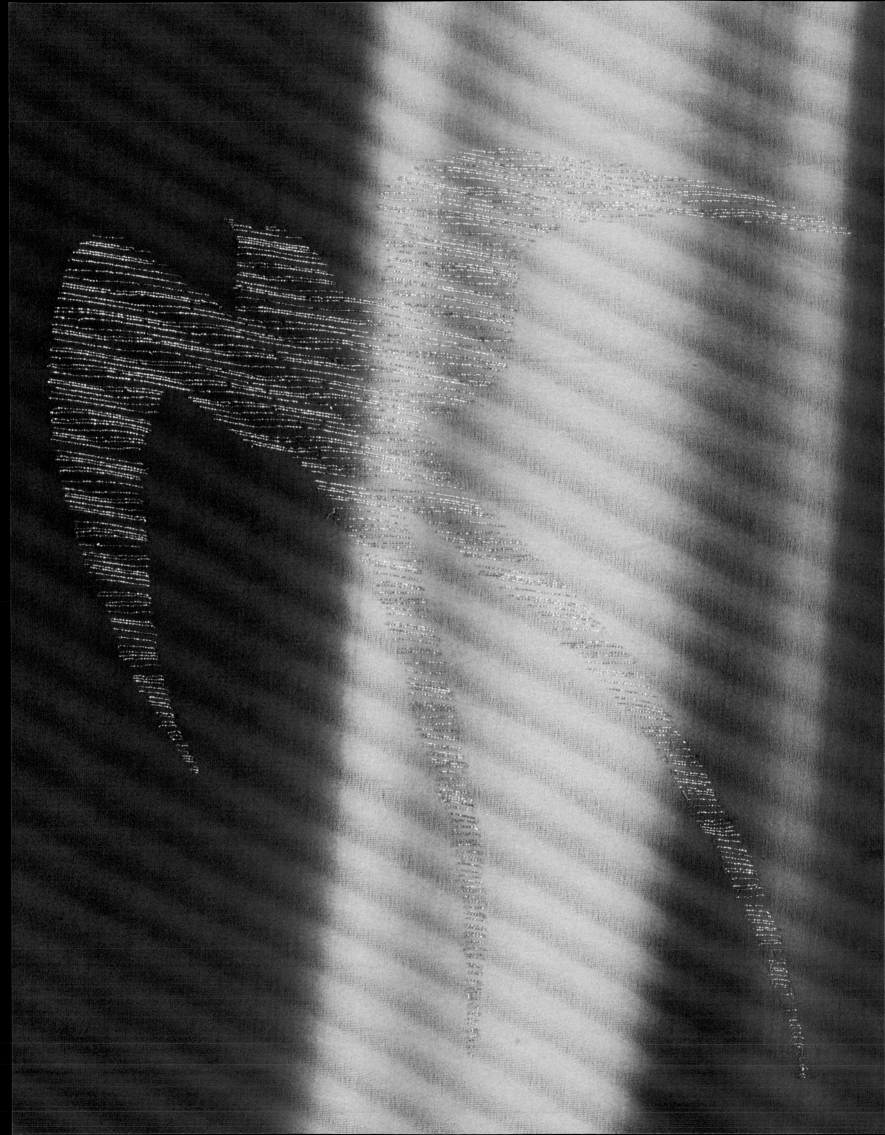

Unlined kimono for a woman (*hitoe*)
Swallows and bamboo

Figured crepe silk (mon-chirimen) with supplementary
wefts; discharge dyeing
Taishō period, 1912–26
154.0 × 121.0 cm
K129

Many of the Taishō and Shōwa kimono in the Khalili Collection are informal garments, but this does not necessarily mean they are unsophisticated, as this supremely elegant example reveals. The fabric is a plain weave silk, in which both warp and weft are twisted, the former very firmly. Tightly and loosely woven areas alternate, shifting in position to create the effect of a diagonal stripe. The gentle, airy quality that results is suitable for the motif of flying swallows, which are executed with supplementary gold and silver wefts. The overall impression of the design is completely transformed, however, by the electric effect of the vertical white bands, produced by the discharge method, whereby bleach or chemicals are used to remove colour from the cloth.

Kimono for a woman
Grapevines
*Plain weave crepe silk (omeshi chirimen) with
supplementary wefts*
Taishō–Shōwa period, 1920–30
148.0 × 124.0 cm
K123

Fashion and art are one in this stunning
kimono, in which grapevines sweep down
elegantly, with broad leaves and twisted
tendrils rendered in a manner that is at once
stylized and naturalistic. The luxurious fabric
has the look of a satin but the texture of a
crepe, while the pattern was produced using
supplementary threads.

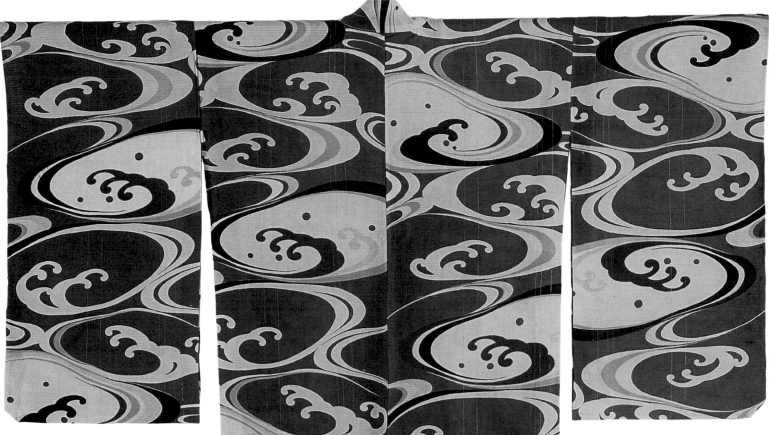

opposite
Unlined kimono for a woman (*hitoe*)
Sailing ships
Plain weave silk and vertical silver thread; stencil-
printing of warp threads (hogushi-gasuri)
Shōwa period, 1930–40
150.0 × 125.0 cm
K13

This kimono has as its motif two-masted,
square-rigged sailing vessels, reflecting
the ongoing fascination with the ships that
carried westerners to Japan from the late
sixteenth to the nineteenth centuries. The
rolling waves create a sense of movement
against the pinstripe ground, while the mix
of fine warps and thick wefts add to the
sense of an undulating surface.

right
Unlined kimono for a woman (*hitoe*)
Swirling water
Gauze weave silk (ro) and vertical silver thread; stencil-
printing on fabric surface (kata-yūzen)
Taishō–Shōwa period, 1910–30
150.5 × 129.0 cm
K30

Water is normally combined with other
motifs, but here it is depicted alone in a
purely decorative manner that recalls the
woodblock prints of Hokusai and Hiroshige,
but which probably also owes something to
the influence of Art Nouveau. The refreshing
motif is appropriate for a kimono designed
for the humid summer months, and the
delicate gauze fabric would have been cool
to wear. The addition of the fine vertical silver
threads lends a luxurious element to the
design.

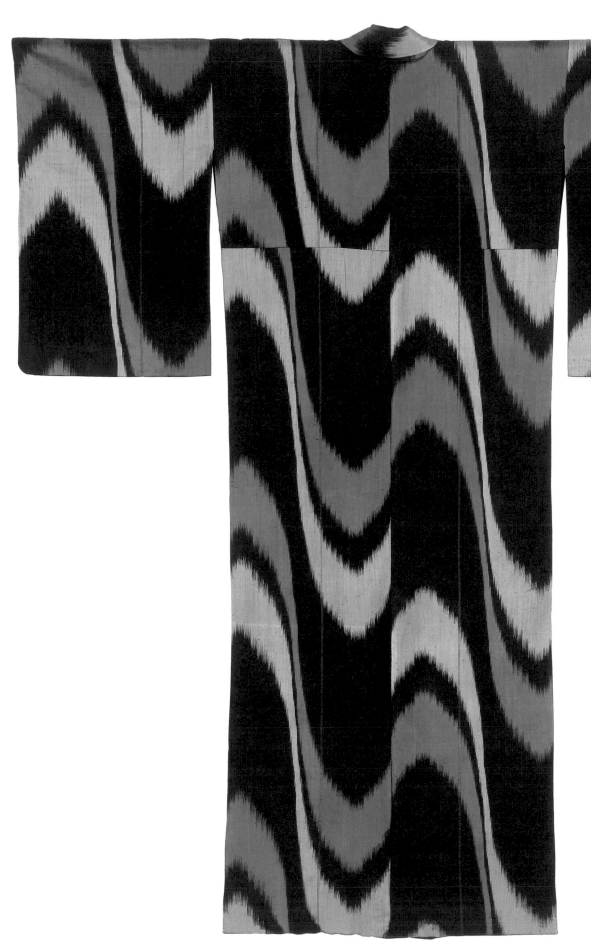

left
Kimono for a woman
Flowing water
Plain weave pongee silk (tsumugi); hand-tied selective dyeing of warp threads (hogushi-gasuri)
Taishō–Shōwa period, 1920–30
145.0 × 124.0 cm
K89

opposite
Kimono for a woman
Flowing water
Machine-spun plain weave pongee silk (meisen); stencil-printing of warp threads (hogushi-gasuri)
Taishō–Shōwa period, 1920–40
140.0 × 126.0 cm
K43

On both of these kimono, the water stream (*ryūsui*) motif has been reduced to its purest form to create a strikingly modern design. K89 (left) is of *tsumugi* silk and has been patterned using the hand-tied *kasuri* technique, resulting in a nubbly textured fabric and a characteristically blurred design. K43 (opposite) is of *meisen* and the warp threads have been stencil-printed, making for a more lustrous and precisely patterned garment.

Unlined kimono for a woman (*hitoe*)
Scrolling wisteria leaves
Machine-spun plain weave pongee silk (meisen);
stencil-printing of warp threads (hogushi-gasuri)
Taishō–Shōwa period, 1920–40
146.5 × 123.0 cm
K11

opposite
Kimono for a woman
Scrolling wisteria
Figured crepe silk (mon-chirimen); with tie-dyeing
(shibori)
Taishō–Shōwa period, 1920–40
148.0 × 123.0 cm
K32

In the kimono opposite, a mandarin-orange
and water pattern has been woven into the
fabric (see K118; pp. 236–7), while the main
design of highly stylized wisteria is produced
with the tie-dyeing (*shibori*) technique. Thus
a more traditional combination of patterning
has been used to create something very
modern. The kimono is similar in style to
K11 (left), but would have been a unique and
more expensive garment.

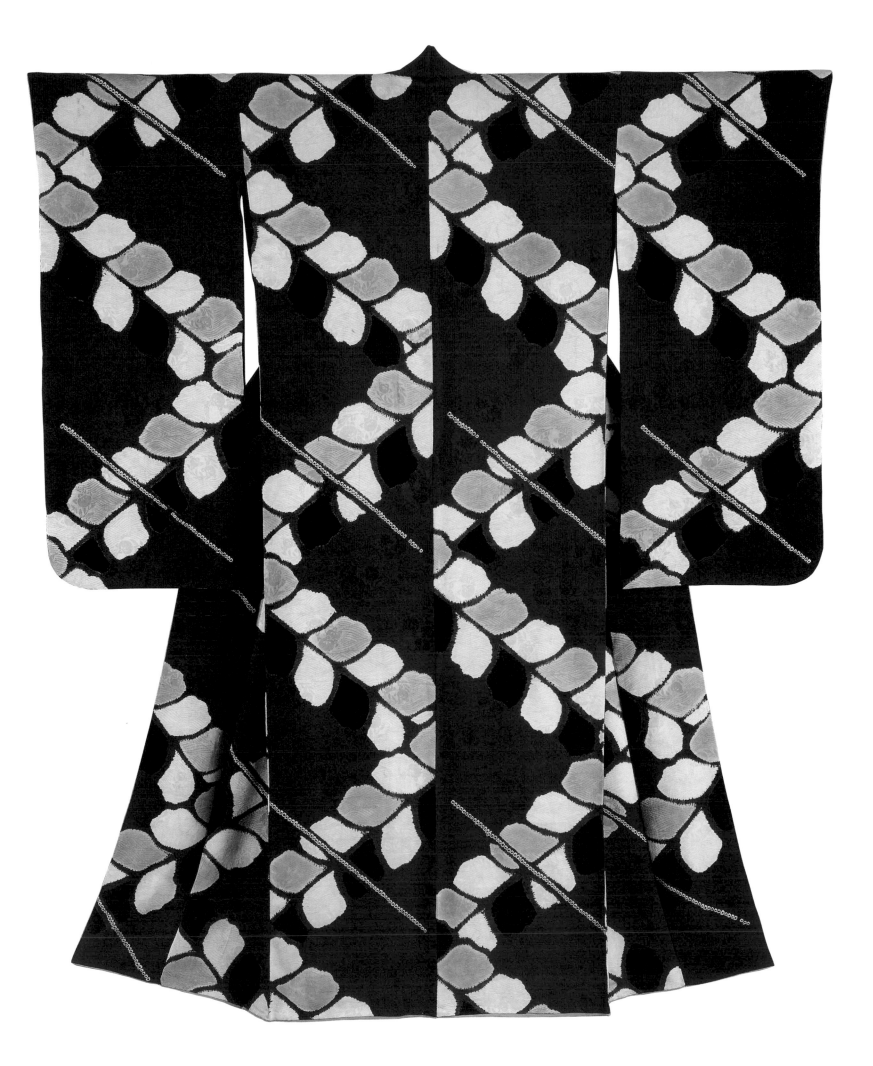

opposite
Kimono for a woman
Peonies and arabesques
Plain weave pongee silk (tsumugi); stencil-printing
of weft threads (yokoso-gasuri)
Taishō period, 1912–26
140.5 × 126.0 cm
K6

right
Kimono for a woman
Arabesques
Figured crepe silk (mon-chirimen); tie-dyed (shibori)
Taishō–Shōwa period, 1920–40
148.5 × 124.0 cm
K132

In this kimono (right), an arabesque
pattern woven into the lustrous fabric has
been overlaid with a larger version of the
motif, created with the tie-dyeing (*shibori*)
technique. Effectively only one colour, a
rich red, was used to produce this dramatic
design. The vine-like *karakusa* ('Chinese
plant') pattern originated in the Islamic
Middle East and was brought to Japan via
the Silk Road and Tang Dynasty China.
Symbolizing longevity and prosperity, it
was often combined with flowers such as
chrysanthemums, morning glories, peonies
(opposite), camellia (see K28; p. 237) and
bush clover (see K66; p. 238).

opposite
Unlined kimono for a woman (*hitoe*)
Mandarin oranges and flowing water
Plain weave crepe silk (chirimen); stencil-printing
of weft threads (yokoso-gasuri)
Taishō period, 1912–26
143.0 × 122.0 cm
K118

In this fine summer kimono, the water
stream motif is combined with mandarin
oranges (*tachibana*), a symbol of longevity.
Both the warps and wefts of the fabric
are twisted, giving the sense, but not the
structure, of gauze.

right
Kimono for a woman
Camellias and arabesques
Plain weave pongee silk (tsumugi); stencil-printing
of weft threads (yokoso-gasuri)
Taishō period, 1912–26
141.5 × 125.0 cm
K28

above
Unlined kimono for a woman (*hitoe*)
Bush clover and arabesques

Plain weave silk; stencil-printing of weft threads
(yokoso-gasuri)
Taishō–Shōwa period, 1920–30
143.0 × 126.0 cm
K66

opposite
Kimono for a woman
Wisteria petals and whirlpools

Machine-spun plain weave pongee silk (meisen);
stencil-printing of warp threads (hogushi-gasuri)
Shōwa period, 1926–40
149.0 × 125.0 cm
K40

From the late 1920s, the patterns on *meisen* kimono became increasingly stylized and abstracted. On this example, the hitherto delicate motif of petals falling into water has been transformed into a design of great energy and colour.

left above and opposite
Kimono for a woman
Leaf arabesques
Plain weave silk and rayon; stencil-printing on fabric surface (kata-yūzen)
Shōwa period, 1930–50
139.0 × 124.0 cm
K52

left below
Kimono for a woman
Floral arabesque
Machine-spun plain weave pongee silk (meisen); stencil-printing of warp and weft threads (heiyō-gasuri)
Shōwa period, 1930–50
149.0 × 124.0 cm
K9

The flower and arabesque motif on this kimono has been rendered in a way that suggests the spontaneity of brush and ink, rather than the mechanics of a loom. The variety of flower may be a rose, but is no longer really discernible, while the arabesque motif has evolved from a scrolling vine into an abstract wave.

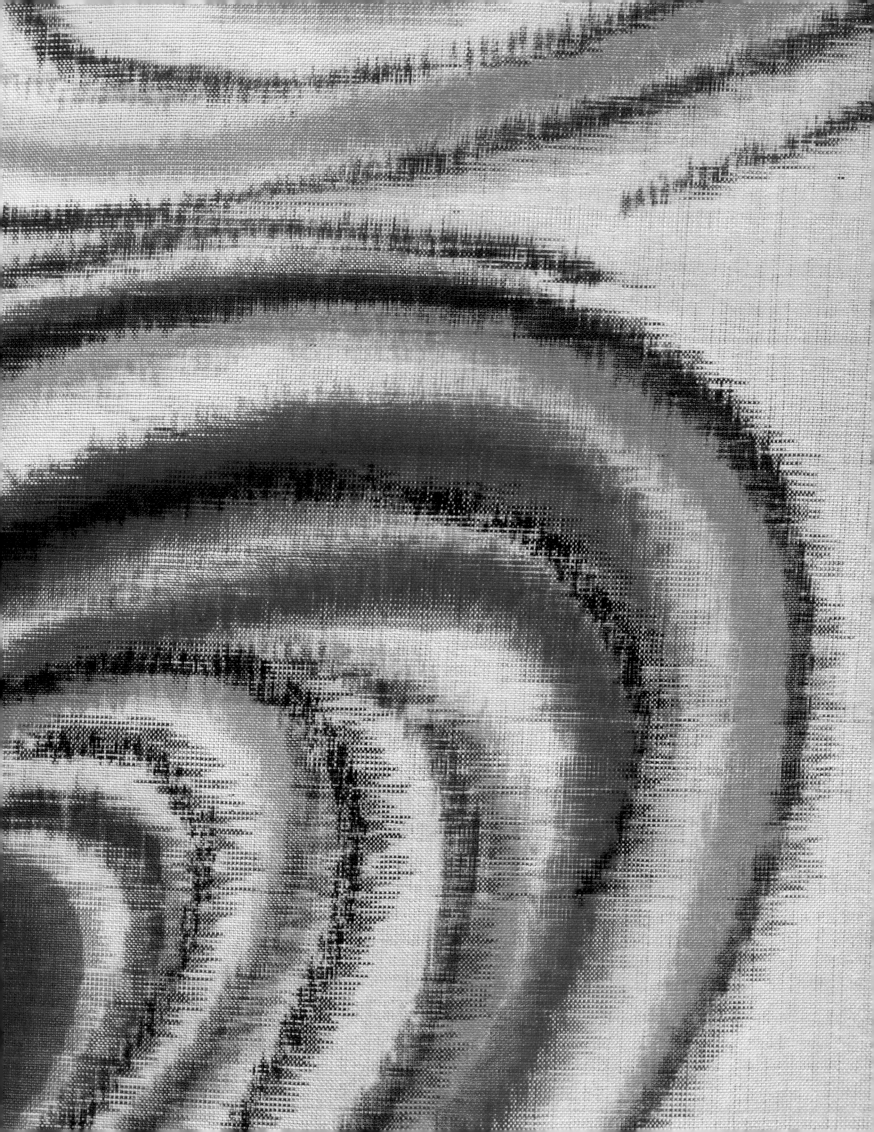

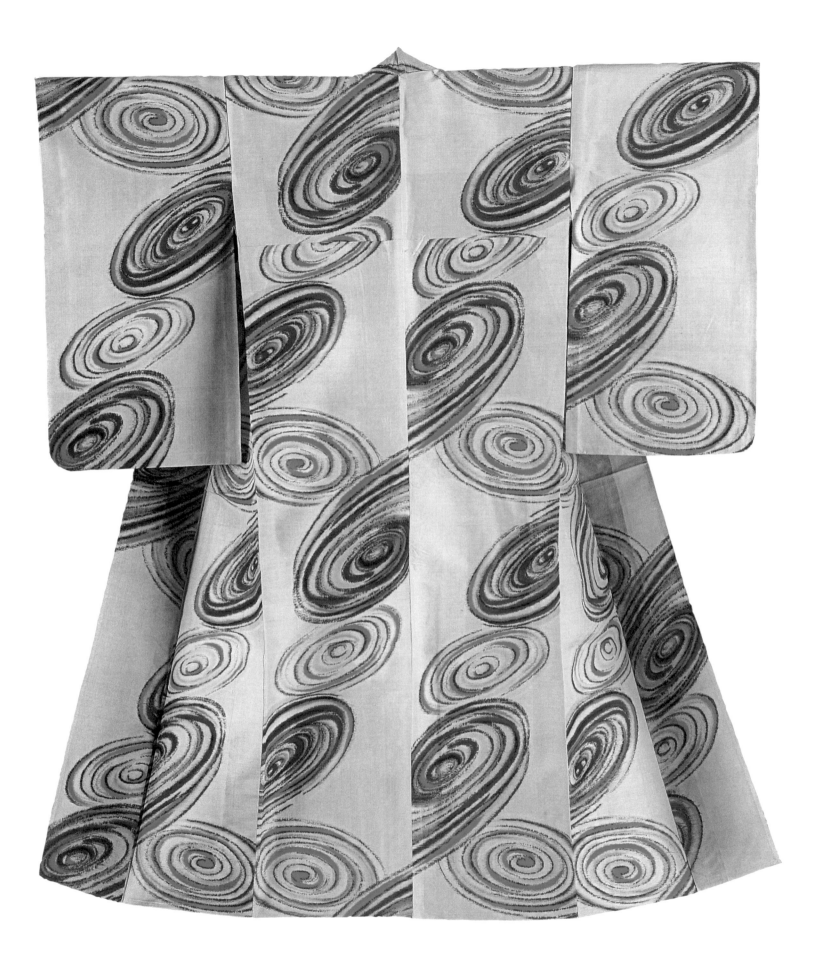

Unlined kimono for a woman (*hitoe*)
Whirlpools

Machine-spun plain weave pongee silk (meisen);
stencil-printing of warp and weft threads (heiyō-gasuri)
Shōwa period, 1930–40
143.0 × 124.0 cm
K16

In this kimono the abstraction of the
whirlpool motif reaches its zenith, as any
impression of water is replaced by the
sensation of pure movement.

left
Kimono for a woman
Tulips on a diagonal stripe
Machine-spun plain weave pongee silk (meisen);
stencil-printing of warp and weft threads (heiyō-gasuri)
Shōwa period, 1926–40
144.0 × 124.0 cm
K84

The interplay between pattern and ground
has always been an important factor in
Japanese textile design. This was increasingly
the case in fashionable kimono of the early
Shōwa period, when the two elements often
seemed to compete for visual prominence.
In this example, bright-pink flowers are
scattered on a dazzling black and white,
diagonally striped ground; the division of this
ground into curved sections lends even more
energy and movement to the design.

opposite
Kimono for a woman
Spinning tops on a diagonal stripe
Figured satin silk (rinzu); stencil-printing on fabric
surface (kata-yūzen)
Taishō–Shōwa period, 1920–40
145.0 × 125.0 cm
K1

As in K84 (left), an energetic motif, here
of spinning tops, is combined with a bold,
diagonally striped ground. The pattern has
been stencil-printed onto fabric, which itself
is woven with a vertical stripe.

Kimono for a woman
**Vertical bands of flowers and abstract
geometric patterns**

*Machine-spun plain weave pongee silk (meisen);
stencil-printing of warp and weft threads (heiyō-gasuri)
Shōwa period, 1930–40*
145.0 × 124.0 cm
K83

Although a combination of the floral and
the geometric, any sense of adherence to
traditional motifs has been abandoned in
this exuberant design. The wearer would
have appeared the dazzling epitome of
urban, contemporary fashion.

Kimono for a woman
Cherry blossom and zigzag pattern
Machine-spun plain weave pongee silk (meisen);
stencil-printing of warp and weft threads (heiyō-gasuri)
Shōwa period, 1926–40
148.0 × 126.0 cm
K76

A series of polka dots, chasing up and down vivid vertical strips (K39) or randomly splashed across a dark zigzag patterned ground (K117), suggest the bright lights of a modern city. While the former is a relatively inexpensive *meisen* kimono, the latter is made from luxurious, figured satin crepe and patterned by hand, using the tie-dyeing (*shibori*) method. These two garments reveal that, regardless of wealth or status, fashionable women of the early Shōwa period shared a contemporary design aesthetic.

The theme of the modern city is explicit in this kimono, which has a skyscraper as its main motif. Its simple but recognizable profile suggests the Empire State Building in New York, which was completed in 1931. The bright strips around the building and the fine lines within the dots evoke shimmering city lights in the night-time.

opposite
Unlined kimono for a woman (*hitoe*)
Abstract cracked ice
Machine-spun plain weave pongee silk (meisen);
stencil-printing of warp and weft threads (heiyō-gasuri)
Shōwa period, 1930–40
140.0 × 125.0 cm
KX140

Although equally abstract and similar in
colour-range to other kimono from the
period, the appearance and impact of this
garment is very different. The pattern,
suggestive of cracked ice, has been skilfully
realized through the use of limited dyes,
which both highlight and shade parts of the
design.

right
Kimono for a woman
Twisting ribbons
Machine-spun plain weave pongee silk (meisen);
stencil-printing of warp and weft threads (heiyō-gasuri)
Shōwa period, 1930–40
142.5 × 124.0 cm
K63

There seems to have been a vogue in the
1930s for black kimono with fairly abstract
patterns in red, yellow and white or cream
(see K47 and K117, previous pages). Simple
and modern in style, chic yet energetic in
design, these garments seem to capture the
spirit of the age. The twisting ribbons that
dance up and down this kimono suggest the
syncopated rhythms of jazz music.

Kimono for a woman
Abstract flowers

Machine-spun plain weave pongee silk (meisen);
stencil-printing of warp and weft threads (heiyō-gasuri)
Shōwa period, 1930–40
146.5 × 128.0 cm
K87

The motif on this garment looks like a
geometric flower or child's pinwheel toy.
Each petal or blade is made up of eight or
nine quadrilateral shapes, striped in white
with yellow, red or silver grey, edged with
white, and connected to the central points
of two flowers. The textile artist has used
the inherent blurriness of the stencil-printed
kasuri technique as part of the design. The
flowers seem to quiver and, with no one
of them contained within a single panel of
cloth, be liable to break out of the fabric
surface at any moment.

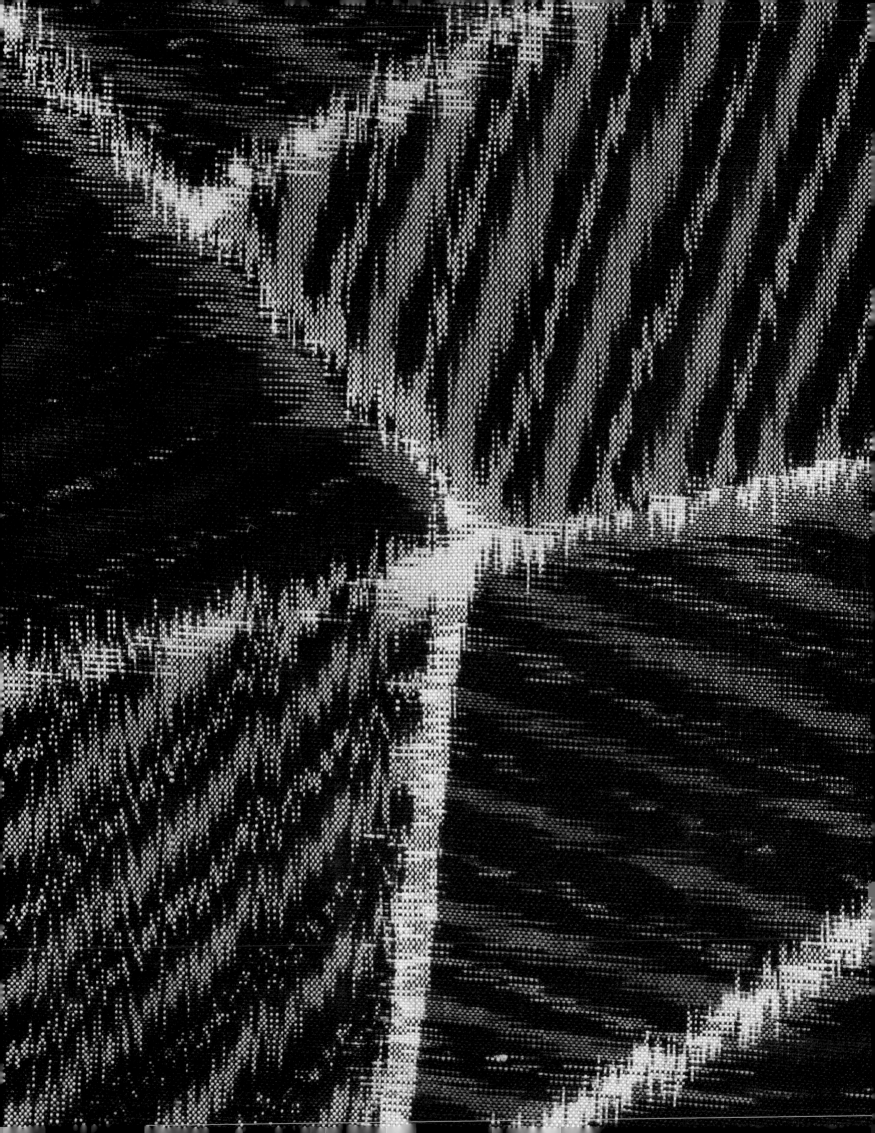

Kimono for a woman
Abstract pattern

Machine-spun plain weave pongee silk (meisen);
stencil-printing of warp and weft threads (heiyō-gasuri)
Shōwa period, 1930–40
146.5 × 126.0 cm
K7

The designs on many of the kimono in the
Khalili Collection reveal the influence of
western modernism in Japan. The surface
of this garment is broken up into irregular
triangular and quadrilateral shapes, which
are filled with stripes, splodges, dashes,
criss-crosses and strange motifs that suggest
some kind of scientific instruments. Another

kimono, K51 (opposite), has a more regularly
structured ground of mottled colours and
white strips augmented by curious dots
and shapes. These designs recall works by
artists such as Wassily Kandinsky, Joan Miró
and Paul Klee, although they may have been
inspired more directly by textiles produced in
Britain and France.

Kimono for a woman
Chequered abstract pattern
Machine-spun plain weave pongee silk (meisen);
stencil-printing of warp and weft threads (heiyō-gasuri)
Shōwa period, 1930–40
148.5 × 124.0 cm
K51

Kimono for a woman
Wavy horizontal stripes

Machine-spun plain weave pongee silk (meisen);
stencil-printing of warp and weft threads (heiyō-gasuri)
Shōwa period, 1930–40
144.5 × 122.0 cm
K46

This completely abstract design conveys a sensation of pure movement and brilliant energy. The colourful lines appear to have been painted directly onto the fabric in a burst of spontaneous creativity, but in fact have been carefully composed and dyed onto the warp and weft threads, before

the cloth was woven on the loom. This dazzling kimono is a tour de force of textile design, and the woman who wore it must have created quite an impact while walking through the streets of pre-war Japan.

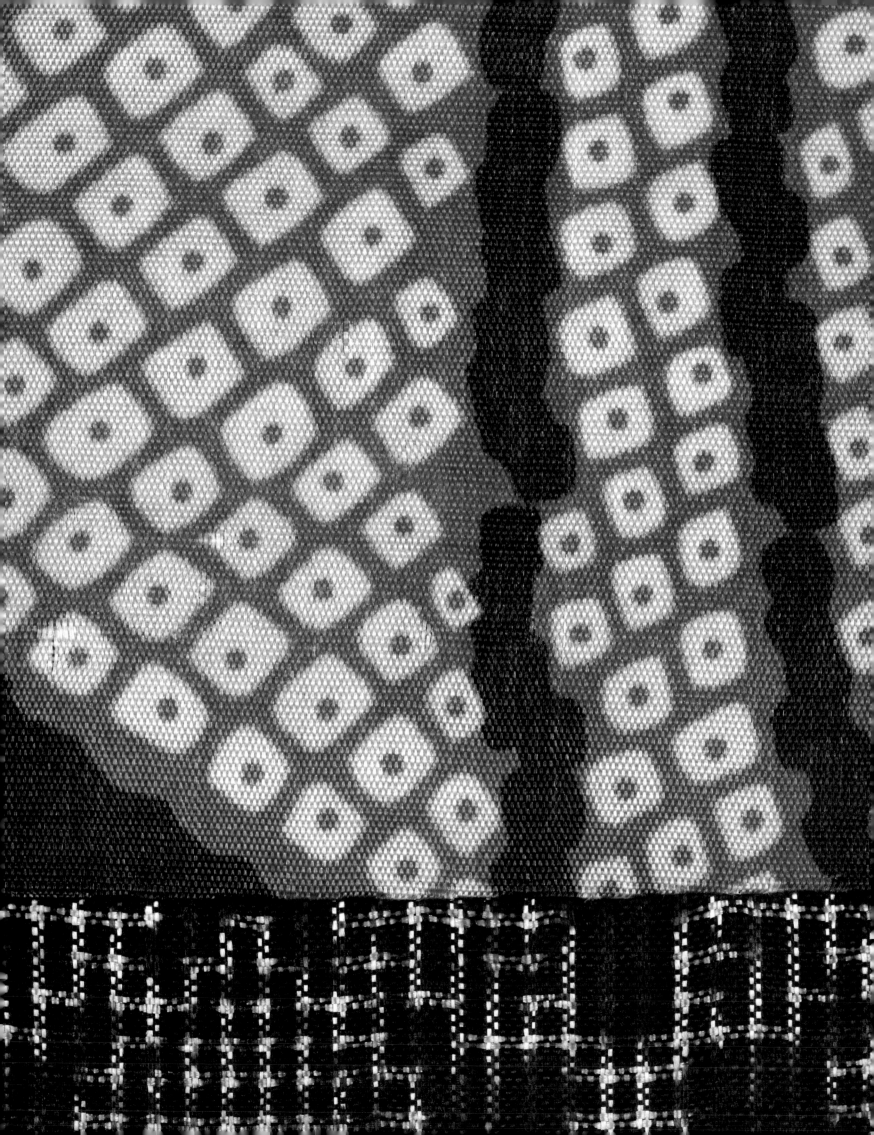

opposite and right above
Kimono jacket for a woman (*haori*)
Geometric diamond pattern
Outer: plain weave pongee silk (tsumugi); block-clamp resist-dyeing of warp and weft threads (itajime-gasuri)
Lining: plain weave silk; stencil-printing on the fabric surface (kata-yūzen)
Taishō–Shōwa period, 1920–40
98.0 × 126.0 cm
K15

The kimono jacket, or *haori*, was an exclusively male item of clothing until the Meiji period, when women began to adopt it. Geisha in Tokyo were the first to appropriate such masculine apparel, and by the mid-1890s other women had begun to wear black *haori* with crests for formal occasions, in direct imitation of male dress codes. By the 1920s, colourful *haori* had become a key ingredient in the wardrobe of most women, who would carefully select both kimono and jacket to create a fashionable ensemble.

This *haori* was made in Amami Ōshima and bears the characteristic mud-dyed, small patterns for which the island is known (see K75; pp. 212–13). The rather sombre exterior conceals a beautiful lining in the upper body and sleeve of purple and red plain weave silk, which has been stencil-printed to look like *shibori* with a motif of bamboo sprigs resembling origami cranes.

right below
Kimono jacket for a woman (*haori*)
Crosses and cartouches on cracked ice
Outer: plain weave pongee silk (tsumugi); stencil-printed warp and weft threads (heiyō-gasuri)
Lining: figured satin silk (rinzu)
Taishō–Shōwa period, 1920–30
76.0 × 126.5 cm
K68

opposite and right above
Kimono jacket for a woman (*haori*)
Mandarin oranges

Outer: machine-spun plain weave pongee silk (meisen);
stencil-printing of weft threads (yokoso-gasuri)
Lining: plain weave silk; printed on the fabric surface
(kata-yūzen)
Taishō period, 1912–26
92.0 × 125.0 cm
K128

This *haori* has a very colourful lining,
showing Chinese boys, toys and flowers
on a diamond chequerboard pattern.

right below
Kimono jacket for a woman (*haori*)
Mandarin oranges

Outer: plain weave silk; tie-dyeing (shibori)
Lining: plain weave silk; printed on the fabric surface
(kata-yūzen)
Shōwa period, 1930–40
93.0 × 126.0 cm
K137

As with men's *haori*, women's jackets often
have colourful linings, but as the exterior
of the garments are far more decorative
than their masculine counterparts, the
two patterns can be equally arresting. The
interior, however, would not be seen by
anyone but the wearer and perhaps a few
intimate friends, as she took her jacket off
once inside. On this example, the lining is of
red, pink and yellow bells, while the exterior
fabric is patterned with a bold, tie-dyed
mandarin-orange motif.

Kimono jacket for a woman (*haori*)
Peonies, wisteria, mandarin oranges and stream
Outer: machine-spun plain weave pongee silk (meisen); stencil-printing of weft threads (yokoso-gasuri)
Lining: plain weave silk; stencil-printing on the fabric surface (kata-yūzen)
Shōwa period, 1930–40
95.0 × 125.0 cm
K69

The turquoise and pink flowers on a lime-green ground make this one of the most striking *haori* in the Khalili Collection. The lining is equally vivid, with fans, bamboo, plum blossoms and stream stencil-printed in red, yellow and green.

Kimono jacket for a woman (*haori*)
Roses
Outer: machine-spun plain weave pongee silk (meisen); stencil-printing of warp threads (hogushi-gasuri)
Lining: plain weave silk; stencil-printing on the fabric surface (kata-yūzen)
Shōwa period, 1926–40
91.5 × 127.5 cm
K33

This *haori* bears the popular western motif of roses, while the lining has a no less bright but more traditionally Japanese pattern of crane and paulownia roundels.

Kimono jacket for a woman (*haori*)
Heian Shrine and plum blossoms
Outer: machine-spun plain weave pongee silk (meisen);
stencil-printing of warp and weft threads (heiyō-gasuri)
Lining: plain weave silk; stencil-printing on the fabric
surface (kata-yūzen)
Shōwa period, 1930–40
78.5 × 126.0 cm
K14

This *haori* features the lakeside buildings of
the Heian Shrine, constructed in Kyoto in
1895 to mark the 1,110th anniversary of the
city, surrounded by trees and blossoms.[3]
That this complex depiction was created
using the stencil *kasuri* technique reveals the
supreme skills of the textile dyer and weaver.
The lining is of more delicate hues, and
depicts flowers and pavilions in cartouches,
surrounded by a water motif.

Kimono jacket for a woman (*haori*)
Tulips and opposing lines with clubs card suit

Outer: machine-spun plain weave pongee silk (meisen);
stencil-printing of warp threads (hogushi-gasuri)
Lining: plain weave silk; stencil-printing on the fabric
surface (kata-yūzen)
Taishō–Shōwa period, 1920–30
94.5 × 126.0 cm
K108

Another western motif, the tulip, adorns this *haori*, bordered by curving vertical lines (a Japanese pattern known as *tatewaku*) and surrounded by shapes representing the suit of clubs in a game of cards. The chic black of the outer fabric contrasts with the bright orange of the lining, which has a diamond chequerboard design featuring linear patterns that relate to the incense game. In this elegant pastime, players must determine different scents, which are recorded using fifty-four geometric emblems that allude to the chapters of the *Tale of Genji*. The two fabrics used in this garment are cleverly combined to celebrate both Japanese and western games.

Kimono jacket for a woman (*haori*)
Scrolling clouds

Machine-spun plain weave pongee silk (meisen);
stencil-printing of weft threads (yokoso-gasuri)
Taishō–Shōwa period, 1920–30
86.0 × 125.0 cm
K67

Underkimono for a woman (*naga-juban*)
Books on horizontal bands
Plain weave silk; tie-dyeing (shibori)
Taishō period, 1912–26
128.0 × 134.0 cm
K10

A *juban* is an undergarment worn by both
men and women, which has the same shape
as a basic kimono. A glimpse of a woman's
underkimono (*naga-juban*), normally as long
as the outer garment, would be seen at the
collar and sleeve edges, and occasionally
at the hem as the wearer walked along, so
alluring colours such as red were a popular
choice. Here, the collar is white, which
gradually became the convention in the
twentieth century (see K12, below; and K94,
p. 268). Although the main body of the
juban would not be seen, they were often
beautifully patterned.

Underkimono for a woman (*naga-juban*)
Paulownia, plum blossoms and arabesques
Plain weave silk; stencil-printed on fabric surface
(kata-yūzen)
Taishō period, 1912–26
124.0 × 128.0 cm
K12

The patterning of *naga-juban* echoed that of
kimono, as can be seen in this lively design
of paulownia and plum blossoms, arranged
in a scrolling arabesque. The white collar on
this garment is of thick satin, figured with a
design of chrysanthemums.

Underkimono for a woman (*naga-juban*)
Shell-matching game and autumn grasses
Gauze weave silk (ro); stencil-printing on fabric surface
(kata-yūzen)
Shōwa period, 1926–40
129.5 × 130.0 cm
K23

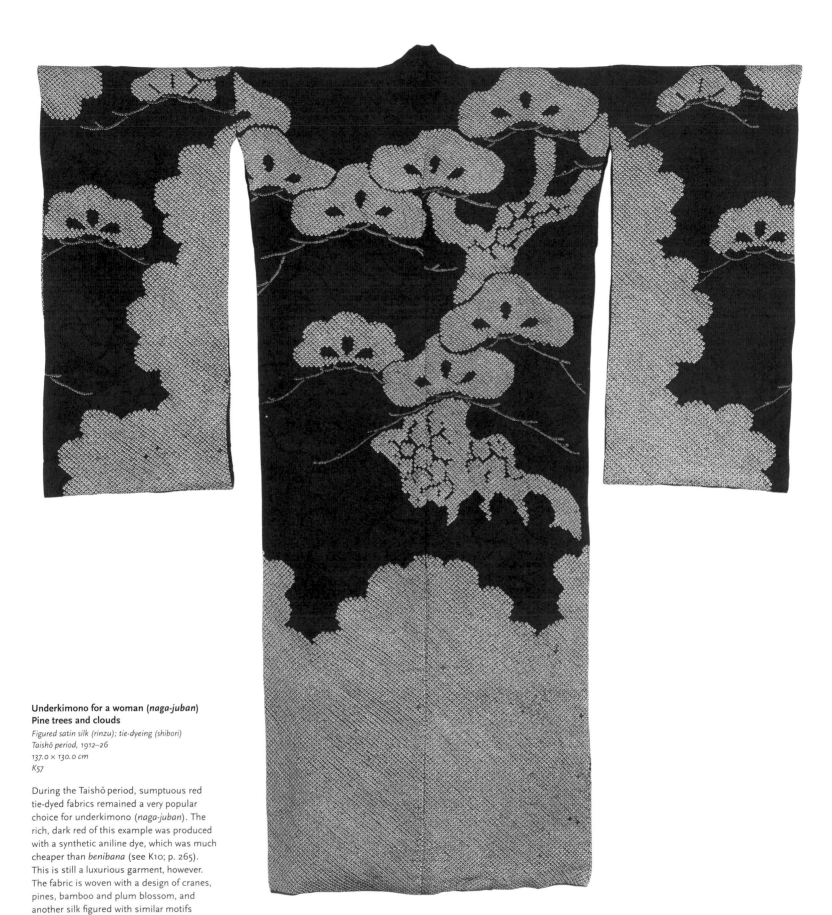

Underkimono for a woman (*naga-juban*)
Pine trees and clouds
Figured satin silk (rinzu); tie-dyeing (shibori)
Taishō period, 1912–26
137.0 × 130.0 cm
K57

During the Taishō period, sumptuous red
tie-dyed fabrics remained a very popular
choice for underkimono (*naga-juban*). The
rich, dark red of this example was produced
with a synthetic aniline dye, which was much
cheaper than *benibana* (see K10; p. 265).
This is still a luxurious garment, however.
The fabric is woven with a design of cranes,
pines, bamboo and plum blossom, and
another silk figured with similar motifs
has been used to line the lower collar and
hem area. The garment was then tie-dyed
with a large pine tree. This combination of
auspicious symbols suggests that it may
have been worn on a special occasion, such
as a wedding.

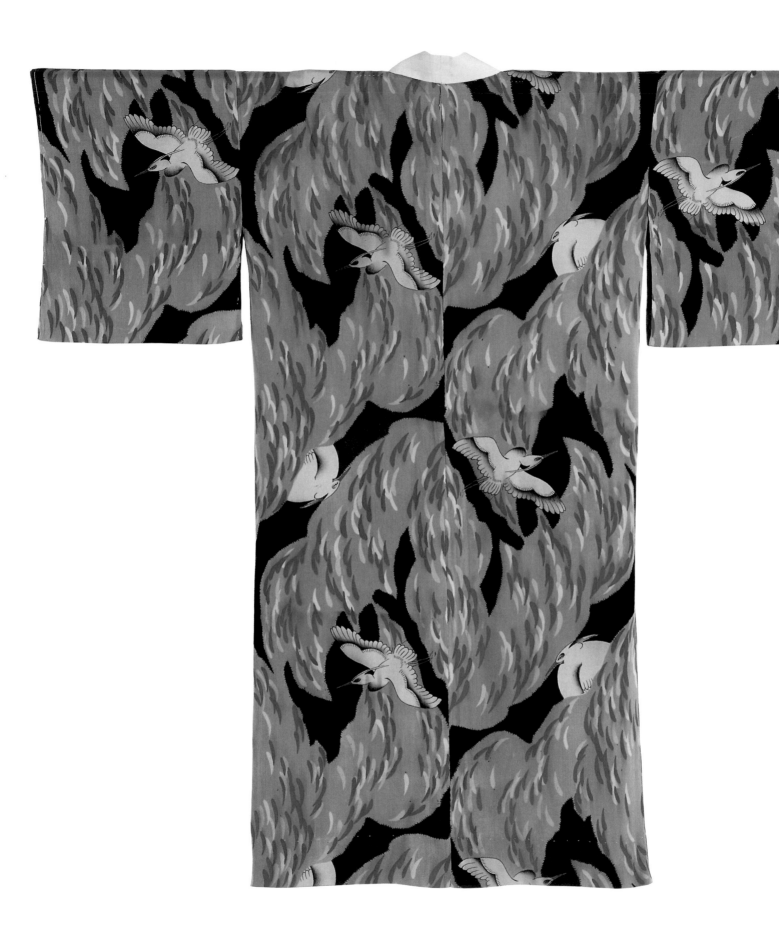

Underkimono for a woman (*naga-juban*)
Herons
Plain weave crepe silk (chirimen); stencil-printing on
fabric surface (kata-yūzen)
Shōwa period, 1926–35
118.0 × 123.0 cm
K94

The depiction of the herons flying across
this underkimono reveals a strong Art Deco
influence. These birds are generally shown
with flowing water, presumably what the blue
sections of the fabric represent, although
they could signify trees or feathery clouds.

Underkimono for a woman (*naga-juban*)
Fans
Plain weave crepe silk (chirimen); stencil-printing on
fabric surface (kata-yūzen)
Taishō period, 1912–26
130.5 × 126.0 cm
K31

Kimono jacket for a man (*haori*)
Daikoku and Ebisu
Plain weave silk (habutae); lining: stencil-printing on the fabric surface (kata-yūzen)
Taishō–Shōwa period, 1920–40
100.0 × 133.0 cm
K95

The restrained, rather sombre garments worn by men often concealed highly decorated linings. This custom had its historical roots in Edo-period sumptuary laws, and even when such rules no longer applied, the taste for hidden designs on *haori* and underkimono continued.

The gods of good fortune, *shichi-fuku-ji*, were a popular choice for *haori* linings in the early Shōwa period (see K98, opposite; K96 and K141, overleaf). This example depicts the common pairing of Ebisu (standing), the god of fishermen and merchants, and Daikoku, the god of wealth and commerce. Here, the pair are shown in a small boat harvesting plants; behind them is an image of a treasure ship (*takarabune*). Some of the treasures are spread among the characters, which read: 'the business went well with this boat, becoming a treasure ship.'[4]

Kimono jacket for a man (*haori*)
Kanzan and Jittoku

Plain weave silk (habutae); lining: ink painting (kaki-e)
Taishō–Shōwa period, 1920–40
105.0 × 126.0 cm
K97

Kanzan and Jittoku are two semi-legendary Chinese Buddhist eccentrics of the Tang Dynasty, frequently depicted in Chinese and Japanese ink painting. Kanzan, whose name means 'cold mountain', was a reclusive poet and is usually shown with a scroll. He was believed to have lived near Mount Tiantai. Guoqingsi, the temple on the mountain, was the home of Jittoku, whose name means 'foundling'. He worked in the temple kitchen, saving food for his friend Kanzan, and is always shown with a broom. The inscription on the lining reads: 'while coming, while leaving.' The signature of the artist is Fusetsu Dojin.

Kimono jacket for a man (*haori*)
Daikoku and Fukurokuju

Plain weave silk (habutae): lining: satin silk; ink painting (kaki-e) and embroidery in silk threads
Taishō–Shōwa period, 1920–40
107.0 × 134.0 cm
K98

Daikoku is normally shown standing or sitting on bales of rice, but here he raises them above his head, much to the concern of the diminutive Fukurokuju. Parts of Daikoku's costume and the ends of the bales have been embroidered, giving extra lustre to the design.

left above
Kimono jacket for a man (*haori*)
Hotei
Plain weave silk (habutae): lining: plain weave silk; ink painting (kaki-e)
Taishō–Shōwa period, 1920–40
105.0 × 139.0 cm
KX141

Hotei, the fat and smiling god of good health and abundance, is carrying his sack of plenty on his head, surrounded by playful children.

left below and opposite
Kimono jacket for a man (*haori*)
Fukurokuju in a treasure boat
Plain weave silk (habutae); lining: ink painting (kaki-e)
Taishō–Shōwa period, 1920–40
102.0 × 131.0 cm
K96

This lining shows another of the gods of good fortune in his treasure ship (*takarabune*). Fukurokuju, god of longevity and wisdom, is distinguished by his large, domed head. The motif is drawn directly onto the silk in ink and colours, its status as a painting confirmed by the artist's signature, Kizan Kazuo (or Kizan Itsuo), and seals. The inscription reads, 'auspicious spirit fills Japan' and 'painted at the Jiungaya'. Like the other formal *haori* in the Khalili Collection, this garment is made from *habutae*, a soft, lightweight plain weave silk.

**Kimono and kimono jacket (*haori*) for a man
Daimyō procession past Mount Fuji**
*Kimono and outer jacket: plain weave pongee silk
(tsumugi); hand-tied selective dyeing of dyed warp and
weft threads (heiyō-gasuri)*
Jacket lining: plain weave silk; ink painting (kaki-e)
Taishō–Shōwa period, 1920–40
141.0 × 137.0 cm (kimono); 87.0 × 134.5 cm (jacket)
K99

This elegant kimono and *haori* jacket
ensemble epitomizes the subtle character of
early twentieth-century male dress. The fabric
is the much-coveted Amami Ōshima *tsumugi*
(see K75; pp. 212–13), which has been woven
with a tiny hatched design using threads
selectively dyed with indigo to produce
three shades of blue. The lining of the jacket
bears a wonderful image of a *daimyō* being
carried in a palanquin, while his samurai
march on foot, all with eyes ahead bar one,
who turns to look at the man behind him.[5]
The linear procession, punctuated only by
two tall standards, is passing Mount Fuji,
which rises up behind it. The inscription tells
us that this is Hara, one of the fifty-three
stations of the Tokaidō, the road linking
the shogunal capital of Edo to the imperial
capital of Kyoto. The famous artist Utagawa
Hiroshige (1797–1858) illustrated the stations
of the Tokaidō in a number of popular print
series during the 1830s–50s, but although
this lining is inscribed 'painted by Hiroshige',
it does not appear to be based on any of his
depictions of Hara. The signature itself is
not like Hiroshige's, so the designer of this
image was presumably just paying homage
to the Edo artist.

Underkimono for a man (*juban*)
Golden Pavilion, Kyoto (Kinkaku-ji)
Gauze weave silk (ro); printed on fabric surface (kata-yūzen)
Shōwa period, 1940–50
130.0 × 128.5 cm
K72

This supremely elegant man's underkimono is decorated, as if on a fan, with a highly painterly image of Kinkaku-ji, the temple of the Golden Pavilion. One of Kyoko's most celebrated sights, here it is shown in the snow – a very cool image on what must be, judging by the gauze weave fabric, a summer garment. The *juban* has been shortened at the waist, so some of the design is missing, although it has been preserved in the seam allowance.

right above and opposite
Underkimono for a man (*juban*)
Christian images
Plain weave silk; printed
Shōwa period, 1930–40
128.5 × 120.5 cm
K48

Christianity was first brought to Japan by Jesuit missionaries in the late sixteenth century, but was banned in the 1630s. Christians were harshly persecuted, but many carried on observing their faith in secret, their descendants coming out of hiding when religious freedom was re-established in the Meiji period. So although Christianity could be openly observed in the twentieth century, it seems appropriate that the person who wore this underkimono kept his faith close to his heart, as the 'Hidden Christians' had once been forced to do. The garment is printed with a repeat pattern of small images of the Holy Family, the Virgin and Child, and angels, some of whom are playing musical instruments. Rather curiously, one of the images appears to be of a woman who looks more like a cabaret star, perhaps a reflection of the more worldly pleasures of the period.

right below
Underkimono for a man (*juban*)
Race horses and betting slips
Plain weave silk; printed on fabric surface
(kata-yūzen)
Shōwa period, 1930–40
127.0 × 130.5 cm
K73

Underkimono for men were often decorated with images that celebrated the delights of modern life, such as a day at the races. This example depicts three horses, in a highly painterly manner, viewed through a monocular, while small horses in silhouette race across the garment below the waist. Betting slips and an enclosure badge also float across the design, bearing the inscriptions *Shoba tohyoken* (winning ticket), *Zenkoku keiba kurabu* (National Horse Racing Club) and *Kinnijuen* (Kinni Park).[6]

Kimono and underkimono for an infant girl
Hōō bird and paulownias

Figured satin silk (rinzu); freehand paste-resist dyeing
(yūzen) and embroidery in metallic threads
Taishō period, 1912–26
124.0 × 87.0 cm (kimono); 124.0 × 86.0 cm
(underkimono)
KX165

That great attention continued to be lavished
on children's kimono in the Taishō and early
Shōwa period is clear from this stunning
garment, which would have been draped on
a baby girl for her first visit to a Shinto shrine
(*miyamairi*). The motif of a *hōō* (phoenix)
is suitably auspicious for this significant
occasion. This mythical bird, the female
equivalent of the dragon, symbolized the
virtues of honesty, benevolence, wisdom,
fidelity and propriety. It is shown flying
across the shoulders of the garment, its
feathers cascading down the front and
back, above a paulownia tree, the only place
where the bird will alight (see KX148; p.
69). Paulownia wood was prized for making
small items of furniture. Being fast-growing,
it was customary to plant a tree on the birth
of a daughter, so that a wedding chest could
be made from the wood. This was believed
to bestow happiness on the union. Thus,
at only a month old, the future prospects
for the infant were being mapped out in
symbolic imagery.

The sumptuous figured satin fabric
was woven with a pattern of a leaf within
vertical curving lines, and the design expertly
executed using the *yūzen* technique, with
the colours delicately shaded on the flower,
leaves and feathers. The ground was then
dyed a magnificent dark pink and the leaves
augmented by tiny flecks of flat gold. Special
stitching (*semamori*) down the centre back of
the kimono would have protected the child
from evil spirits. The long sashes at the front,
attached to the garment with auspicious
stitches (*kazari-nui*), would have been tied
around the neck of the adult, traditionally the
grandmother, who carried the baby to the
shrine. The kimono is the outer part (*uwagi*)
of a layered set; the undergarment (*shitagi*)
is of the same fabric but undecorated. The
outer kimono has a store label that reads,
in Japanese characters and Roman script,
'H. Inoue. Daimaru. Kyoto'. Like other
department stores, Daimaru, founded in
Kyoto in 1717 by Shimomura Hikoemen,
started as a dry-goods store selling kimono.

Kimono for a young girl (*furisode*)
Lilies

*Plain weave pongee silk (tsumugi); freehand paste-
resist dyeing (yūzen) and embroidery in metallic
threads*
Taishō period, 1912–26
96.0 × 107.0 cm
K105

Lilies were another popular motif for
kimono. Admired for their beauty, they also
symbolized prosperity. Here, they grow up
a girl's kimono, elegant yet striking against
the mauve ground. Executed in a painterly
style using the *yūzen* technique, an extra
shimmer has been achieved through the
splashes of silver.

Kimono for a young girl
Chinese boy, drums, fans and flowers

Figured crepe silk (mon-chirimen); freehand paste-resist dyeing (yūzen) and embroidery in silk threads
Taishō period, 1912–26
124.5 × 117.5 cm
K19

On a shaded ground of pale green and warm orange, a chubby Chinese boy plays around the tassels of a hand-drum, surrounded by flowers and fans. This motif symbolized future family prosperity, but the boy also resembles the *gosho ningyo* (court dolls) given as gifts by the nobility to *damiyō* passing through Kyoto on their way to Edo. Their popularity spread to the general populace, and in the twentieth century were adopted as kimono motifs to represent a child's innocence. On this garment, the child's costume and the petals of one chrysanthemum have been embroidered with silk thread. Mirroring the style of adult dress, this one-crested kimono is semi-formal attire (see K77; p. 170).

left
Kimono for a young girl
Decorated shells and hexagonal boxes,
fans and flowers
Plain weave crepe silk (chirimen); stencil-printing on
fabric surface (kata-yūzen)
Taishō period, 1912–26
81.0 × 74.0 cm
K111

opposite
Kimono for a young girl
Decorated shells, peonies and stream
Pongee silk (tsumugi); stencil-printing on fabric surface
(kata-yūzen)
Taishō period, 1912–26
94.0 × 82.0 cm
K112

Kimono worn by young girls often had very
dense, highly colourful patterns. Flowers
were generally featured, while the shell-
matching game (*kai-awasei*) was another
favoured motif (see K92; pp. 168–9). Such
designs were very pretty, as befitting a female
child, and carried wishes for a future happy
marriage

Young girl in an opulent kimono
Photograph, silver gelatin print, c. 1920s
Ikjeld.com

Here, the very bold pattern almost
overwhelms the small garment, but clearly
demonstrates that girls' dress could be just as
fashionable as that for adult women.

This extraordinarily striking kimono is one
of the most arresting twentieth-century
garments in the Khalili Collection, and must
have been worn by a very stylish young
woman. The pattern is stencil-printed, but is
designed to look like *kasuri*.

Kimono and vest for a young girl
Diagonal bands
Plain weave silk; tie-dyeing (shibori)
Shōwa period, 1930–40
69.0 × 77.0 cm (kimono); 46.0 × 35.0 cm (vest, from seam to seam at hem)
K85

This kimono and vest are patterned with the traditional tie-dyed (*shibori*) technique, but the vibrant colour combination and dynamic design of the ensemble make it highly modern. Both garments have been heavily padded for extra warmth, and the collar of the vest is edged with ruffled silk.

Kimono and kimono jacket (*haori*) for a girl
Abstract oval shapes

Machine-spun plain weave pongee silk (meisen);
stencil-printing of warp and weft threads (heiyō-gasuri)
Jacket lining: plain weave silk; stencil-printing on fabric
surface (kata-yūzen)
Shōwa period, 1930–40
110.5 × 111.0 cm (kimono); 70.0 × 112.0 cm (jacket)
K59

Like her older sisters, the girl who wore
this eye-catching ensemble had forsaken
traditional feminine floral motifs in favour of
something bold, abstract and totally modern.

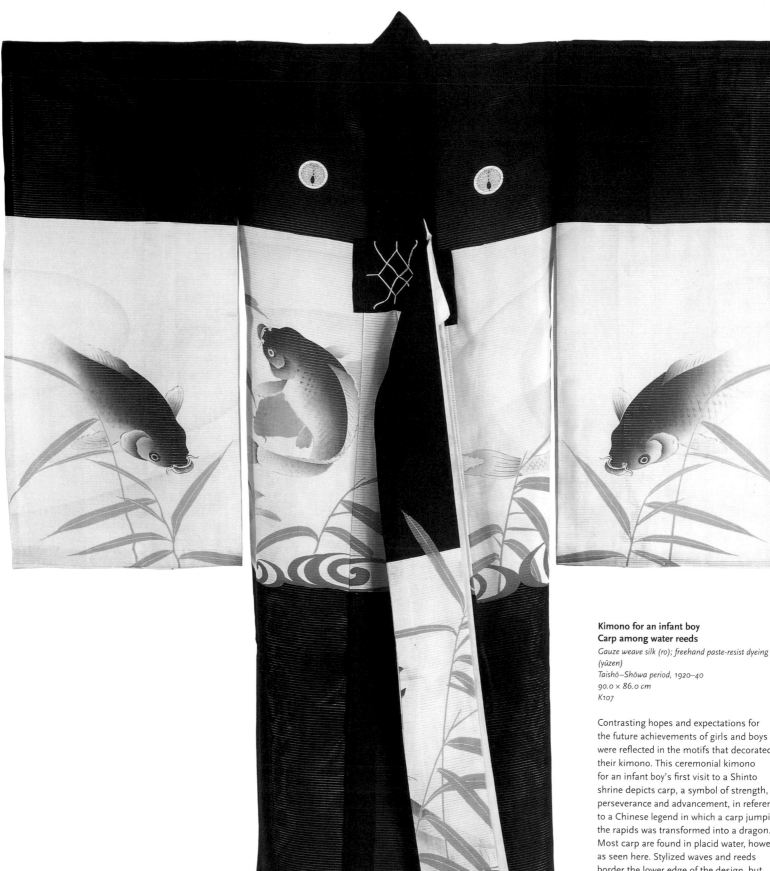

Kimono for an infant boy
Carp among water reeds
Gauze weave silk (ro); freehand paste-resist dyeing (yūzen)
Taishō–Shōwa period, 1920–40
90.0 × 86.0 cm
K107

Contrasting hopes and expectations for the future achievements of girls and boys were reflected in the motifs that decorated their kimono. This ceremonial kimono for an infant boy's first visit to a Shinto shrine depicts carp, a symbol of strength, perseverance and advancement, in reference to a Chinese legend in which a carp jumping the rapids was transformed into a dragon. Most carp are found in placid water, however, as seen here. Stylized waves and reeds border the lower edge of the design, but otherwise it is incredibly naturalistic, with the fish swimming in and out of view. The cool waters of the imagery are in harmony with the rippling open stripe of the soft gauze fabric. The infant who wore this kimono must have been a summer baby. Like much formal dress for boys, the garment has a dark ground, a restrained colour palette and patterning concentrated at the waist.

Kimono for an infant boy
Cranes in reeds

Gauze weave silk (ro); freehand paste-resist dyeing
(yūzen)
Taishō–Shōwa period, 1920–40
100.5 × 91.0 cm
K82

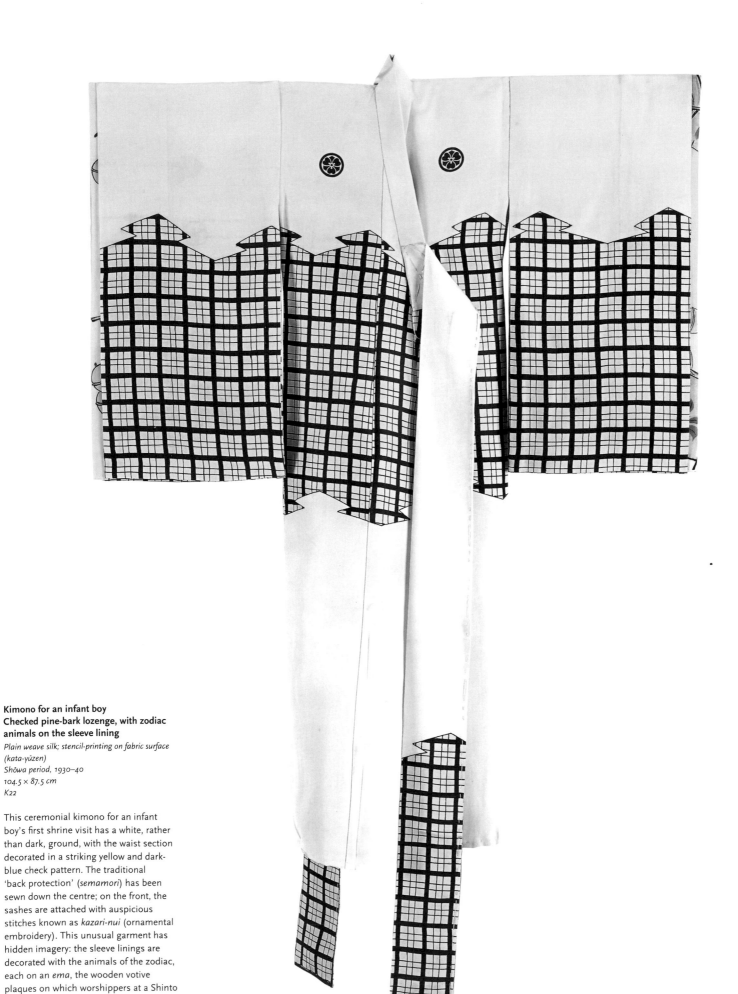

Kimono for an infant boy
Checked pine-bark lozenge, with zodiac
animals on the sleeve lining
Plain weave silk; stencil-printing on fabric surface
(kata-yūzen)
Shōwa period, 1930–40
104.5 × 87.5 cm
K22

This ceremonial kimono for an infant
boy's first shrine visit has a white, rather
than dark, ground, with the waist section
decorated in a striking yellow and dark-
blue check pattern. The traditional
'back protection' (*semamori*) has been
sewn down the centre; on the front, the
sashes are attached with auspicious
stitches known as *kazari-nui* (ornamental
embroidery). This unusual garment has
hidden imagery: the sleeve linings are
decorated with the animals of the zodiac,
each on an *ema*, the wooden votive
plaques on which worshippers at a Shinto
shrine express their prayers and wishes.

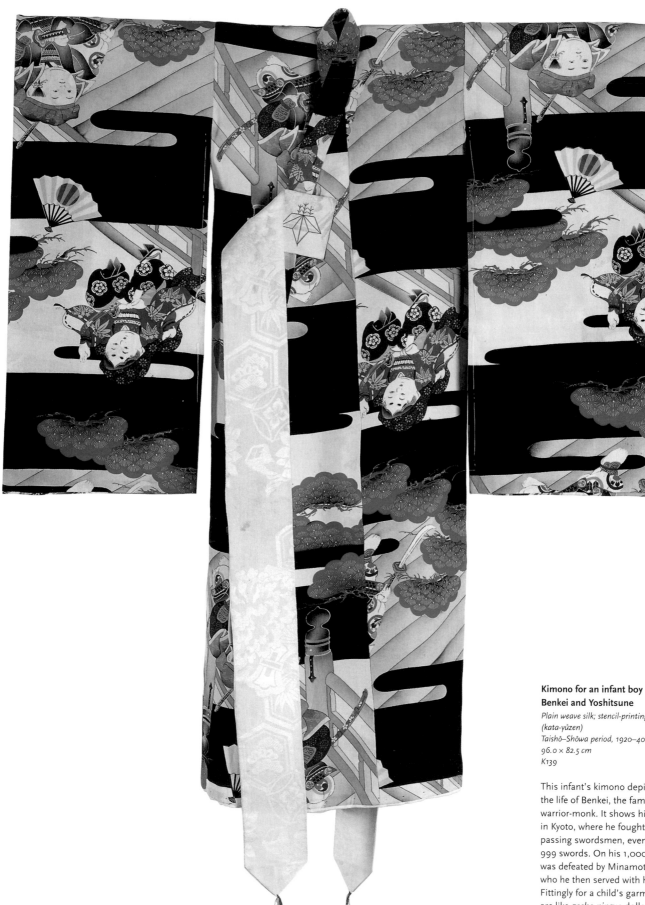

Kimono for an infant boy
Benkei and Yoshitsune

Plain weave silk; stencil-printing on fabric surface
(kata-yūzen)
Taishō–Shōwa period, 1920–40
96.0 × 82.5 cm
K139

This infant's kimono depicts an episode from
the life of Benkei, the famous twelfth-century
warrior-monk. It shows him on Gojō Bridge
in Kyoto, where he fought and disarmed
passing swordsmen, eventually collecting
999 swords. On his 1,000th duel, Benkei
was defeated by Minamoto no Yoshitsune,
who he then served with honour and loyalty.
Fittingly for a child's garment, the figures
are like *gosho ningyo* dolls. Black areas break
up the design into a chequerboard pattern,
while pine trees and fans patterned with the
Japanese rising sun complete the scene.

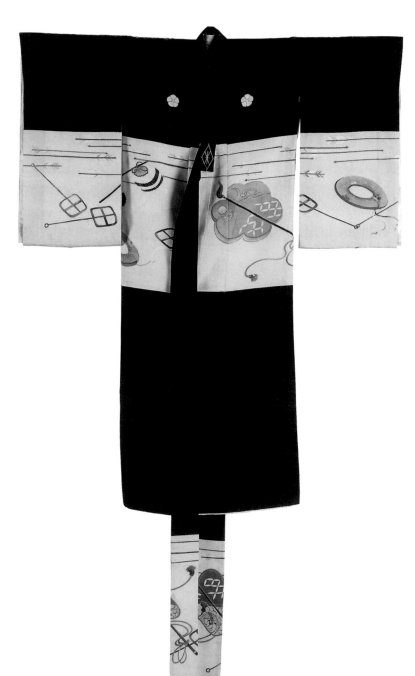

Kimono, kimono jacket (*haori*) and underkimono for a young boy
Samurai accoutrements
Plain weave silk; freehand paste-resist dyeing (yūzen) and embroidery in metallic threads; sleeve lining of figured satin silk (rinzu)
Shōwa period, 1930–40
123.5 × 104.5 cm (kimono); 98.0 × 105.0 cm (jacket); 125.0 × 104.0 cm (inner kimono)
K138

This splendid ensemble for a young boy is decorated with suitably masculine imagery. The samurai sword, helmet, fans, horse trappings and arrows – the latter whizzing past at the back of the otherwise static design – carry the wish that the child be blessed with the strength, valour and honour of a warrior. The depiction of the helmet is particularly detailed, and shows an iron bowl, stencilled leather sections with dragonflies (known as the 'victory insect'), and chrysanthemums, applied metal bosses and stitched, lacquered iron plates. Magnificent hoe-shaped crests (*kuwagata*) and a dragon ornament – which would normally be at the front on the helmet, rather than on top – burst above the demarcation line of the central design, looking suitably striking against the black ground, while the edge of the sword guard (*tsuba*) glistens in gold.

The sleeves of the kimono have an extravagant inner lining of cream figured satin, woven with *hōō* birds flying among clouds of gold, which is adhered to the fabric surface. The *haori*, too, has sleeve linings of satin, woven with a design of cranes. The inner kimono is of cream plain weave silk, with sashes edged with the same design as the main garments.

Kimono and kimono jacket (*haori*) for a young boy
Rats and *noshi*

Plain weave silk; freehand paste-resist dyeing (yūzen), hand-painted and embroidered in silk and metallic threads
Taishō period, 1912–26
114.0 × 105.0 cm (kimono); 69.0 × 103.5 cm (jacket)
K104

This charming formal kimono and *haori* ensemble for a young boy is decorated with rats, which are seen nibbling auspicious folded paper ornaments (*noshi*). Each rat is different, delicately depicted and full of character. The garments are likely to have been made for a boy born in the year of the rat, the first animal in the East Asian zodiac. The kimono has protective stitching (*semamori*) at the back, while the *haori* has ties of silk and gold brocade at the sleeve openings.

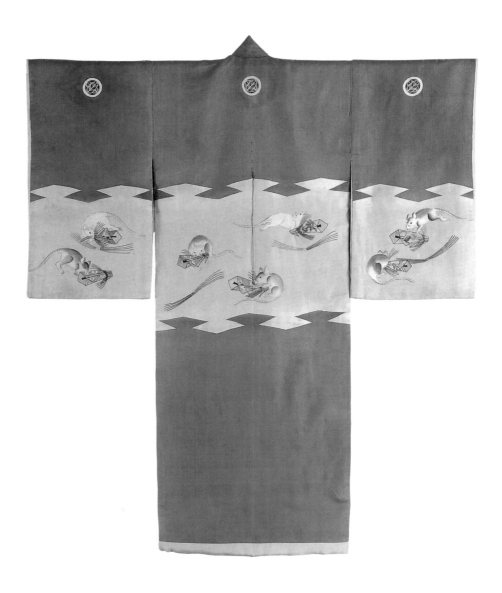

Kimono and kimono jacket (*haori*) for a boy
Well frame; auspicious motifs

Outer: plain weave pongee silk (tsumugi); hand-tied
selective dyeing of warp and weft threads (heiyō-gasuri)
Lining: plain weave cotton; printed
Shōwa period, 1920–40
109.0 × 110.0 cm (kimono); 81.0 × 112.0 cm (jacket)
K110

This kimono and *haori* ensemble is of finely
textured *tsumugi* silk, woven with hand-tied
selectively dyed yarns with a motif known
as *igeta*, or 'well frame', as it resembles the
wooden structure placed on a Japanese well.
Echoing the garments worn by adult men
(see K99; pp. 274–5), the subtly patterned
exterior of the *haori* hides a colourful lining
of cotton, which is printed with a design of
treasure ships, temples, drums, pine trees
and cranes.

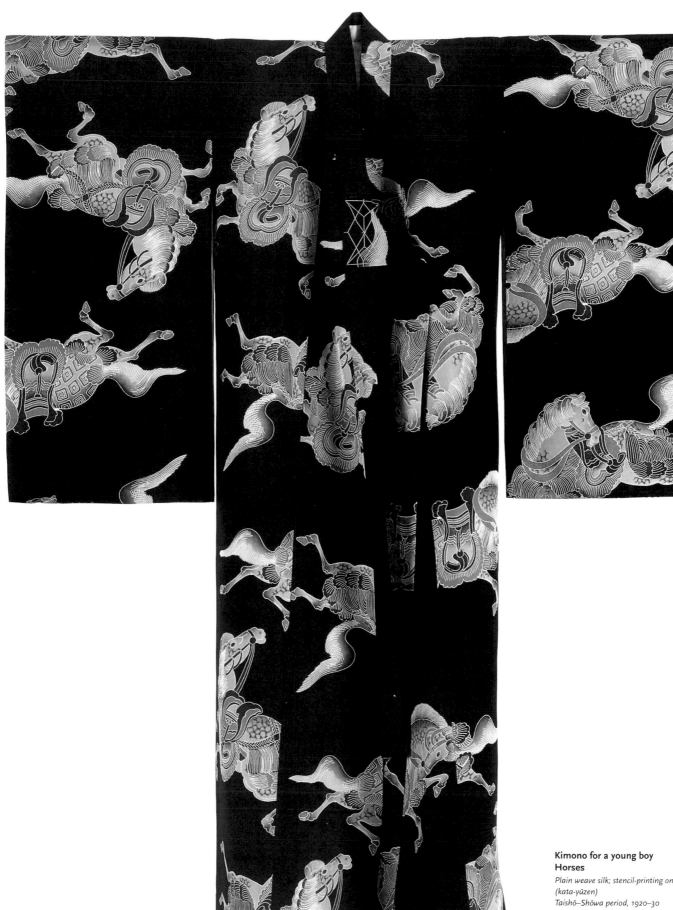

Kimono for a young boy
Horses
Plain weave silk; stencil-printing on fabric surface
(kata-yūzen)
Taishō–Shōwa period, 1920–30
103.0 × 82.0 cm
K81

Shrine horses in elaborate trappings prance
across the surface of this young boy's
kimono. Rendered in detailed shades of grey
against a black ground, the design is striking
yet playful.

Kimono for a young boy
Dragons in the clouds

*Plain weave silk; stencil-printing on fabric surface
(kata-yūzen)*
Taishō–Shōwa period, 1920–40
K109

Powerful dragons emerge from the clouds
on this young boy's kimono. The magical
beasts not only act as an auspicious motif,
carrying wishes for strength and good
fortune, but also symbolically wrap the child
in divine protection. Depicted in shades
of grey, the design looks like an ink painting
and recalls the work of artists such as
Katsushika Hokusai.

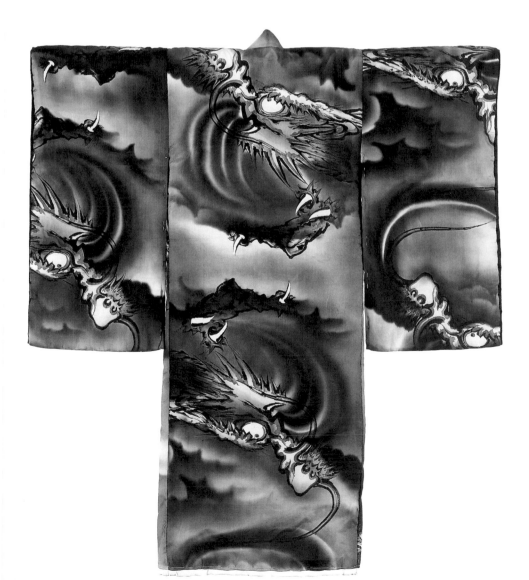

Katsushika Hokusai (1760–1849)
Dragon and Clouds

Hanging scroll, ink on paper
Freer Gallery of Art, Smithsonian Institution,
Washington, DC

above
Underkimono for a young man (*juban*)
Battleships, bomber planes, tanks and
Mount Fuji on a chequered ground
Plain weave wool; printed
Shōwa period, 1930–45
118.5 × 125.0 cm
K61

In the 1930s, the patterning of male
garments became increasingly nationalistic.
The style of the designs was consistent with
others that celebrated modern Japan, but
cars and trains were replaced by tanks, and
passenger planes and luxury liners by fighter
jets and battleships.

opposite
Kimono for an infant boy
Planes, battleships and submarines
Gauze weave silk (ro); printed on fabric surface
(kata-yūzen)
Shōwa period, 1930–45
73.0 × 76.5 cm
K21

This garment, of delicate *ro* gauze, was
probably designed for an infant boy's first
shrine visit. Historic motifs of samurai have
been supplanted by ones that celebrate
modern military might, wrapping the young
child in wishes for both his own, and the
nation's, future.

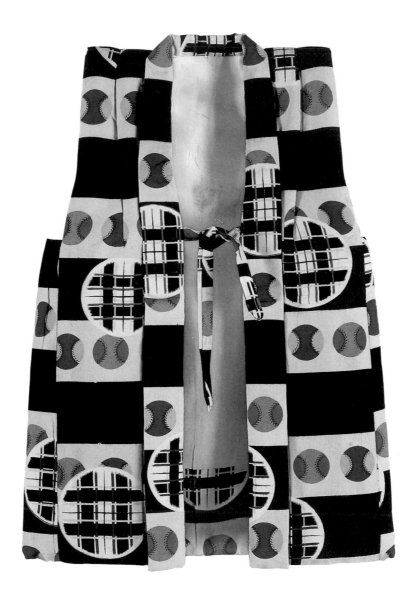

Kimono and vest for a young boy
Baseballs and well frames on horizontal bands
Plain weave silk; printed
Shōwa period, 1930–50
76.0 × 81.0 cm (kimono); 51.0 × 35.0 cm (vest, from side to side seam at hem)
K20

Circular motifs have been combined with broad horizontal stripes in this colourful kimono and vest ensemble. Closer inspection reveals that the small, round motifs are baseballs. First introduced to Japan in 1872, the sport became one of the most popular in the country. A professional baseball league was established in 1936.

Kimono Today: A Modern Master

ANNA JACKSON

The turmoil of the Asia-Pacific War and its aftermath caused irrevocable changes to Japan's social, economic and cultural landscape. Faced with enormous physical destruction, the trauma of defeat and the increasing Americanization of culture resulting from occupation, the country looked to its past to provide stability and a sense of national identity. In the early 1950s the government promulgated a number of laws that aimed to protect both tangible cultural properties, such as buildings and works of art, and 'intangible cultural products', such as drama, music and the applied arts, which have 'high historic or artistic value'.[1] A system was established whereby individuals were designated as holders of each of the identified Important Intangible Cultural Properties, these appointees being popularly known as Living National Treasures.

Such efforts ensured the preservation of traditional weaving and dyeing practices, but they also accentuated a shift in the status and meaning of kimono from the practical to the symbolic. In the second half of the twentieth century, the wearing of kimono dramatically declined. Although still worn by those engaged in the restaurant and entertainment business, for most people the kimono ceased to be an item of everyday dress and became instead a codified ceremonial costume, worn only on special occasions or by those conducting specific cultural activities, such as the tea ceremony or flower arranging. The kimono became treasured as a cultural relic, and revered as the essence of what was Japanese in an increasingly globalized world. The beginning of the twenty-first century has witnessed something of a revival, however, with vintage kimono being adapted and re-styled by a younger generation, while in the summer shops are full of casual *yukata*. Wearing a kimono can again be a fashionable choice, just as it was in the Edo period.

Contemporary textile designers who employ historic techniques still use kimono as the primary format for their artistic expression. Moriguchi Kunihiko (b. 1941) was designated a Living National Treasure in 2007, following in the footsteps of his father Moriguchi Kakō (1909–2008), who received the honour in 1967, and employs the methods of *yūzen* dyeing developed in the seventeenth century. The kimono is temporarily assembled and the design drawn onto the silk with pale blue, soluble tracing liquid. The garment is then unstitched, the individual panels area stretched onto bamboo frames and rice paste is squeezed through a fine nozzle along the lines of the drawing. Areas within the resisted outlines are then sized with soya-bean extract (*gojiru*), before dyes are brushed on in stages, often with intermediate applications of rice paste to protect already patterned areas.

Moriguchi also uses a technique, first developed by his father, called *makinori* (sprinkled rice paste). Zinc dust is added to the paste, which is then dried and pulverized into small particles that are fixed to the surface of the fabric prior to and between applications of the background colours. After dyeing, the cloth is washed and the *makinori* scraped off, leaving a dramatic speckled effect. Moriguchi is known for his abstract and geometric patterns, which are first carefully delineated on paper, reflecting his training as a graphic designer in Paris in the early 1960s. His technical mastery and bold imagination are revealed in this garment, which was displayed at the 52nd Dento Kogeiten (Traditional Crafts Exhibition) in 2005 and at the Fine Art Society in London in 2013.

Through his very individual creative process, Moriguchi respects historical traditions while exploring the contemporary possibilities they offer. His work is prized internationally and collected by private individuals and public institutions. Yet Moriguchi is acutely aware that he is not only making objects of art for preservation and exhibition, but also items of dress that will be animated by the movement and personality of the wearer. As he has himself stated: 'We have to answer the challenge of modernity: what is a kimono, or what will it become, if it ceases to be a thing worn.'[2]

Moriguchi Kunihiko (b. 1941)
Kimono, entitled *Beyond (Tōkō)*
Plain-weave crepe silk (chirimen); freehand paste-resist dyeing (yūzen)
2005
175.0 x 130.0 cm
KX224

NOTES

14–19

1. Shiba Kōkan, letter to Yamaryō Kazuma, *c.* 1813, in Nakano Yoshio, ed., *Shiba Kōkan kō* (Tokyo, 1986), p. 40.
2. Kimuro Bōun (Nikyōtei Hanzan), *Mita kyō monogatari [The Kyo(to) I Have Seen]*, in *Nihon zuihitsu taikei*, series 3, vol. 4 (Tokyo, 1976), pp. 565–81.
3. Ibid.
4. Sadly the only English translation is highly inaccurate, see Ihara Saikaku, *The Life of an Amorous Man*, trans. Harada Kengi (Rutland, Vermont, and Tokyo, 1963).
5. Men designated for death would act as in Europe, bending forward to indicate they were ready and to expose the jugular; the difference was that in Japan this extending of the neck was notionally a movement forward to reach for a dagger to stab themselves. However, it was all but unheard of for a man actually to do so.
6. Yuasa Genzō, *Kokui ron [Medicine of this Realm]*, in *Nihon zeizai daiten*, vol. 22 (Tokyo, 1927), p. 7.
7. Ōta Nanpo, *Ichiwa ichigon [One Story, One Talk]*, in *Nihon zuihitsu taikei*, supp. vol. 4 (Tokyo, 1978), p. 197.

20–7

1. Quoted in Donald Shively, 'Sumptuary Regulation and Status in Early Tokugawa Japan', in *Harvard Journal of Asiatic Studies* 25 (1964–5): 124–5. The title of Saikaku's book is sometimes translated as *The Eternal Storehouse of Japan*.
2. For a detailed analysis of the weaving, dyeing and embroidery techniques used in Edo kimono, see Amanda Mayer Stinchecum, *Kosode: 16th–19th Century Textiles from the Nomura Collection* (New York and Tokyo, 1984), pp. 26–38.
3. In plain weave (*hira-ori*), the simplest way of weaving fabric, the weft (horizontal) thread is passed over and under each successive warp (vertical) thread. The general term for crepe in Japanese is *chijimi*, where the wefts and/or the warps are highly twisted. Strictly speaking, *chirimen* is a type of crepe in which the twist direction changes with every two wefts. Ibid., p. 20.
4. There is no English term that comprises all the techniques covered by the word *shibori*, but it is normally translated as 'tie-dyeing'.
5. Quoted in Maruyama Nobuhiko, *Yūzen Dyeing* (Kyoto, 1993), p. 93.
6. For discussion of the importance of red, see Monica Bethe, 'Reflections on *Beni*: Red as a Key to Edo-Period Fashion', in Dale Carolyn Gluckman and Sharon Sadako Takeda, eds, *When Art Became Fashion: Kosode in Edo-Period Japan* (Los Angeles, 1992), pp. 133–53.
7. Quoted in ibid., p. 2.
8. Rinpa painting is distinguished by its highly decorative, stylized forms, while the work of Maruyama Ōkyo and his followers was more naturalistic. Nanga is a literati style inspired by Chinese ink painting.
9. Silk had been cultivated in Japan since the third century AD, but until the early eighteenth century the finest quality thread was imported from China. Cotton was introduced to Japan in the sixteenth century,

transforming the clothing of the general populace.
10. There were separate workshops for weaving, dyeing and embroidery.
11. About 180 *hinagata-bon* were published between 1662 and 1820. See Nagasaki Iwao, 'Designs for a Thousand Ages: Printed Pattern Books and Kosode', in Gluckman and Takeda, op. cit., pp. 95–113; and Terry Satsuki Milhaupt, *Kimono: A Modern History* (London, 2014), pp. 46–52.
12. For the standard account of fashion as uniquely European, see G. Lipovetsky, *The Empire of Fashion: Dressing Modern Democracy*, trans. C. Porter (Princeton, New Jersey, 1994). Lipovetsky states: 'The Japanese kimono remained unchanged for centuries'; p. 19.
13. See Monica Bethe, 'Color: Dyes and Pigment', in Stinchecum, op. cit., pp. 61–2.
14. Shively, op. cit., p. 128
15. Ibid., p. 125

28–103

1. *The Tale of Genji* is a celebrated work of Japanese literature written by Murasaki Shikibu in the early years of the eleventh century. It is often considered the world's first novel. Nō, a classical form of musical theatre, first developed in the fourteenth century and was patronized by the military elite.
2. Dyes are soluble in water and penetrate the fibres of the fabric, while pigments are insoluble and adhere to the surface. On the whole, dyes are extracted from vegetable sources and pigments from minerals, but pigments can also be created from vegetable dyes. The properties of indigo, *murasaki* (purple) and *beni* (red) make them most suitable for immersion dyeing. If they were to be brushed on, they were made into pigments. See Bethe, op. cit., pp. 59–76.
3. The Eight Views are: returning sails at Yabase; the evening glow at Seta; the autumn moon at Ishiyama; the clear breeze at Awazu; the evening bell at Mii; the evening rain at Karasaki; returning geese at Katata; and the snow on Hira mountains.
4. I am grateful to John T. Carpenter, Metropolitan Museum of Art, New York, for identifying and translating the poem.
5. *Tales of Ise: Lyrical Episodes from Tenth-Century Japan*, trans. Helen Craig McCullough (Stanford, California, 1968), p. 76.
6. Edo-period dyers became skilled at using other sources of red, particularly *suō* (sappanwood) to imitate *beni*. Without dye analysis, it is not always possible to be certain what plants have been used to colour kimono.
7. The fabric is similar to seersucker, but in silk rather than cotton.
8. I am grateful to John T. Carpenter, Metropolitan Museum of Art, New York, for translating these characters.

106–11

1. For general overviews of the period, see W. G. Beasley, *The Meiji Restoration* (Stanford, California, and Oxford, 1973); Marius B. Jansen and John Whitney Hall, eds, *The Cambridge History of Japan*, vol. 5 (Cambridge,

1989); and Marius B. Jansen, ed., *Changing Attitudes Towards Modernization* (Princeton, New Jersey, 1965).
2. Marius B. Jansen, 'Cultural Change in Nineteenth-Century Japan', in Ellen P. Conant, ed., *Challenging Past and Present: The Metamorphosis of Nineteenth-Century Japanese Art* (Honolulu, 2006), p. 32.
3. T. Fujitani, *Splendid Monarchy: Power and Pageantry in Modern Japan* (Berkeley, California, 1998).
4. Satō Dōshin, *Modern Japanese Art and the Meiji State: The Politics of Beauty*, trans. Hiroshi Nara (Los Angeles, 2011), pp. 103–24.
5. Fujita Haruhiko, 'Notomi Kaijiro: An Industrial Art Pioneer and the First Design Educator of Modern Japan', in *Design Issues* 17:2 (2001): 26.
6. Frederic A. Sharf, Anne Nishimura Morse and Sebastian Dobson, *A Much Recorded War: The Russo-Japanese War in History and Imagery* (Boston, 2005), p. 32.
7. David Howell, *Geographies of Identity in Nineteenth-Century Japan* (Berkeley, California, 2005), p. 131.
8. James Hoare, *Japan's Treaty Ports and Foreign Settlements: The Uninvited Guests, 1858–1899* (Folkstone, Kent, 1994).
9. On tourist photographs, see Allen Hockley, 'Felice Beato's Japan: Places, An Album by the Pioneer Photographer in Yokohoma', http://ocw.mit.edu/ans7870/21f/21f.027/beato_places/fb1_essay01.html accessed on August 30, 2013.
10. Ian Nish, ed., *The Iwakura Mission in America and Europe: A New Assessment* (Richmond, Surrey, 1998).
11. Hiroaki Satō, trans., *A Brief History of Imbecility: Poetry and Prose of Takamura Kōtarō* (Honolulu, 1992), p. 3, as cited in Christine M. E. Guth, 'Takamura Kōun and Takamura Kōtarō: On being a Sculptor', in Melinda Takeuchi, ed., *The Artist as Professional in Japan* (Stanford, California, 2004), pp. 171–2.
12. Koyama Shizuko, *Ryōsai Kenbo: The Educational Ideal of 'Good Wife, Wise Mother' in Modern Japan* (Leiden and Boston, 2013), p. 7.
13. E. Patricia Tsurumi, *Factory Girls: Women in the Thread Mills of Meiji Japan* (Princeton, New Jersey, 1990), p. 29.
14. John S. Brownlee, *Japanese Historians and the National Myths, 1600–1945: The Age of the Gods and the Emperor Jinmu* (Vancouver, 1997).
15. Thomas Smith, 'Peasant Time and Factory Time in Japan', in *Past and Present* 111:1 (May 1986): 165–97.
16. This is a term used by Miriam Silverberg, 'Constructing the Japanese Ethnography of Modernity', in *Journal of Asian Studies* 51:1 (February 1992): 31.
17. Nakano Makiko, *Makiko's Diary: A Merchant Wife in 1910 Kyoto*, trans. Kazuko Smith (Stanford, California, 1990), pp. 84, 90, 95, 96, 114, 126, 129, 153, 172.
18. Quoted in David Gordon, *Fabricating Consumers: The Sewing Machine in Modern Japan* (Berkeley, California, 2012), p. 80.
19. Ibid., p. 17.

112–19

1. Quoted in Liza Dalby, *Kimono: Fashioning Culture* (New Haven and London, 1993), pp. 66–7.

2. Julia Meech-Pekarik, *The World of the Meiji Print: Impressions of a New Civilization* (New York and Tokyo, 1986), p. 72
3. Ibid, pp. 64–71
4. Dalby, op. cit., p. 71.
5. She was known posthumously as Empress Shōken.
6. Meech-Perarik, op. cit, p. 129.
7. Yōshū Chikanobu is how this artist normally signed his work, but he is also known as Hashimoto Chikanobu and Toyhara Chikanobu.
8. 'Japanese Art Wares', in *Woman's World*, 1888, p. 94. Quoted in Elizabeth Kramer, 'Re-Evaluating the Japan Mania in Victorian Britain: The Agency of Japanese and Anglo-Japanese Wares', in Fiona Hackley, et al., eds, *Networks of Design* (Florida, 2009), pp. 169–74.
9. Kimono-clad women appear in the art of James McNeill Whistler, James Tissot, Claude Monet, Pierre-Auguste Renoir, William Merritt Chase, Charles Sprague Pearce, and many others.
10. See Anna Jackson, 'Orient and Occident', in Paul Greenhalgh, ed., *Art Nouveau 1890–1914* (London, 2000) pp. 100–13.
11. Such attitudes are common in cultural appropriation; while the West could be inspired by the East, it needed the East to remain 'pure' and untainted.
12. It was at this time that the term *gosho-doki*, which describes one of the major styles of samurai dress, was first used.
13. Amy Reigle Newland, *Time Present and Time Past: Images of a Forgotten Master, Toyohara Kunichika, 1835–1900* (Leiden, 1999), p. 19.
14. Meech-Perarik, op. cit, p. 183.
15. For full details of the changes to weaving and dyeing practices see Tetsuro Nakaoka, et al., 'The Textile History of Nishijin (Kyoto): East Meets West', in *Textile History* 19:2 (1988): 117–42.

160–5

1. The basis for this chapter formed a lecture presented at the symposium 'The Greater Taishō Period: Years of Irony and Paradox', organized by the Society for Japanese Arts and held at Leiden University in January 2013. This was later published; see Anna Jackson 'Fashioning the Greater Taishō Era', in *Andon* 97 (2014): 105–16.
2. Although the samurai class had been abolished in the 1870s, elite families continued to wear their family crest on clothing.
3. I am grateful to Mami Shinozaki for this information and for giving permission to use the image of her grandparents. The kimono is now in the collection of the Victoria and Albert Museum (FE.138-2002).
4. See Penelope Francks, 'Was Fashion a European Invention? The Kimono and Economic Development in Japan', in *Fashion Theory* 19:3 (June 2015): 331–62, and Reiko Mochinaga Brandon, *Bright and Daring: Japanese Kimono in the Taishō Mode* (Honolulu and Tokyo, 1996), pp. 11–15. A tan is the amount needed to make a kimono (about 12m, or 39 ft).
5. Until recently another event was also credited with speeding up the introduction of western dress. In 1932 a fire broke out at the Shirokiya department store and fourteen people lost their lives. Those trying to escape made their way down from the upper floors on makeshift ropes. It was reported that shop assistants wearing kimono, and thus not western-style underwear, in struggling to maintain their modesty and keep their garments from flying up, had lost their grip and fallen to their deaths. When the store was rebuilt, it was claimed that female staff were paid to wear western dress. The story has proved to be false, however. See Inoue Shōichi, *Pantsi ga mieru: shūchishin no gendaishi [My Panties are Visible: The History of Being Ashamed]* (Tokyo, 2002).
6. See Elise K. Tipton, 'The Cafe: Contested Space of Modernity in Interwar Japan', in Elise K. Tipton and John Clark, eds, *Being Modern in Japan: Culture and Society from the 1910s to the 1930s* (Brisbane, Queensland, 2000), pp. 119–36.
7. See Ewa Machotka, 'For Girls and Wives: Narrating "Tradition" and "Modernity" Through Gendered Publications of the Taishō Era', in *Andon* 97 (2014): 91–104.
8. A move pioneered by Matsuzakaya.
9. See Anna Jackson, 'Art Deco in East Asia', in Charlotte Benton, Tim Benton and Ghislaine Wood, eds, *Art Deco 1910–1939* (London, 2003), pp. 370–81.
10. The Vienna Secession, the Austrian Art Nouveau movement, was founded in 1897 and included artists Gustav Klimt and Josef Hoffmann.
11. See Jacqueline M. Atkins, *Wearing Propaganda: Textiles on the Home Front in Japan, Britain and the United States 1931–1945* (New Haven and London, 2006).

166–309

1. This was sometimes allowed for, with a change in direction of the pattern made at the shoulder. However, this could only be done with specially commissioned kimono, not with garments made up from bolts of cloth produced in quantity.
2. *Tales of Ise: Lyrical Episodes from Tenth-Century Japan*, trans. Helen Craig McCullogh (Stanford, California, 1968), p. 75.
3. My thanks to William H. Coaldrake for identifying the buildings.
4. The text on the *haori* linings was originally translated by Annie Van Assche and published in *Fashioning Kimono*, op. cit., pp. 132–6.
5. For information about these processions, see p. 16.
6. Translations by Annie Van Assche, *Fashioning Kimono*, op. cit, p. 128.

310–11

1. Quoted in Rupert Faulkner, *Japanese Studio Crafts: Tradition and the Avant-Garde* (London, 1995), p. 13.
2. Judith Thurman, 'Letter from Japan: The Kimono Painter', in *New Yorker* (17 October 2005): 127. Quoted in Terry Satsuki Milhaupt, *Kimono: A Modern History* (London, 2014), p. 224.

BIBLIOGRAPHY

Atkins, Jacqueline M., *Wearing Propaganda: Textiles on the Home Front in Japan, Britain and the United States 1931–1945* (New Haven and London, 2006).

Beasley, W. G., *The Meiji Restoration* (Stanford and Oxford, 1973).

Monica Bethe, 'Reflections on Beni: Red as a Key to Edo-Period Fashion', in Dale Carolyn Gluckman and Sharon Sadako Takeda, eds, *When Art Became Fashion: Kosode in Edo-Period Japan* (Los Angeles, 1992).

Brandon, Reiko Mochinaga, *Bright and Daring: Japanese Kimono in the Taishō Mode* (Honolulu and Tokyo, 1996).

A Brief History of Imbecility: Poetry and Prose of Takamura Kōtarō, trans. Satō Hiroaki (Honolulu, 1992).

Brown, Kendall, H., ed., *Deco Japan: Shaping Art and Culture, 1920–1945* (Alexandria, Virginia, 2012).

Brown, Kendall, H. and Sharon A. Minichello, *Taishō Chic: Japanese Modernity, Nostalgia and Deco* (Honolulu, 2002).

Brownlee, John S., *Japanese Historians and the National Myths, 1600–1945: The Age of the Gods and the Emperor Jinmu* (Vancouver, 1997).

Bunka Gakuen Fukushoku Hakubutsukan, ed., *Bunka Gakuen Fukushoku Hakubutsukan zōhin: Nihon fukushoku no bi [Masterpieces of Japanese Dress from the Bunka Gakuen Costume Museum]* (Tokyo, 2005).

—————, *Mitsui-ke no kimono [Kimono from the Mitsui Family]* (Tokyo, 2006).

—————, *Mitsui-ke no kimono to shitae: Maruyama-ha ga motarashita dezain no sekai [Kimono and Designs from the Mitsui Family: The Maruyama School's Influence]* (Tokyo, 2009).

Dalby, Liza, *Kimono: Fashioning Culture* (New Haven and London, 1993).

Dees, Jan, *Taishō Kimono: Speaking of Past and Present* (Milan, 2009).

Downer, John W., et al., *The Brittle Decade: Visualizing Japan in the 1930s* (Boston, 2012).

Francks, Penelope, 'Was Fashion a European Invention? The Kimono and Economic Development in Japan', in *Fashion Theory* 19:3 (June 2015).

Frederick, Sarah, *Turning Pages: Reading and Writing Women's Magazines in Interwar Japan* (Honolulu, 2006).

Fujita Haruhiko, 'Notomi Kaijiro: An Industrial Art Pioneer and the First Design Educator of Modern Japan', in *Design Issues* 17:2 (2001).

Fujitani, T., *Splendid Monarchy: Power and Pageantry in Modern Japan* (Berkeley, California, 1998).

Gluckman, Dale Carolyn and Sharon Sadako Takeda, eds, *When Art Became Fashion: Kosode in Edo-Period Japan* (Los Angeles, 1992).

Gordon, David, *Fabricating Consumers: The Sewing Machine in Modern Japan* (Berkeley, California, 2012).

Guth, Christine M. E., *Japanese Art of the Edo Period* (London, 1996).

Guth, Christine M. E., 'Takamura Kōun and Takamura Kōtarō: On Being a Sculptor', in Melinda Takeuchi, ed., *The Artist as Professional in Japan* (Stanford, California, 2004).

Harootunian, Harry, *History's Disquiet: Modernity, Cultural Practice and the Question of Everyday Life* (New York, 2000).

Hoare, James, *Japan's Treaty Ports and Foreign Settlements: The Uninvited Guests, 1858–1899* (Folkestone, Kent, 1994).

Hockley, Allen, 'Felice Beato's Japan: Places. An Album by the Pioneer Photographer in Yokohoma', http://ocw.mit.edu/ans7870/21f/21f.027/beato_places/fb1_essay01.html.

Howell, David, *Geographies of Identity in Nineteenth-Century Japan* (Berkeley, California, 2005).

Ihara Saikaku, *The Life of an Amorous Man*, trans. Harada Kengi (Rutland, Vermont, and Tokyo, 1963).

Ishimura, Hayao, and Maruyama Nobuhiko, *Robes of Elegance: Japanese Kimonos of the 16th–20th Centuries* (Raleigh, North Carolina, 1988).

Inoue, Shōichi, *Pantsi ga mieru: shōchishin no gendaishi [My Panties are Visible: The History of Being Ashamed]* (Tokyo, 2002).

Jackson, Anna, 'Art Deco in East Asia', in Charlotte Benton, Tim Benton and Ghislaine Wood, eds, *Art Deco 1910–1939* (London, 2003).

—————, *Country Textiles* (London, 1997).

—————, *Japanese Textiles in the Victoria and Albert Museum* (London, 2000).

—————, 'Orient and Occident', in Paul Greenhalgh, ed., *Art Nouveau 1890–1914* (London 2000).

Jansen, Marius B., 'Cultural Change in Nineteenth-Century Japan', in Ellen P. Conant, ed., *Challenging Past and Present: The Metamorphosis of Nineteenth-Century Japanese Art* (Honolulu, 2006).

Jansen, Marius B., ed., *Changing Attitudes Towards Modernization* (Princeton, New Jersey, 1965).

Jansen, Marius B. and John Whitney Hall, eds, *The Cambridge History of Japan: The Nineteenth Century*, vol. 5 (Cambridge, 1989).

Joshi Bijutsu Daigaku, ed., *Edo kimono artsu: kimono bunka no bi to yosooi [Edo Kimono Art: Aesthetics in Japanese Fashion]* (Tokyo, 2011).

Kawakami, Shigeki and Yoko Woodson, *Four Centuries of Fashion: Classical Kimono from Kyoto National Museum* (San Francisco, 1997).

Kennedy, Alan, *Japanese Costume: History and Tradition* (Paris, 1990).

Kimuro Bōun (Nikyōtei Hanzan), *Mita kyō monogatari [The Kyo(to) I Have seen]*, in *Nihon zuihitsu taikei*, series 3, vol. 4 (1976).

Kokuritsu Rekishi Minzoku Hakubutsukan, ed., *Edo mōdo daizukan: kosode mon'yō ni miru bi no keifu [Edo à la Mode: Aesthetic Lineages Seen in Kosode Kimono Motifs]* (Tokyo, 1999).

Koyama Shizuko, *Ryōsai Kenbo: The Educational Ideal of 'Good Wife, Wise Mother' in Modern Japan* (Leiden and Boston, 2013).

Kramer, Elizabeth, 'Re-evaluating the Japan Mania in Victorian Britain: The Agency of Japanese and Anglo-Japanese Wares', in Fiona Hackley, et al., eds, *Networks of Design* (Florida, 2009).

Kyoto Kokuritsu Hakubutsukan, ed., *Miyako no mōda: kimono no jidai [Kyoto Style: Trends in 16th–19th Century Kimono]* (Kyoto, 1999).

Liddell, Jill, *The Story of the Kimono* (New York, 1989).

McClain, James, *Japan: A Modern History* (New York, 2002).

McDermott, Hiroko T., and Clare Pollard, *Threads of Silk and Gold: Ornamental Textiles from Meiji Japan* (Oxford, 2012).

Machotka, Ewa, 'For Girls and Wives: Narrating "Tradition" and "Modernity" through Gendered Publications of the Taishō Era', in *Andon* 97 (2014).

Maruyama Nobuhiko, *Yūzen Dyeing* (Kyoto, 1993).

Meech-Pekarik, Julia, *The World of the Meiji Print: Impressions of a New Civilization* (New York and Tokyo, 1986).

Milhaupt, Terry Satsuki, *Kimono: A Modern History* (London, 2014).

Nagasaki Iwao, 'Designs for a Thousand Ages: Printed Pattern Books and Kosode', in Dale Carolyn Gluckman and Sharon Sadako Takeda, eds, *When Art Became Fashion: Kosode in Edo-Period Japan* (Los Angeles, 1992).

————, *Furisode* (Kyoto, 1994).

————, *Kimono Beauty: shikku de modan na yosooi no bi - Edo kara Shōwa [Kimono Beauty: The Beauty of Chic and Modern Clothing from Edo to Shōwa]* (Tokyo, 2013).

————, *Kimono: kosode ni miru hana: dezain no sekai [Kimono: Flowers on Kosode: World of Design]* (Tokyo, 2006).

————, *Kosode* (Kyoto, 1993).

————, *Kyōritsu Joshi Daigaku korekushon: Nihon fukushoku hen [Kyoritsu Joshi Daigaku Collection: Japanese Dress]* (Tokyo, 2009).

————, *Kyōritsu Joshi Gakuen korekushon: kosode, kimono hen [Kyoritsu Joshi Gakuen Collection: Kosode and Kimono]* (Tokyo, 2005).

Nakano Makiko, *Makiko's Diary: A Merchant Wife in 1910 Kyoto*, trans. Kazuko Smith (Stanford, California, 1990).

Nakano Yoshio, ed., *Shiba Kōkan kō* (Tokyo, 1986)

Nakaoka Tetsurō, et al., 'The Textile History of Nishijin (Kyoto): East Meets West', in *Textile History* 19:2 (1988).

Newland, Amy Reigle, *Time Present and Time Past: Images of a Forgotten Master, Toyohara Kunichika, 1835–1900* (Leiden, 1999).

Nish, Ian, ed., *The Iwakura Mission in America and Europe: A New Assessment* (Richmond, Surrey, 1998).

Nishiyama Matsunosuke, *Edo Japan: Daily Life and Diversions in Japan, 1600–1868* (Honolulu, 1997).

Ōta Nanpo, *Ichiwa ichigon [One Story, One Talk]*, in *Nihon zuihitsu taikei*, supp. vol. 4 (Tokyo, 1978).

Parmal, Pamela A., 'The Impact of Synthetic Dyes on the Luxury Textiles of Meiji Japan', in *Textile Society of America Symposium Papers* (Lincoln, Nebraska, 2004).

Rimer, J. Thomas, ed., *Since Meiji: Perspectives on the Japanese Visual Arts, 1868–2000* (Honolulu, 2011).

Satō Dōshin, *Modern Japanese Art and the Meiji State: The Politics of Beauty*, trans. Hiroshi Nara (Los Angeles, 2011).

Schenking, J. Charles, *The Great Kanto Earthquake and the Chimera of National Reconstruction in Japan* (New York, 2013).

Screech, Timon, *Obtaining Images: Art, Production and Display in Edo Japan* (London, 2012).

Seidensticker, Edward, *Tokyo Rising: The City Since the Great Earthquake* (Cambridge, Massachusetts, 1991).

Seiroku, Noma, *Japanese Costume and Textile Arts* (New York and Tokyo, 1974).

Sharf, Frederic A., Anne Nishimura Morse and Sebastian Dobson, *A Much Recorded War: The Russo-Japanese War in History and Imagery* (Boston, 2005).

Shively, Donald, 'Sumptuary Regulation and Status in Early Tokugawa Japan', in *Harvard Journal of Asiatic Studies* 25 (1964–5).

Silverberg, Miriam, 'Constructing the Japanese Ethnography of Modernity', in *Journal of Asian Studies* 51:1 (1992).

————, *Erotic Grotesque Nonsense: The Mass Culture of Japanese Modern Times* (Berkeley, California, 2006).

Slade, Toby, *Japanese Fashion: A Cultural History* (Oxford and New York, 2009).

Smith, Thomas, 'Peasant Time and Factory Time in Japan', in *Past and Present* 111:1 (May 1986).

Stinchecum, Amanda Mayer, *Kosode: 16th–19th Century Textiles from the Nomura Collection* (New York and Tokyo, 1984).

Tales of Ise: Lyrical Episodes from Tenth-Century Japan, trans. Helen Craig McCullough (Stanford, California, 1968).

Tansman, Edward Alan, ed., *The Culture of Japanese Fascism* (Durham, North Carolina, 2009).

Tipton, Elise and John Clark, eds, *Being Modern in Japan: Culture and Society from the 1910s to the 1930s* (Honolulu, 2000).

Tsurumi, E. Patricia, *Factory Girls: Women in the Thread Mills of Meiji Japan* (Princeton, New Jersey, 1990).

Van Assche, Annie, *Fashioning Kimono: Art Deco and Modernism in Japan* (Milan, 2005).

Vlastos, Stephen, ed., *Mirror of Modernity: Invented Traditions of Modern Japan* (Berkeley, California, 1998).

Weisenfeld, Gennifer, *Mavo: Japanese Artists and the Avant-Garde, 1905–1931* (Berkeley, California, 2002).

Yoshioka Sachio, *Sarasa: Printed and Painted Textiles* (Kyoto, 1993).

Yuasa Genzō, *Kokui ron [Medicine of this Realm]*, in *Nihon zeizai daiten*, vol. 22 (Tokyo, 1927).

LIST OF KIMONO

page number indicates page on which illustration appears
dimensions given are length from base of neck to hem × width across the shoulders

AUTHOR BIOGRAPHIES

Anna Jackson is Keeper of the Asian Department at the Victoria and Albert Museum, London. She has particular responsibility for the Museum's collection of Japanese textiles and dress, and her publications on the subject including *Japanese Country Textiles* (1997), *Japanese Textiles in the Victoria and Albert Museum* (2000), and numerous essays in journals and catalogues. Her other major research interest is the cultural relationship between Asia and the West and she has contributed to a number of V&A exhibitions and their related publications, including *Art Nouveau 1890–1914* (2000), *The Victorian Vision* (2001) and *Art Deco 1914–1939* (2003). In 2004 she was co-curator of the exhibition *Encounters: The Meeting of Asia and Europe 1500–1800*, and in 2009 lead curator of *Maharaja: The Splendour of India's Royal Courts*, which subsequently toured to Germany, North America and, in revised form, the Palace Museum in Beijing. Other publications include *Expo: International Expositions 1851–2010* (2008).

Kendall H. Brown is Professor of Asian Art History in the School of Art at California State University, Long Beach. His books include *The Politics of Reclusion: Painting and Power in Momoyama Japan* (1997), *Kawase Hasui: The Complete Woodblock Prints* (2003) and *Quiet Beauty: The Japanese Gardens of North America* (2013). Also active as a curator, he has edited several exhibition catalogues including *Deco Japan: Shaping Art and Culture, 1920–1945* (2012), *Traditions Transfigured: The Noh Masks of Bidou Yamaguchi (2013)* and *Water and Shadow: Kawase Hasui and Japanese Landscape Prints* (2014).

Christine M. E. Guth is Senior Tutor at the Royal College of Art, London, where she leads the Asian design specialism in the postgraduate History of Design Programme, run jointly with the Victoria and Albert Museum. Her publications include *Art, Tea and Industry: Masuda Takashi and the Mitsui Circle* (1993), *Longfellow's Tattoos: Tourism Collecting and Japan* (2004) and *Hokusai's Great Wave: Biography of a Global Icon* (2015).

Nagasaki Iwao is Professor of Apparel Science and Director of the Center for Interdisciplinary Studies of Science and Culture at Kyoritsu Women's University, Tokyo. Formally the Curator of Textiles at Tokyo National Museum, he is one of the world's foremost authorities in the field. His publications include *Japanese Textile Collections in American Museums* (1995) and *Kimono Beauty* (2013), and he has also contributed essays to a number of exhibition catalogues, including *When Art Becomes Fashion: Kosode in Edo-Period Japan* (1992), *Kazari: Decoration and Display in Japan 15th–19th Centuries* (2002) and *Miracles and Mischief: Noh and Kyogen Theater in Japan* (2002).

Timon Screech is Professor of the History of Art at the School of Oriental and African Studies, University of London. An expert on the art and culture of the Edo period, including its international dimension, he has published many books on the subject, most notably *The Lens Within the Heart: The Western Scientific Gaze and Popular Imagery in Later Edo Japan* (1996; rev. ed., 2002), *Sex and the Floating World: Japanese Erotic Imagery, 1700–1820* (1999; rev. ed., 2010) and *Obtaining Images: Art, Production and Display in Edo Japan* (2012).

PHOTO CREDITS

INDEX

ACKNOWLEDGMENTS

This publication would not have been realized without the generous help and kind support of a number of people. I am particularly grateful to Dror Elkvity, for his unwavering dedication and enthusiasm, and to Ando Kyoko for her skilful translation of Japanese texts.

I am greatly indebted to the authors Kendall H. Brown, Christine M. E. Guth and Timon Screech for their valuable contributions, and particularly to Nagasaki Iwao for so generously sharing his expertise in answering my innumerable questions. Many others have also given their time, knowledge and encouragement, and my warm thanks go to Jacqueline M. Atkins, John T. Carpenter, Sarah Cheang, William H. Coaldrake, Rosemary Crill, Edwina Erhman, Rupert Faulkner, Francesca Henry-Pierre, Gregory Irvine, Andrew Keelan, Elizabeth Kramer, Jenny Lister, Beth McKillop, Jeffrey Montgomery, Helen Persson, Shikama Naohito, Shoji Tsumugi, Sudo Ryoko, Philip Sykes, Takagi Yoko, Annie Van Assche and Yoshimura Kohka.

Special thanks go to Hugh Kelly for his beautiful photographs and to everyone at Thames & Hudson for turning the words and images into such a handsome volume, particularly Philip Watson, Elain McAlpine and Alexandra Boalch, and to Karin Fremer.

Finally, and most importantly, my deepest gratitude is due to Professor Nasser David Khalili, for entrusting me with the role of honorary curator and thus providing me with the wonderful opportunity to both research his remarkable collection and to share with him a mutual passion for the art and artistry of kimono.

Kimono: The Art and Evolution of Japanese Fashion
© 2015 The Khalili Family Trust

Designed by Karin Fremer

First published in 2015 in hardcover the United States of America by Thames & Hudson Inc., 500 Fifth Avenue, New York, New York 10110

thamesandhudsonusa.com

Library of Congress Catalog Card Number 2015932482

ISBN 978-0-500-51802-1

Printed and bound in China by C & C Offset Printing Co. Ltd